MW01248435

ON THE VERGE

A novella by GSeverino

ON THE VERGE

bookofawriter.wixsite.com/bookofawriter

Book Cover by GSeverino. Editing by Jeri Marie

Independently published

Paperback: 9798387974984

Hardcover: 9798387975394

eBook: B0BZXCLL4H

First edition: 2023

Trigger Warnings: Mental illness (anxiety & depression), Gaslighting (self-gaslighting), Grief, Panic attacks/disorders

To those who, like me, have felt lost at some point.

To those who feel like they have nowhere to go.

To those who don't know how to ask for help.

To those who don't know who to trust.

To those who deserve everything!

∞

This is for you...

on · the · verge

at the point when [something] is about to happen or is
very likely to happen, but it never does.

CHAPTER I

IRASCIBLE

iras·ci·ble

(adj.) marked by hot temper and easily provoked anger

"He who gets the better of an irascible temperament conquers his worst enemy." — Publilius Syrus

Anger, hatred, disdain. Have you ever felt so much of it at once? An irrational amount of it. Not the kind that requires medication to handle it—just plain, irrational anger bubbling inside.

I refuse to believe I'm the only one having trouble controlling those irrational thoughts and feelings, those random bursts of hatred for no apparent reason.

But, at the same time, I feel so alone in this sentiment. Alone, abandoned, isolated—however you want to call it.

Am I doing this to myself? Are people doing that to me? How can I even know? I keep most of it bottled up inside, too afraid to let it out from how damaging it can be.

Sometimes, some of it slips through the cracks, and I seem rude. I don't mean to be, I swear, I don't. I just don't know how to handle all of it.

It might merely be a little thing, something very minute. And yet, it triggers a wave of burning irritation within me. Crying uncontrollably doesn't even provide relief. I've felt *on the verge* of exploding, just as I'm on the brink of bursting now.

Why? Why do I have this constant hatred and disdain inside? Why can't I control it or let it go? *Why, why, why?*

But, what's so wrong with allowing these feelings to exist if they're not hurting anyone? Not anyone besides myself. I'm tired all the time, exhausted from having all these emotions roaming free in my mind, in my heart.

Why can't we have an off button for emotions? Why can't everything stop, just for a second?

I need time to stop, breathe, and submerge in that blank space. A blank space that doesn't exist, not in my reality. I know there's meditation, but I can't empty my mind; it's busy all the time. It's a non-stop cycle of emotions, anxiety, and overthinking.

And that makes me mad again, the fact that I can't stop my constantly running mind. I don't want to be angry; I don't. My emotions control me, sometimes, and I hate it. I'm an emotional person, and I try to live with it, but it's hard.

Music helps. When I feel I'm on edge, right *on the verge* of combusting, I listen to music. I put on my headphones and play whatever I'm in the mood to listen to. But sometimes, it only makes me angrier—lonelier. And loneliness makes me angry, makes me hateful again.

I then get angry at *time*. When time moves slowly, when time moves fast, and the fact that it doesn't stop. Why is it that when we want time to slow down, it seems to speed up? Or vice versa?

And yet, it doesn't stop, doesn't freeze. I'm not asking for days, weeks, or months. But seconds, only a couple of seconds of everything stopping, so I can breathe.

I'm always reading novels where the characters are having a moment, and all they want is for time to stop for a second. And in those moments, it feels as if I am them; I am the character. I, too, wish for time to stop, for feelings to stop. It's irrational because that can't happen; it won't happen.

We're not in a movie, it's not real. I despise the fact that it isn't. *I'm always going back to hate.*

I don't know how to stop it, I don't know how it starts, I don't know how to heal. I don't know. I hate that I don't know. I hate that I feel like crying all the time, not even knowing why.

Impotence: not being able to do something but wanting to do it so badly. My hands are tied, and I don't know how to break the knot.

I hate that I have so much more to say, express, and let out, but I don't know how to. Words are not enough to explain the pain, the pressure on my chest. Words themselves are pushing against every fiber of my being, but I push back.

And then I get angry at myself. Angry for hating myself: hating that I don't ask for help, for staying quiet, for venting to someone who doesn't care, for oversharing. Blaming myself for all the wrongs and rights that make up who I am, the things I do or say.

And yet, there's nothing more I can do—nothing else but stay silent, carrying the contempt inside. Silently praying, begging, yearning, too afraid to voice it out for real.

But, how do I even cry for help when I don't even know what I need? And how would they listen if they don't even

know what to listen *for*? Who do I talk to, pray *to*? Who's
on the other side, who's willing to listen?

An endless void of irrational hatred, unanswered
questions, and forgetful pleas, that's what burns inside.
What I'm *on the verge of* but can never quite reach: the
end of my *irascibility*.

CHAPTER II
ALEW

a·lew

(n.) [obsolete, rare] a cry of despair

"Allow despair to empty you so that an appetite for life may return." — Bobby Dasgupta

Have you ever reached a point of no return? That point of being *on the verge* of breaking, of desperation? Where all you can do is sit there and take whatever's coming and there's nothing else you can do? That moment when pain, agony is all there is, and no matter what you do, everything keeps going south?

I can't seem to find a healthy way to cope with my emotions when things don't go my way. I'm desperate for a way out, a release from this anguish apart from crying in the shower or alone in bed.

Can't I know peace? Can't I have a break from losing my mind? Can't my heart stop being in a constant cry of despair?

The worst thing is that I know I'm not on my own, not really, but it still feels that way. I know. *I know.* But sometimes, I *don't* know. What if someone's reaching for me, but I can't see it?

My heart aches, my head's spinning, and my body hurts. And I don't see the light at the end of the tunnel, but am I not seeing it unconsciously?

All I want to do is *go*, go somewhere else than where I am now, far away from it. But everything seems to be working against me, time seems to move slower, and nothing's happening. I *need* to leave, but I don't seem to be able to. I'm desperate for a sign, for a chance at a brighter future.

Do you remember when you were a kid, and all you wanted to do was grow up? Be like the successful grown-ups. What a foolish dream to have, right? Because now that we are becoming adults, all we want to be is a kid again. *That's an even more foolish idea, isn't it? We can't turn back time.*

I'm stuck. I'm stuck in that in-between where I wish to be a kid without responsibilities, but I want my freedom, my bright future. I'm stuck at that point of having no control.

Oh, that awful despair when we lose control. I don't want to cry; I don't want to feel useless or pathetic. I don't want to *see* myself crying anymore. Yet I don't know how to stop, how to take control again.

Did I ever even have control of anything? That's the thing: I hate not having control or lacking the feeling of it. But have I ever, truly? I don't know.

When you're *on the verge*, that's when you lose the most control. You're at your breaking point, and any little thing can give you that last push. I'm *on the verge* of despair and frustration right now, and one more thing will break me. *I don't want to break.*

But maybe, just maybe, that's what will help me heal. Because, before the clarity, comes the storm—the pain.

Before we can rise, we need to fall. But what's going to be that *thing*? What's going to break me, finally? That's what I'm afraid of; I already feel like breaking, but I'm not.

I can't turn back but can't move forward; I'm stuck in place, waiting. Waiting, waiting, waiting—just waiting for the next thing to go wrong, to mess me up. I'm bracing myself for it, keeping my emotions in check, bottling everything up.

How I'll hate to see that bottle break; when I'll break.

Life isn't fair, isn't it? We crave things, and we hope for the light to shine through, yet we don't allow ourselves to hope when we're down. We've hit rock bottom; we can't be any lower than that.

We soak in that despair, the desperation, and we allow it to drown us. We trick ourselves into believing we deserve it at that point, that the dawn won't come.

Now we're back on the cycle—a cycle of despair and sorrow, from which I don't see a way out. The sun won't shine tomorrow, *or so we think*. We cry, and cry, and cry; what's the use of smiling now? We're alone in our misery, believing that hoping is not worthwhile.

Despair is a dangerous emotion to have, a dangerous game to play. Despair is when you reach the point in which all you can do is sob, as if you've got nothing left to lose. I think it's worse than hate or anger. Those fade, be it with time, help, or even the realization that it's worthless.

"A cry of despair," because you have nothing else to give, only lose. *But I don't want to lose any more than I already have.* I don't want to repeat the cycle: anger, hate, despair, loneliness. How do I break it? How do I get out of something that's never-ending? *How, how, how.*

I'm not in control, not at all, and I want—*need*—it
back. I crave the feeling of it, the knowledge that things
are happening because I want them to. The power of not
allowing the dark to come in and take control of the light—
my light. But, how do I gain it? And if I do, how do I keep it
in check?

Do *you* have the answer to that question? I don't, and
maybe I never will. And maybe that's the beauty within this
darkness—the not-knowing, the 'blissful' ignorance.

You just wallow in your despair, and at that point,
that's all you know, all you feel: left alone to lament with
loud *alews*.

CHAPTER III
LORN

lorn

(adj.) lonely and abandoned, desolate or forsaken; left alone and forlorn

"The whole consciousness of my life lorn, my love lost, my hope quenched, my faith death-struck, swayed full and mighty above me in one sullen mass." — Charlotte Brontë

Lorn, what a strange word. It even lives up to its definition, seeming very lonely and forsaken. Have you ever felt that way, or is that only me and Charlotte Brontë? Struck by a loneliness so pronounced that it's not only that, it's abandonment—left behind, forgotten.

It's as if everyone close to you—the world—has moved on and left you. And it didn't matter how hard you kicked, screamed, or tried to pull them back, they still went away and are not coming back for you.

That hollowness, that emptiness that you feel inside as you watch them leave, what do you call that?

Why do they leave? Why can't they stay? Is there something wrong with me, am I not worthy enough for them? How can I even lift myself from this cold, hard floor?

Forsaken, abandoned, and pained as I watch the scene

unfold before my eyes. It doesn't make any sense. How can the world be so heartless? How can one live when it feels as if life itself is against you? How is that fair?

Plot twist: it's not.

I don't want to be alone, not like this, not forgotten by the ones I love or even the ones who don't truly know me. The strange thing is that it doesn't make me angry.

But I feel like screaming, not from anger, but anguish. Still, screaming won't be enough, not while they continue to walk away without looking back—without a goodbye.

No turning of the head, not a glimpse of a sad smile, not even a small wave; nothing. I don't know what hurts more: that they left or that they didn't care enough to say goodbye. A goodbye means some sort of closure, a sliver of a path to healing the pain.

Can you at least explain why? What reason could you possibly have that will justify you leaving me sobbing, heartbroken, and *lorn*? But they don't give me a reason, leaving me to my devices with a whirlwind of emotions.

Every piece of me aches with every dark emotion in existence. I can't move, I'm stuck in place and no one but myself can help me now. I don't know how. I don't know how to fix my broken self. I don't know how to mend the pieces back together.

No amount of tape is enough. No amount of medicine can heal my wounds. Nothing can help when it feels like my world is coming to an end.

If I stop caring, if I turn off my emotions, will that make it easier? What if I forget about them? Do I stop feeling so empty? Will I ever get answers to my questions?

More importantly, why *should* I care when they didn't

even think twice about leaving *me*? It was as if their bags were already packed, as if it was planned ahead of time.

Their actions didn't seem hasty: they seemed calm and collected. How can you be calm while abandoning someone, abandoning a home?

But is this even a home if there's no one but you in it? How can it be a home if it feels like pain? How can it be of comfort to anyone when all it does is remind them of everything they've lost?

Isn't home supposed to be the place where you feel safe, protected, and surrounded by warmth? All it is now is a cold and endless void where silence is louder than noise, where color has turned gray, and light has turned into darkness.

The memories that made you smile only bring you sorrow, and heartache. What once was my source of comfort is now the source of my pain.

This home is not my own anymore, but it's also no one else's. But can it still be my home even though I don't recognize it anymore, when it doesn't feel like it is?

It's empty, hollow, forsaken, forgotten...like me. *Maybe it is my home, just a different version of each other*.

People say change is good, that it's always for the better. Would you consider losing everything you knew, being abandoned, and feeling lost as something *good*? I wouldn't, no one should.

What, am I supposed to smile even though I'm broken? There aren't even any clouds in the sky, even they left me.

How will I be okay? How is any of this okay? What's the use of smiling if I have no reason to do so?

There's no use in trying when hope is gone, when all there's left is agony.

No, I'm not okay, this is not okay. None of this is, and I'm not *fine*; I'm tired of saying I'm *fine* when I'm not. Will I be okay someday? I don't know, I hope so—though I don't believe it myself. *Who am I lying to now? There's only me and my thoughts.*

All I know, all I am now are broken pieces of my soul, my heart that I don't know how to fix. All I see when I stand in the mirror is a distorted vision of myself: *lorn* and somber, a far cry from who I used to be.

CHAPTER IV

LACUNA

la·cu·na

(n.) a blank space or a missing part

"I seem to enjoy telling stories with a central absence,
with a lacuna tunneled into them." — Junot Díaz

When was the last time you felt whole, complete? I can't remember, not exactly when. It's a distant memory, a foggy thought of a "happier time" that I'm not even sure existed.

But I shouldn't complain, I've lived a good life so far. I've had comfort, a home, food, not many money problems, and a great education.

Why *should* I complain? Is it even a question I should be asking myself: why am I complaining when I've had more than most people have?

But then, why do I still feel empty? Why do I feel incomplete, as if something's missing within me? What burdens me enough for me to write about it? What's creating this *lacuna* inside?

*How do I find that answer, and where do I start looking?*I think this is one of those unanswerable situations in life: the big questions.

Sometimes, if I try hard enough, I can feel myself being

on the verge of finding the truth. But have I said that life is unfair? It's one step forward and two, three steps back—stuck in place

How do I heal a wound when I don't know where it came from? How do I feel complete when I don't know what's lacking? How do I find answers when all I come up with are more questions? How do I stop crying when I don't have a reason to?

How, how, how—all I have are hows. I *want* to let go, I *want* to move on and find peace, I *want*. And I wish it were easier, easier to express myself, to go for what I need, to *be*.

Can someone tell me what or how to do it? Is there an answer key, or a cheat sheet? *Am I just scared of finding out the truth, is that it?*

Everything I do or try feels wrong, like a sin, like I can't have forgiveness. I try, and I try, and I try, but it's still not enough to heal what's broken. How is it even helping when the whirlwind of thoughts never stops, and I'm still left feeling empty?

I want to ask for help. But when I'm feeling everything and nothing at the same time, what do I say? Will anyone even understand the hurt?

Am I the one to blame? Am I the problem? Am I hating myself enough to cause the emptiness, to push people away? Is the surrounding quiet a product of my creation, of my doing?

Telling myself I'm doing fine when I'm not. Praying for an answer to someone I'm not sure if I still believe in, and only getting silence in return. A silence so loud that it gives the doubts a free pass to occupy every space.

"It's okay not to be okay." But who is that for and who's

listening? I want to say that I agree, that it *is* okay *not* to be okay, but I don't. I'm still *not okay*, I'm still hurt, and I still feel broken and empty.

I'm not myself anymore...*but did I ever know who I am?* How do I know what "being complete" means when I have no knowledge of what's missing? It's as if I'm working on a puzzle that has no bigger picture, no guide; doing it blindly.

To which I ask myself: what's the point, then? What's the goal of putting together the pieces? What do we gain in return? A place in society as a fully functioning human being—a pawn on a board.

I refuse to experience a sense of inadequacy, worthlessness, or being discarded. Why should I work on "my better self" when further down the line I'll be back at the start? Why should I find the perfect puzzle pieces when no one really cares about the final picture?

Who says I have to dry my tears when not even I recognize myself in the mirror? I already feel empty, why should I break my heart and soul repeatedly when the result will be the same? Why should I change the lenses through which I'm watching myself when all I'll see is the same *lacuna*?

Was there even something to fix to begin with? Would I be complete then? What if, by obsessing over feigning completeness, I broke myself? I don't know, I don't *need* to know—I don't *care*, not anymore.

Empty, whole, glass-half-full: at the end of the day, it's all the same; I'll be judged anyway. And I wonder how long it will take humanity to realize that we're all floating in the same insignificant *lacuna*.

CHAPTER V

ABDITORY

ab·di·to·ry

(n.) a place into which you can disappear, a hiding place

"An abditory for every soul is ultimately within the soul itself."
— *Asma Beeran*

Where do you go when you want to run, but have nowhere to run off *to*? Where do you go when you want to hide? What's your *abditory*? *I don't think I have one.*

When everything goes wrong, when life hits, and you wish to escape, where do you go? I have nowhere to go, nowhere to run; just an endless road that leads to nothing. *Is this what my life's become, a prison?*

A prison of my rambling thoughts, of my caged heart and mind, of misunderstood feelings and sleepless nights. With nowhere to escape, to hide.

What am I supposed to do when I have no one to keep me company, only my whimpering soul? What am I supposed to do when I'm spiraling out of control, when my feelings go numb, to block out the pain?

Why am I even saying all this? Who cares, who's listening? The sun won't shine brighter above me solely because I express how I feel. Just as this road won't lead me to my *abditory*.

I'm tired of running, my legs are shaking from carrying the weight of my thoughts and aching heart. My breath is bated, coming out short. But I don't stop, I can't; not until I have somewhere *to* stop.

Can someone tell me where to stop or rest? I don't know where I'm going, or where my pain is taking me.

It's as if the longer I stay running on this path the harder it gets to breathe, to keep going, as if the road itself is closing in on me.

Why won't this path come to an end? Why do I have to keep pushing myself to the brink of self-destruction? Where is my *abditory*, my safe space to hide? Please, someone, answer me, whoever is listening.

Am I alone in this? Am I the only one searching for that hiding place to no avail? Am I the only one tearing myself apart in the quiet?

My lungs don't even have the strength to yell out anymore, the surrounding silence would swallow it if they did. And who would listen if I did? The God above whom I've neglected, who I stopped praying to?

Would he even notice if the sky above me is so dark that not even the sun rays shine through? How can I even have hope when the darkness surrounding me consumes it?

What about dreams...I can't even remember the last time I dreamt, they're all nightmares.

Praying, waiting, hoping, running... An endless cycle of disappointing myself for expecting things that will never come to rescue me. Is my soul even worth rescuing anymore?

How far is too far gone for salvation, for redemption?

Am I even moving forward, or am I only going backward? Which direction am I supposed to follow when the path breaks into multiple ones? *What's my yellow-brick road? Should I even care at all?*

Here I am talking about finding my *abditory* when it feels as if I'm running in place: neither forward nor backward—stuck. Where's my escape, my salvation? An emergency exit, anything to help me get out of this hell I'm in. Nothing?

How much longer until I can't keep going, until my body gives out? How much more can I bear? Should I put myself out of my misery...*is that even an option?*

This world is cold, laughing at my misery. It doesn't knock me down or encourage me to reach the stars; it just mocks. It pushes me to the point where my heart continues to break, my breathing fails, and my body aches.

Why can't this misery let me go? When I lose my way and drift away, it keeps holding on. But to what? There's nothing left of me, no more fighting. Only a hiding place could free me from the brink of insanity.

I used to be a dreamer, the one to imagine wonderful places to which I could escape. But all I did then was break my own heart, lying to myself that I would reach those places.

The sound of silence is all I know now, taking up the space where the light lived...*maybe this is my abditory.*

CHAPTER VI
ATELOPHOBIA

a·tel·o·pho·bia

(n.) the fear of imperfection, the fear of never being good enough

"The bright sorrow is always ringing, always ringing, and fading into forgetting." — "atelophobia," Jonathan Chan

What happens when you burn out? After the curtain has closed and you can't keep up the appearance anymore. Is my *atelophobia* actually real or just an excuse to appease my fears of vulnerability?

Am I hiding behind a mask of perfection because that's how the world molds us? Or did I grow up in an environment that did not allow anything *but* perfection? Why do I laugh out the uncomfortable moments of truth? Why do I put up a smile when all it does is hurt me inside?

If I ran away, would I be judged for escaping reality? *Why do I even care, who would care?*

If I left it all behind because I couldn't take the pressure of perfection anymore, who would I hurt? Myself? I can't hurt myself more than I already have by not being who I truly am.

Why can't I leave that mask behind? And when I look

at my reflection, why don't I like what I see—who I see? I hold on to this "meaning" of perfection, this self-imposed definition of who I am—who I'm *supposed* to be.

Maybe that was me at some point, maybe I did look at myself in the mirror and recognized the image in front of me. But what if that image expired and I just kept going?

I'm holding on to that version of myself, as if my self-worth depended on it. As if no other option would be good enough. *As if I wouldn't be good enough.*

What would happen if I stepped into the light without that mask of perfection? Would my *atelophobia* bring me back down? Would people even recognize who I am without it, who I've become?

Does it all define me, these ghosts of my past and my life? Is this why I keep going, this fear that ties me down? Living life on autopilot, not recognizing that each step I take is a step further into losing myself to the motion of it all.

Why doesn't anyone stop me? Does no one realize that I'm stuck on this endless path of self-destruction? Are they as lost as I am in their own *atelophobia* that they can't see past it?

Why do we create different versions of ourselves that others will accept? Why are our true selves not enough? *Why am I not enough?*

All I want is to be proud of myself, proud of who I am and what I have become. All I want is to be released from this caging prison. Isn't the first step to acknowledge the problem, admitting the fear? Why isn't *that* enough?

What if it's always been enough, *I've* always been enough, and I've just never let the fear go? Did I do this to myself, or was it done to me? Have I become *something*, a never-ending machine? Or was I molded into that?

If I am *so perfect*, then why do I hide my thorns, my flaws? Why am I so afraid to show my vulnerability, to show myself as I truly am? I am so confined to people's points of view that I have lost mine, lost my sense of humanity.

It's hard to leave that version of myself in the past. But perfect's just too much to ask, and that's hard to say. Why do I put so much pressure on myself, keeping up appearances just to please others' unrealistic expectations of me?

Why should I be the one crying myself to sleep? Why should I be the one covering my tracks so no one sees the truth? Why can't I allow myself to show what's beyond the surface, below the shallow end? Is the pill that hard to swallow?

Am I putting myself out of reach? Am I so afraid of rejection that I don't even try anymore? What's so wrong with being good enough for *me*?

Are the scars I hide under my skin so horrible to see? Layer after layer, my true self is buried so deep inside that I haven't even seen her in a while.

I can feel myself withdrawing from the world, hiding behind that wall of perfection. And I don't even know if I care... I've barely even lived, and I'm already scared of living life for myself.

There are so many things I want to do, so many things I want to write. And yet, I lean against that wall in restriction—my crippling *atelophobia*.

CHAPTER VII

MARCID

mar·cid

(adj.) withered; shrunken; wasted away

"Who is to decide which is the grimmer sight: withered hearts, or empty skulls?" — Honore de Balzac

How much is too much? How do you know when you've had enough? Is it when you hit a wall? When your *marcid* soul has gone far beyond repair? When your heart has been torn to pieces?

I've learned that time waits for no one, especially for those who have no more stories left to tell. How do I rush against time when my mind, my creativity, has withered; *marcid,* and useless? Do I fight against my survival instincts, or do I just give up?

But how can I avert my eyes and pretend it's not happening when it's all that surrounds me? *Is this the best I can do? Have I reached my limits? Am I really this unable to exceed my own [unrealistic] expectations?*

Is this all I've become? A withering heart and soul, wasting away on the floor. Why am I even trying, looking for a reason? If I'm running out of time...maybe I should let the good things die.

I can't summon up any more energy or hope when it's

not even in me in the first place. Does it make me cry? Yes, all the time, but what's the point? Do I stop wishing for more time, for forever, if nothing lasts?

This feeling that things are ending...makes me want to say goodbye. *To what? To whom?* And how do I even say goodbye when I'm too weak to get up, too tired and resigned?

Who do I trust with this pain? Who can I count on to help me heal? *Is there even anything to heal, any hope left? Are there any more tears left to cry...does it even matter?*

And if it does...who's left to care? Who will help me bear, help me carry, the weight of my pain?

Why is there always a trigger, a breaking point? And what's mine...? What causes me to become this? What pushes me over the edge, to the point where there's nothing left but remnants of who I was?

How do I know if I'm too far gone? Or how much I have left to save?

And yet...I don't think there's anything I can do to stop it, to plant my feet firmly on the ground and not bend. I'm not sure if I'm strong enough, don't know if I can handle it.

I'm not sure if it even hurts, as if I'm now numb to the pain.

It's as if life has dealt me so many blows that I've now learned to expect it, doesn't even catch me off-guard. And I'm so used to it that I can't tell how bad it is.

Is being numb part of becoming *marcid*? Or is numbness my newfound survival instinct? Is this how I'll handle the pain from now on, phasing through it as if it means nothing? *As if I mean nothing...?*

What's *life* anymore, what's it worth? What's my meaning, my purpose? *If* I even have one...would I know how to use it, *what* to do with it? Would it even be useful if I can't muster up the energy to water my soul, to give life back to it?

Are these tears running down my face? How can I still be able to cry, able to hurt? *What else did I expect? And what more could I bear, handle?* Is this what I've come down to, an insignificant, withered entity?

How can I turn back to who I was? Is it too late? Will time wait for me? *But time waits for no one...not even for those willing to try. ...am I willing?*

Does time even want anything to do with me? Does it remember I exist, acknowledge me?

Can time forget...ignore? I don't know, I don't know anything at this point. Am I even worth anything to *life* at all now?

There's nothing left for me to do. My hands are tied and I can't escape. *At least I think they are.* Is it all in my head? Am I seeing things that aren't there?

Am I doing this to myself? Do I have some kind of debt to pay, am I punishing myself for it?

Who would even know? Who would even care, notice? Who can help me free myself from my self-imposed barriers? Is there even anything left to be saved? Is my now *marcid* soul worth redeeming or healing?

Too many questions, too few answers. Too much pain, heartache. Too much quietness. Too much everything, too much nothing.

No one to answer them, no one to help me heal, no one to break the silence, too much...

CHAPTER VIII

UKIYO

uki·yo

(n.) "the floating world" – living in the moment, detached
from the bothers of life

"Live only for the moment...drifting, always drifting."
— *Shōgun, James Clavell*

Ukiyo, "the floating world;" how is this supposed to
feel? Is *Ukiyo* known to be a peaceful escape, of feeling
free? Is this what "living your best life" means? If it is...
then why do I just feel lost, floating in nothingness?

I don't know what I'm doing, or how I got here. It feels
like this escape has been wasted on me, as if I don't deserve
it. But how do I get out, or give it up to someone else who
needs it, deserves it, more?

*Do I even have a fighting chance against the "forces of
the universe"?* And who are those forces? Are they tangible,
are they spirits? Who am I even asking...and who can
answer me?

What do I do with this opportunity? Is this a chance to
fix myself, to put my broken pieces back together? I don't
think I can, I'm not sure that I have enough strength left in
me. I'm not sure if *I'm* enough...

I have scars around my heart, wounds that haven't
healed and might never do. So how can I be in *Ukiyo*? How

can I be "living peacefully in the moment" when I'm not even sure I'm deserving of peace?

What did I do right? And how can it be right when it all feels wrong? Maybe in another life, this is exactly where I'd rather be...maybe it would be where I'm *supposed* to be.

Maybe I would've taken this chance and made the right use of it. But I'm not in another life, I'm in this one. *Whatever that may be...*

Does this mean that there's hope? That I might get through this, see the other side? Or am I being led astray? Can someone just tell me what to do—how to get through this?

What if I'm dreaming? If I held my breath, would I wake up? Would I find myself back on the floor holding myself together? Or if I close my eyes, would it keep me hidden from what's hurting me?

What if I open my eyes and I'm still here? What if this is my "new home"? Surely someone will lend a hand and lead me to a safe place to land.

But what if no one does... If this *is* a safe place...why don't I know how to be in it? Would I fall? Would someone catch me if I did? *Who would... Should I pray for peace instead?*

And if I do, would He listen? Would *He* grant me peace of mind? Would *He* allow me to rest in my newfound *Ukiyo*? Or would *He* send me back down to reality? ... *would He punish me instead?*

What if I don't want to let go? I want to stay here, explore this place, and what I'm supposed to do with this second chance. *If it even is a "second chance..."*

I just need a sign! Something telling me, proof, that I'm

not just going crazy—losing my mind. Is this the window of opportunity I've been waiting for after all my doors closed? What if I'm already missing it by being too much into my head, drowning in my thoughts?

The stars and planets aren't aligning. There's no "light at the end of the tunnel." There's no one calling my name, being there for me. The universe doesn't care that I'm hurting. This *Ukiyo* is just a figment of my imagination— I'm not here, it's not real.

So, what, life's merely playing a sick, twisted game with me? Having a laugh at my expense? Or am I being too cynical and this is truly happening, I'm getting a second chance at turning my life around?

But how do I stop my mind from spinning? How do I stop myself from self-sabotaging the one thing I've been waiting—praying—for?

Can I really do this on my own? Can I allow myself to breathe, to soak in the peace and quiet? Can this moment calm the turmoil in my soul, my heart?

Have I been doing this to myself all along, wallowing in my misery? Have I been sent here to be reborn?

Maybe I *should* allow myself to dive in, to stop hiding away, to stop swimming in my head. Maybe all love and hope are not lost. Maybe life is not what I've been thinking. Maybe I *can* mend my own heart. Maybe everyone's misunderstood, not just me.

Maybe I can stop pushing myself away, pushing away the help of others. Maybe someone is out there—has been out there all along.

Maybe, this *is* my *Ukiyo*. And maybe, *just maybe*, I can remember what it is to be human.

CHAPTER IX

WHELVE

whelve

(v.) to bury or hide something deeply inside oneself

"The secret was whelved so deeply in her heart." —
Unknown

Do you sometimes get flashbacks of your past life, of who you used to be—flashbacks to when you didn't use to *whelve* your true self? To a life where everything seemed fine, when everything didn't seem lost; *when you didn't overthink everything.*

I don't, I'm not even sure that time existed. *Or am I blocking it from my mind, ignoring it?* I can say "I love me," but words are not enough anymore.

How am I supposed to make others believe that when I'm not even sure myself, when I whelve that too deep down...? Is it possible to feel hollow while hiding everything deep inside?

Why am I like this? Why do I overthink to the point where I can no longer distinguish what's real, and what's just in my head? Why can't I stop myself? Why do I let my thoughts run wild and for too long?

Why does my true self only surface when I'm alone? What am I trying to hide from others? Is there something so deeply wrong or disturbing about myself?

Am I afraid that showing who I truly am might make others scurry away from me? Have I been hurt so badly in the past that I can't even let the sunlight in?

And here I am, *whelving* my true self between my walls, hiding behind my pains and sorrows. Is it the stares, the laughter, the fake smile, and the masks people wear?

How can I show up, heart on my sleeve, when I know all I'll feel is judgment? They don't love this version of me, the one I built through the years. Why would they love the real one?

Does that mean that I might not love myself enough? ...am I not worthy of love, not even mine? Or am I just overthinking over and over again until there's no other thought left?

Have I been telling myself that I'm fine, that I'm okay, long enough to believe? Was I lying all these years to the point where it's now out of control? But lying about what: that I'm fine, or that I had to hide? *Which one is it, how do I even know?*

Have I been gambling my soul away for a piece of society, to fit in with the crowd? It's a fine line between faking it and becoming it if you do it long enough.

When did I cross it? When did I finally bury all of me and become numb to life? And how far away am I from that line? Do I have time to go back? *Do I deserve this...to have my life back?*

What would "going back" look like? What could be my first step? How can I see myself, see who I was, and become that person once again? Is there any strength or fight left in me?

I don't want to do this alone...why am I always alone?

Is there anyone out there, anyone who "sees" me? I don't see myself.

Does this mean my growing part is over? No more colors to discover, just black and white. Fear is all there will be now: afraid of slipping, always living in perfection, no freedom, no healing—an endless cycle.

"Don't be so hard on yourself," is what I want to hear. "Look up," something inside me would be screaming. And when I do, something would shift, would change.

There would be light, something to follow, somewhere where my spirit would live again. Would I believe it? Would I follow it, or would I stay behind my walls?

Would I trick myself into thinking it's just a figment of my imagination? Would I be able to accept it and make the change? Would I be capable of tearing down the walls and letting my true self out?

Could I rip the masks off, and snap them into unfixable pieces? Could I start over—let the darkness out and the sunlight in? Could I face myself and accept that loneliness is part of the process? *Would I be enough for myself?*

And if I took that chance, what if the sun sets on it, on me? What if time runs out while overthinking my options? What if by the time I realize that I *can* do this on my own, life has already passed me by?

What would life even be? What does the world look like when you release who you are? How would I feel if I stopped living as a prisoner inside my own mind?

All these questions and the million more to come can only be answered if I *un-whelve* who I am...

CHAPTER X

NEPENTHE

ne·pen·the

(n.) something capable of causing oblivion of grief or
suffering

"It takes away my memory like a cup of nepenthe."
— *Théophile Gautier*

Wouldn't that be poetic, drinking a cup of *nepenthe*
to obliviate the memories of grief and sorrow? To be able
to start from scratch—a clean slate from the pain that
held you back. How else am I supposed to move on? What
options do I have?

Can I hide the pain away, bury it deep inside until
it's nothing but a faint memory? Would it work, would it
resurface?

I wish this existed: a poison that could turn suffering
into oblivion. Would the mind be powerful enough to block
it out, erase it from memory? Make it so distant that I'll
forget it was there at all, *forget what loneliness feels like.*

Should I ask for help? Or is it too late to save me
from myself? Am I still redeemable, or am I just my most
beautiful regret? How can I, when even I have run out of
expectations for myself? And if I'm worth holding on to,
why have I already let go?

Am I abandoning myself? Am I ignoring the signs? Am

I letting my sorrows drown me when I can try to reach the surface? Can I carry this pain with me for the rest of my life? Is there truly no way to leave it behind?

Every step I take, every attempt I make to move forward, is being held down by the wrath of my anguish— haunting me.

How can I have peace when there's not even a moment of silence in my mind? The memories chase me, follow me like a shadow.

If I bury them, how long will it take until their withering scent resurfaces and drags me back down with it? How long would I be able to hold on? Wouldn't it be safer to stay here, where I'm surrounded by it and It's already hurting me?

Why would I allow myself the ephemeral respite, only to succumb to it once again somewhere down the line? This cruelty of life is never-ending, isn't it? Laughing in my face, kicking me while I'm already down. When will it be enough? When can I break free from these chains?

Why do I have to keep hiding away? Why do I push others—myself—away? If all is lost, why am I still breaking my own heart? If *I'm* lost, why am I trying so hard to be found?

If I just get a little taste of what's waiting ahead, the tiniest slice of life, maybe it wouldn't all be for nothing. If I could get a sign, maybe I can keep going. If I could get my hands on something, anything, that can help keep the pain at bay, maybe I'm not hopeless yet.

If I could catch a flicker of sunshine, maybe there's no need to stay trapped in the dark, for my true self to stay hidden. If I catch a glimpse of Spring or Summer, maybe

Winter won't be eternal. *Too many ifs, too many maybes...*

I can feel myself going out of my mind, slowly losing it with each passing second. What if I just take the keys and lock the door?

Would that be possible, to lock it in and lose the key? Would it eventually return, find its way back to me, and make the pain resurface?

Was this an option all along, a silver lining underneath the despair? Have I been wallowing so much that I forgot how to breathe it out? But that's how I've always been, feeling sorry for myself until it eventually numbs.

But is there still a chance? Is there hope of remembering how to live again? Did I ever even know how to live, or did the pain make me forget?

Could I make new memories, try to erase the old wounds? Could it be a replacement for *nepenthe*—an actual answer to my worries?

Maybe it's not all lost after all...

CHAPTER XI

MELIORISM

me·lio·rism

(n.) the belief that the world gets better; the belief that humans can improve the world

"Perhaps I don't deserve nice things 'cause I'm paying for sins I don't remember." — milk and honey, Rupi Kaur

Is my feeble *meliorism* just a cowardly attempt at lying to myself? Is holding on to this belief helping me heal...or is it destroying me further? If nobody's listening, what's the point of believing it gets better?

Isn't it part of our humanity to go through pain and sorrow? Isn't it normal to feel scared, to hide away? *Why am I blaming and punishing myself for these things when it's all part of being alive?*

Everything I do feels like a *sin...but is it, really?* If I'm already open to pain, why can't I be open to experiencing happiness?

Am I closing myself off when it should be the opposite? Am I neglecting myself the experience of freedom? Could the world truly get better, can humanity?

Could my sins be forgiven? ...are they sins, or just human behavior?

If questioning myself over and over what it feels like to be human—to be alive—then I'm not sure if I still want it.

*Is it even my choice? ...what if I'm not the only one? What
if there are others out there experiencing loneliness?*

But how can I find them, where do I even start, when
I can't pick up my own pieces? How do I help others pick
up theirs when I'm broken myself? How can I trust my
meliorism if I don't fully believe in it?

What if this is just a distraction, tricking my mind into
thinking it's healing when, in reality, it's destroying me
further—a mirage? Or has my pain been a facade all along,
have I always held hope?

Have I poured all my hopes and dreams into my fears,
keeping them hidden until I felt it was safe to let them
out? Am I ready to cross that faint line between faith and
sorrow? Am I ready to refill the empty parts of me, to
believe—begin— again?

I'd be lying if I said I wasn't scared anymore, that I was
free. Every day feels like I'm nonstop running from fire,
like I'm surrounded—consumed—by it. But am I ready to
force myself to stop, to take a breath, and put it out?

What if breaking free from my chains makes me lose
myself again? What if this light just leads me to more
darkness? Is it worth the risk? It won't be easy, that's the
only thing I'm sure of.

What if I'm *on the verge* of something great, and yet, I
can't give myself the final push?

What if I can't jump, take the leap? What if this all
goes to waste? What if this was all for nothing? Would I get
another chance? Could I have that choice again?

Am I stealing my ability to light up my own life, self-
sabotaging? Have I been doing it for the sake of a comfort
zone? Have I been caging myself behind walls built under

my own hands? *It's all lies...*

How am I just now realizing this? How could I have failed myself so much? Have I held myself to such a high and unfair standard that I've forgotten how to live?

Did I overthink to the point of betraying my own mind—believing it was done to me instead?

Was it supposed to go this way, go this wrong? Was I supposed to escape it, and how long ago? Was I supposed to extinguish the flames instead of lighting them further? *Is it my fault...?*

How can this be living when I was merely surviving? How can I believe in the light again when all I've had is darkness? How can I open my eyes when all I've done is blind them? How can I have faith when all I've experienced is doubt—doubt in myself, in the world?

Should I trust humanity again? Should I hold on to hope, even if I can't see that far ahead? Should I believe there's a tomorrow after only having a today for so long?

And if it's human experience to feel hurt, maybe it's also human to open myself to happiness. Maybe, *just maybe*, there's hope after all. And maybe, somehow, *meliorism* is not a hopeless belief to have.

And maybe...just a sliver of it...losing myself was the new becoming of who I was meant to be.

CHAPTER XII

KOMOREBI

ko·more·bi

(n.) sunlight that filters through the leaves of trees

"Don't call it uncertainty—call it wonder. Don't call it insecurity—call it freedom." — Osho

Is this what hope feels like? Is this what they call freedom? Have I found my place of serenity—my *komorebi*? Or am I just dreaming...? Would I wake up back in my dark place? Or is this finally it—my safe haven?

I'm done holding onto the past, the pain; it's no longer here to stay. I no longer deserve pain. I should accept this love for myself, and let my heart move along with it.

Maybe this loneliness has been a sign that I've been in desperate need of myself all along.

And maybe I wasn't born to fall and fail, it was just preparing me with the strength to rise. I should be thanking the universe instead of blaming it. It has taken what it needed to take, and now it's giving me everything I need to thrive.

I don't want to see myself crying anymore. I don't want to keep catching my reflection, crumbling down on the floor. But it'll be tough to believe and accept: Accept that tomorrow will come, that it's possible.

Maybe today will be difficult, but I finally believe I can get through this.

The hurting will pass, and I'll be able to move forward. All I needed to do was give it time: time to heal, time to let it go, time to let it break, time to feel complete.

Is this me accepting myself as I was designed?

Maybe the world has given me so much pain so I could eventually make something out of it. Maybe it's what I was supposed to do all along and I took too much time.

Is it too late? Do I turn around, go back to what I was before? Not when I found my *komorebi*, I found the place where I'm supposed to be: where I can wonder and be free.

If the sun can dance through the leaves, so can I. If nature can keep itself company, so can I. If music can be its own melody, so can I.

If memories can heal, so can I. And if they all can make it through the trauma—the pain—and pick up the pieces, so can I.

Maybe it's not supposed to be easy, maybe it never was. Maybe I was supposed to fight through the pain, not succumb to it. Maybe the sun was always shining, and I just hid from it, believing I had to.

Maybe I was supposed to kick those old habits aside. Maybe I should've been trying harder. There are always too many *maybes*, but they don't matter anymore, not when I've made it this far.

I don't have to "fill the empty parts of me," I'm already complete on my own. *Maybe I always was...* How much time did I lose—waste—kicking myself down, hating parts of myself?

Maybe if I knew what safety felt like I would have

spent less time falling deeper into the darkness. Maybe I wouldn't have sadness living in places where they shouldn't be. There's no bigger illusion in the world.

I've replayed the pain so many times that I forgot how to live. But now it's over... I'm no longer at war with myself. I no longer have to hold on to my sorrow.

I no longer have to give in to the lies I've told myself. I no longer have to succumb. No longer is the shadow of who I used to be.

Isn't that freeing? Isn't it a relief to break free of the chains that were holding me down? Isn't it liberating to breathe in the air of what my future holds? Isn't it hopeful to not be going backward?

It makes me think...what comes next? What does tomorrow look like for me? What lies ahead? And maybe that can't be put into words.

Maybe it can't be translated. Maybe this feeling can't be expressed.

What if, perhaps, I am my own *komorebi*? And, what if, I can relish in it for eternity?

on the verge

CHAPTER XIII

EUDAEMONIA

eu·dae·mo·nia

(n.) "human flourishing;" a content state of being happy, healthy, and prosperous

"Bloom beautifully, loudly, bloom softly; however you need, just bloom." — milk and honey, Rupi Kaur

"Eudaemonia," human flourishing; what a beautiful term, and maybe what I needed all along. It's the reason for believing that not all hope is gone, that life goes on—worth living.

But I had to change, or let life change me. *But is that enough? Will it last? Will I lose it again?*

No, no more self-doubt, no more second-guessing; it's my time to bloom, to allow myself to dream again. *I can't even remember the last time I let myself fly free. Has this really been me all along, just hiding?*

Maybe if I would've stayed strong from the beginning... who knows? Doesn't matter, there's no space to dwell on the past anymore—all that's left is space for growth, for blooming; time to bridge the gap that's been broken apart in my mind.

And maybe my dreams will just be dreams now, instead of my haunting past—my new beginning.

But where will I go next, what's my home now? It's

been a long, long time. Do I go back to where I came from, and risk drowning in my memories? Or do I move forward and find someplace new to call home?

What if it's not a place, it's a someone...? Could that be the answer I've been looking for?

Maybe I'm strong enough now, strong enough to grow, to bloom into someone new. And maybe these new flowers will lead me to where I'm supposed to be—who *I'm* supposed to be.

There's so much I don't know, so much left to explore of the world, of myself. I've always thought I had to be alone, but who said it's true?

Growing doesn't have to happen on my own. The highs, the lows; maybe I can grow as I go, take it slow.

I am now a work in progress, unfinished but with so much new space for change. And, who knows, maybe I'll encounter someone whose purpose is to join me on my journey.

I don't know who I'll become. That might be the point of all of this, the point of "what's next." Maybe what's next it's freedom. Freedom to branch out, to break free from fear, to find a place where I belong without regrets.

Maybe it was written in the stars, maybe not. Once it's done, I know it will be better. A change is what I needed to push forward, to inch closer toward the dream life.

Have you ever dreamed of a perfect life—a life in which you are truly happy and fulfilled? But what does that "dream life" look like exactly? What am I walking and aiming towards?

Is it love? Is it success? Is it health? Is it a career? Is it all of the above? *Can I even have it all?*

All paths are open. It's not just one "yellow-brick road" anymore. I can choose and walk them all. Or I could pick one and change my mind later—it's up to me now.

It's not about *surviving*; it's about *living*. How else can I appreciate my new life if all I'm doing is trudging along one day at a time?

Rupi Kaur explains it best: "Stay strong through your pain, grow flowers from it, you have helped me grow flowers out of mine."

So then, maybe, *eudaemonia* can be more than just a state of mind. Maybe, hopefully, we can aim higher than wistful thinking and let ourselves bloom, flourish.

CHAPTER XIV

ATARAXIA

at·a·rax·ia

(n.) a state of serene calmness

*"Freedom from irrational fears and anxieties of all sorts –
in brief, peace of mind." — Epicurus*

Ataraxia, is this what makes life worth living after
surviving the chaos—the calm after the storm? *Is this
happening? Am I truly allowing myself to experience
some peace of mind?*

It feels like this is the beginning of something— of my
brighter future.

I deserve more, *I've always deserved more,* maybe
I'm just finally accepting that. I deserve to be one with my
surroundings, not fighting against them.

Could this be my *ataraxia,* my peace? I've been so
used to believing that all my days would be the same, like
a broken promise. *Maybe some promises are meant to be
mended back together.*

Time, time was all I needed—all I wanted to have. Time
to stop and smell the roses, to hear the birds sing, to see
the trees dance with the wind, time to let nature heal me
how it heals itself.

I am who I am now, and I'm okay with that. I've left
behind what no longer fits me, and I'm okay with that.
Maybe I should've accepted this a long time ago, or maybe

it wasn't the right time and now it is.

If I wasn't supposed to be here...then I wouldn't be here, right now, in the first place. And that's a beautiful thought to have.

This moment, this sense of calmness, roots me. It roots me to the ground I walk on, to the tears I shed for myself, to the stars that guide me in my new path.

I can finally stop searching, stop looking for the "why" behind my past self. The "now" is enough for me, and all I desire is to keep exploring it.

Of course, I want a future. But what is a future if I don't build it in the present? What used to terrify me to the very core, pushing me back into my shell, I now struggle to understand. *The power of time and finding calmness.*

And maybe I should crumble, succumb back into the darkness. But my heart and soul yearn for a new life, for *ataraxia. And nothing sounds safer to me.*

Safety...what I would've given to know what that truly felt like.

The feeling of safety now fills the parts of me that used to be empty, that didn't seem like my own. That security makes me feel complete, as if the whole world has opened up to me.

I understand now that life is meant to be lived, to be enjoyed, to be beautiful. Who am I to neglect life's wishes? And if that's its desire for me, then I must oblige—I must *live.*

Yes, I'm still growing, still learning, and finding myself. But I'm not the only one, we're all unfinished. And there's nothing wrong with being unfinished. It only means that we have ways to go, we're not written in the stars...yet.

Life and the future it holds will come in due time. And when it does, it will call my name, it will hold me close in its arms, and it will soothe the pain away because it knows the past has been hard enough.

And I'd be lying if I said that I doubt the peace, the calm protecting me now. I might still be weak when the time comes. I might wish to go back.

But I won't...because peace is all I know now, it has freed me. And now that I've tasted freedom, there's no way my chains can hold me back again. *Ataraxia* is my new state of mind, my new state of being.

CHAPTER XV

SELCOUTH

sel·couth

(adj.) unfamiliar, rare, strange, and yet, marvelous

"A selcouth soul, dark and beautiful." — Amoret

A *selcouth* soul, is that what I am now? Is that what I'm meant to be, something so unfamiliar and yet tastes so freeing? Light and lively, while also dark and alluring.

It's as if I've uncovered the secrets behind the complexity of life, of a soul. So close yet so far out of reach, I can almost smell it in the air, can almost feel it in my fingertips.

What lies beyond those doors? What are they hiding? What's so worthy of such mystery?

If I take the next steps toward freedom, toward true peace, will I stumble? Am I meant to keep going further than I've reached so far? What's keeping me from going?

Whatever it is, it lures me forward, tempting me with promises of a better tomorrow. Should I embrace the unknown, the uncharted territories, and surrender myself to unfamiliarity? Would it be too much to ask for a clear answer, a clear mind?

Like a siren song, it calls my name. A melody strong enough to keep me entrapped in its tune but foggy enough to not recognize the words, yet. A *selcouth* game of life.

Do I play? Or do I quit and sit in my freedom, in my new space, unchanging? Do I let this newfound thirst for life consume my will, or do I quench it?

And if I wait too long, what happens then? Will the decision be made for me? Or will it exist for as long as I can hear its song? Do I bring my guard up or do I succumb to the pull?

Two paths, both mine to choose, and both honorable at their core. *Isn't this what I was searching, longing, for? Isn't this a result of my treacherous past?*

The answer should be clear...but why isn't it? Nothing should be holding me back anymore—nothing but a blurry vision of a past long gone.

This life is my own to take, to do as I wish and make it what I hoped to be. Its *selcouth* allure shall not make me quiver, it shall make me thrive. I shall discover what lies beyond, unbury the secrets of life, and accept the unknown.

Is there anything more beautiful than not knowing? For what's purer than walking through the threshold with an open mind and a desire for adventure?

And maybe that's what we all should be looking for, a *selcouth* life. A life of uncertainty, a thrilling life ready for the taking. Maybe we *should* embrace the unexpected, the messiness of being human—not knowing where it'll lead us.

Maybe that's the big message, the deep, dark secret that lies underneath our skins. I choose to believe that it's always been within us. I choose to push through, to keep the momentum going.

For a door is just a door until we break it down. Then it becomes nothing but an insignificant memory of what was keeping you out of your destiny.

What would *you* do if faced with a life-changing decision? Would you squander it or accept it? Would you stand still or move on with it?

I know *my* answer, traveling down this *selcouth* path. Do *you*?

CHAPTER XVI

SERENDIPITY

ser·en·dip·i·ty

(n.) the occurrence of making pleasant and desirable
discoveries by pure accident

"Sometimes serendipity is just intention unmasked."
— *Elizabeth Berg, The Year of Pleasures*

What if venturing into this path was not a coincidence
at all? What if, all along, *serendipity* had been waiting for
me on the other side?

What if breaking down the door was the best decision
I've ever made? What if...*serendipity* was just waiting to be
unmasked, ready to show me the beauty of life?

And if I had rushed in, would I have gotten the same
result? Would life have been kinder to me then, or would I
have missed the window at its right time?

Serendipity, my hidden gift. Maybe it was lost in time
while I found myself, while I searched for it. And now it's
mine to keep, mine to cherish.

I might have stumbled upon you, but you have found
me. Be it to guide me or help me relearn who I am, I will
never be the same again—or who I was before.

My heart sings of new life, of new adventures to
be chased. My lungs breathe in the new air, an air of
mysticism. *Serendipity* has set me ablaze and I don't want

to put it out.

Perhaps these are now the nice things I deserve, regardless of pain and sins. No longer can I hold onto my past, it does not want me anymore, and neither do I. This is now the birth, the start, of my strength—my brightest of futures.

Perhaps the universe never meant to keep its secrets. Perhaps it was waiting for them to be found, to be sought after. Perhaps that's the deeper meaning of *serendipity*: discovering that the universe's secrets were just hiding in all of us.

And perhaps, those thousands of unanswered questions were just waiting behind closed doors. The doors we were too afraid to open. Is that what I'm supposed to do now, find the answers? And what will I do with them? How do I carry them with me?

Maybe they'll help me embrace the truth, and my resilience, and accept myself as I was designed. For the hurt came and went, and now comes the happiness— there's nothing purer than that.

Perhaps *serendipity* will help me plant my roots so deep into the ground that I can't help but grow in love, in happiness. Perhaps it'll help me appreciate human connection, appreciate who I love and who loves me back.

And maybe now I can stop searching. Maybe I can realize that I am enough for myself, as I always have been. Maybe my art can be about myself, for myself, for my soul. Maybe the journey was always supposed to lead me here.

Is my *serendipity* discovering that my fate was always in my hands? The hurting, the breaking, the treacherous paths, the loneliness, the journey to healing, and now the loving and understanding.

In the mosaic of my experiences, is this the revelation that my fate was always cradled in my hands? The journey woven with threads of pain, breaking, loneliness, and healing, now paints the canvas of love and understanding.

As I contemplate the winding path ahead, I realize that perhaps I stood in my own way—a guardian obstructing the view of endless possibilities. The prelude to a symphony of self-discovery encourages me to cease the relentless search and recognize that I am enough for myself.

With newfound clarity, my art becomes an ode to the soul, a celebration of the journey that led me to this moment. Serendipity, the overture to a story that unfolds not by chance but by the deliberate strokes of fate.

Perhaps there's still so much more to uncover. And, perhaps, *serendipity* was only the start of so much more than just pure coincidence.

CHAPTER XVII

ALEXITHYMIA

alex·i·thy·mia

(n.) inability to describe or express emotions in a verbal manner

"To uncloak these unconscious desires, the things that your mind tries to repress, those secrets of your soul."
— *Allan Dare Pearce*

What if the words that dance on my tongue, imprisoned, are not a result of a lexical deficiency, but rather an intricate design woven into the fabric of my being?

What if the silence I carry within me is not a void but a language in its own right, waiting to be deciphered by a patient soul?

What if the inability to articulate the symphony of emotions within is not a curse, but a unique dialect spoken only by those initiated into the enigmatic realm of *alexithymia*?

What if, within this seemingly desolate landscape, lies a garden of emotions, wild and untamed, waiting for someone with the courage to navigate its intricate maze?

If I had possessed the right words to convey the storm raging inside me, would I have discovered this hidden sanctuary of self-exploration? Would I have forged this intimate connection with the unspoken, the ineffable, the visceral essence of my existence?

Alexithymia, my elusive companion. Perhaps, like a shadow cast by the moonlight, you are not meant to be grasped but to be observed, to be embraced.

In your wordless embrace, I find solace, a refuge from the cacophony of a world that insists on verbal confessions.

I might have yearned for fluency in the language of emotions, but you have bestowed upon me a silent eloquence that transcends the limitations of mere words. Be it to shield me from the overwhelming storm or to reveal the quiet beauty of emotional landscapes, you have become an unexpected guide on this introspective journey.

My heart beats to the rhythm of unsung melodies, resonating with the pulse of emotions too profound for verbal expression. My soul breathes in the silence, an air thick with the poignancy of unspoken narratives.

Alexithymia has ignited a flame within, a flame that flickers with the warmth of self-acceptance.

Perhaps these unspoken emotions are the uncut gems of my existence, hidden beneath the surface, waiting to be unearthed. No longer can I cling to the illusion of linguistic mastery, for in the realm of *alexithymia*, vulnerability is not a weakness but a profound strength—a vulnerability that births resilience.

Perhaps the universe, in its infinite wisdom, intentionally veiled the language of emotions, challenging us to seek beyond the superficial, to delve into the nuanced layers of our own humanity. What if that's its hidden purpose: an invitation to explore the uncharted territories of our emotional selves?

And maybe, behind the closed doors of verbal expression, lie the answers to questions I've been hesitant to ask. Is it now my destiny to confront these unspoken queries, to unearth the emotions that have lingered in the shadows for far too long?

Maybe, as I unlock these concealed chambers of my heart, I will discover the key to embracing the truth with open arms, cradling it like a fragile blossom. Perhaps this will guide me to plant the seeds of understanding so deep that they blossom into a garden of self-love and acceptance.

And maybe, just maybe, this is the end of the relentless search. Maybe the realization dawns that I am complete within myself, even in the absence of words.

Perhaps my art is not about communicating to others but a silent conversation with my soul. Maybe this journey was destined to bring me to this point all along.

Is my *alexithymia* an unveiling of the autonomy I hold over my own narrative? The struggle, the introspection, the winding paths, the solitude, the journey to self-awareness, and now the embrace of self-love.

Perhaps it was always me standing at the crossroads, choosing the direction of my journey. Perhaps there is still more to be uncovered, more layers to peel away.

Perhaps, *alexithymia* is not just a linguistic quirk but the prelude to a symphony of self-discovery orchestrated by the hands of fate.

CHAPTER XVIII

METANOIA

met·a·noi·a

(n.) the journey of chasing one's heart, self, mind, or way of life

"Sometimes the dreams that come true are the dreams you never even knew you had." — *Alice Sebold, The Lovely Bones*

In the quiet alcove of my thoughts, I find myself on the precipice of a journey, a metamorphosis of the self. *Metanoia*, they call it, is the pursuit of one's heart, mind, and the very essence of existence.

How did I stumble upon this path, or did it, in its cosmic design, find me? What if the threads of destiny were interwoven with the fabric of my choices?

What if every step I took, every door I opened, was a note in the symphony of my own becoming? It whispers through the corridors of my mind, a serenade to the seeker in me.

The decision to break down the doors, was it a rebellion against the monotony or an embrace of the unknown? What if, in that moment of liberation, I unknowingly unleashed the dormant forces of change?

Metanoia, perhaps, was waiting patiently on the other side, ready to reveal the kaleidoscope of life.

As I walk this path, I sense a shift within. A subtle awakening of the spirit, a realization that the journey itself is the destination. The dance of self-discovery, a choreography of introspection that leads to the revelation of one's true nature.

The doors I once feared to open were gateways to uncharted territories within myself. *Metanoia*, the silent companion, guided me through the labyrinth of my fears, showing that the shadows concealed treasures waiting to be unveiled.

The call to chase not just dreams but the essence of being. Was it a mere coincidence that I found myself on this trail, or was it a predestined alignment of stars, a celestial conspiracy leading me to my true north?

In the echoes of my past, I hear the resonance of a person I used to be. The shedding of old skin is both liberating and disorienting.

What if this journey is not just about finding oneself but also about creating a self that one aspires to be? The sculptor's chisel is in the hands of destiny, shaping and molding the contours of my existence. I am not merely a traveler; I am the architect of my own becoming.

The questions, like constellations in the night sky, are both numerous and elusive. What if the answers lie not in the destination but in the pursuit itself?

My new compass, pointing not to a place but to a state of being—an ever-evolving state that beckons me forward.

The hurts, the stumbles, the scars—they are not relics of the past but stepping stones on this odyssey. *Metanoia* is the alchemy that turns wounds into wisdom, pain, into resilience.

The journey is not devoid of darkness, but it is in embracing the shadows that I discover the brilliance of my own light.

What if this is not a stroke of luck but a cosmic collaboration between the universe and the seeker?

A partnership in the grand design of a life unfolding. Each revelation is a chapter in a story written not by fate alone but by the choices I make along the way.

The pursuit of happiness, they say, is a universal endeavor. Perhaps happiness is not a destination but a byproduct of the continuous pursuit of authenticity.

As I pen down these thoughts, I realize that the journey of chasing one's heart, self, mind, or way of life is not a linear path but a mosaic of experiences, each contributing to the masterpiece of my own evolution, my *metanoia*.

CHAPTER XIX

REDAMANCY

red·a·man·cy

(n.) the act of loving the one who loves you; a love returned
in full

*"I was just a flawed person trying to find redamancy, but
you turned out to be the dawn of my life."* — Shivangi

In the quiet corners of my heart, I find myself
immersed in the gentle embrace of *redamancy*, the
sweet surrender to a love that echoes in the chambers of
reciprocity.

A journey not just towards another, but towards the
sacred temple of self-love, where the tendrils of affection
intertwine, weaving a tapestry of completeness.

What if the essence of *redamancy* is not just about
receiving love, but discovering the reservoirs of love
within? What if, in returning the gaze of affection, I find
not only solace in the arms of another but also a mirror
reflecting the love I harbor for myself?

Redamancy: the dance of souls entwined, a celestial
waltz where hearts echo each other's beats. As I traverse
this path, I wonder if every step forward is a step deeper
into the sanctuary of mutual adoration, a shared voyage
toward love.

As I tiptoe through the corridors of my mind, I stumble

upon a truth—a revelation that perhaps the love I sought in the eyes of another was always nestled within the alcoves of my own being.

The gentle whisper of self-love, a hymn that harmonizes with the symphony of reciprocal affections.

Love, like a delicate petal, unfolds in layers. Yet, beneath it lies the uncharted territory of self-love, waiting to be unearthed. It is not a selfish act but a necessity, a communion with the depths of my own soul.

What if loving oneself is not vanity, but a profound acknowledgment of one's worth? A recognition that, in the vastness of my existence, love is an indispensable thread, weaving its way through the intricate design of my being.

It's a love that blooms in the soil of self-discovery, blossoming into a garden of acceptance. Every flaw, every scar, becomes a testament to the resilience of my heart, a canvas painted with the strokes of self-appreciation.

In the reflection of another's love, I find the courage to embark on a journey of self-exploration. The insecurities that once cast shadows now stand illuminated by the light of self-love.

The echoes of *redamancy* reverberate not only in the exchanges with others but also in the quiet moments of introspection. It is in the chambers of solitude that I learn to whisper words of affirmation.

This journey is not without its challenges. The weeds of self-doubt may threaten to overrun, but with each passing storm, the roots grow stronger. Redamancy is not a destination; it is a commitment to nurture the love within.

Maybe this is the revelation—the key to *redamancy* is not solely in the hands of another but lies in the sacred covenant I make with myself.

It's an oath to cherish, to protect, and to cultivate the garden of self-love so that it may bloom abundantly, casting its fragrance on the winds of existence.

So, I tread this path, hand in hand with *redamancy*, embracing the reciprocal dance of love. In loving the one who loves me, I find not only a companion for the journey but a confidante within—a love that emanates not just from the world around me but from the depths of my own heart.

CHAPTER XX

QUERENCIA

que·ren·cia

(n.) a place from which one's strength is drawn, where one feels at home; the place where you are your most authentic self

"Always returning to the same spot as if it is a place of safety."
— *Chloe Thurlow*

How do you yearn for something that you've never actually known? How can you feel as if you've loved something for a million years? How can *querencia* be what I'm feeling? For what is home to me now?

Life must've known that I was lonely, that I was craving that place that makes me feel at home, for it came to my rescue.

If opening my heart to the opportunity was all I had to do, if I had known, then I would've done it from the beginning.

I thought home was a person, someone to hold me at night when the nightmare came. But maybe home is something else...not *someone* else.

Now I know the truth... Since life has come, silence doesn't swallow me anymore, it hugs me. It coincides with the noise and they make a new symphony.

Since life has become a possibility, it feels like I'm cheating time, as if I have all of it. As if now the sun shines down on me, smiling and casting away the shadows.

I feel like the luckiest girl in the world. Everything has changed, and now my heart is open. It's as if happiness and strength are all I know. As if the heavens live inside me, as if we are now one.

Life might not have been my first love, but it makes the past feel irrelevant. It's as if life has touched me without actually doing it, and I turn to it, for its overflowing inspiration.

Querencia ignites all the senses. It smells like heaven, it feels like home, it tastes like happiness, I can hear its soothing tones, and I can see it bloom within me.

It's as if it knows my struggles, but decides to give me strength instead. Life found me in my mess, it saw me struggle, but it has pulled me out of it. It caught me as I fell and made me land somewhere safe.

Life has made me figure out who I am, reminded me of where I came from and where I'm going. I am hopelessly a dreamer. And while I had thought it would've been the death of me, it has shown me that it is the way to my future.

Fate has brought me to life's feet. It has brought me promises of a better life. It has proven what I've known all along but has just kept it hidden all this time.

Life whispered in my ear and told me the words I needed, not wanted, to hear. Its soothing, lovely voice made me feel warm inside. As if my true self had finally awakened and taken its rightful control.

And as time goes by, I will hold on to this version of myself—hold on to life itself. In my past, life had ended before it had begun. But now I can feel it restarting, as if it was *paused*, not *finished*.

Sometimes I forget, forget that there's no one single, physical place that I belong to. There's nowhere that I *have* to return to. And sometimes I forget that I can allow myself to be in that mental space of not knowing.

But what I'll never forget is that my lonely days are over. For now, I've found my dreams, I've found my happiness, I've found a way to break the spell.

And it didn't take much searching to realize where the answer was hiding. The truth was hidden in me, deep within my walls. Waiting to be rediscovered, for the right questions to be asked.

Where is my *querencia*? Home is a feeling, a place I carry with me wherever I go. Home is not a fixed location. Home changes as I change, it grows and evolves around me—within me.

I am my own *querencia*. I am my own home. I am my own sounding board. I am my own soulmate. *And what a beautiful feeling to carry with me...*

ACKNOWLEDGMENTS

To my mom for being my rock, for guiding me in bringing out my passion, and for being my sounding board.

To my dad for his mentorship, for being my anchor, and for always reminding me of where my dreams come from.

To my siblings and my best friend for their inspiration and their never-ending love.

To my grandpa...the literary legacy lives on!

To my partner for not letting me shy away from my love for writing and my ambition.

To my editor for helping me ground the story.

To my colleagues, friends, and family for cheering me on.

To my readers for taking a chance on me.

I wouldn't be here without you!

Love this book? Don't forget to leave a review!

Every review matters, and it matters a lot! Head over to my website and see where you can leave a review for me.

I thank you endlessly!

MORE FROM THE AUTHOR

"Book of You & I"
Publishing in 2024

GSeverino

Contemporary—New Adult Writer

An avid reader, obsessed with fantasy worlds, and with a burning passion for writing, embarking on a journey of self-discovery through her words.

She was born in Miami, Florida, and is of Dominican and Puerto Rican descent.

Currently, her greatest desire is to read and write while traveling the world, coffee in hand.

"With endless stories to tell and a desire to bring in a new vision, light, and energy as a way to connect with others."

Visit her website for updates about her current and upcoming projects.

Jacob sat in the mall's security office with his adopted father seated next to him and a security guard standing off to the side. In silence, the trio watched the surveillance footage. Thanks to the ability to rewind, they saw the attacker's failed attack and subsequent fall for the third consecutive time.

Douglas cried out, "How many times do we have to watch this? Obviously, my son was trying to walk away but was being harassed. The bully slipped trying to push him. We saw his legs come out from under him while Jake doesn't even move."

Sullenly, the mall cop responded. "Then why did he run?"

Doug harshly laughed. "He's a kid! Some bully tries to pick a fight but hurts himself. Then a brawny adult in a uniform is chasing after him. Why wouldn't he run? You're lucky I just want to forget this ever happened, instead of throwing a fit over the injury my son suffered after being chased by an overzealous security guard. Maybe the local news would like to cover the rampant bullying and the harassment of victims down at the galleria?" Rising in disgust (much of it feigned to escape the situation), he turned to his child. "Jake, grab your stuff. We're leaving."

The guard made no move to stop them. His instructions had been simple. He was not to hinder their exit, if the boy did not admit to any instigation and Jacob stubbornly refused to change his story.

On the other hand, the assailant and his girlfriend had told a drastically different version of events until the camera footage was revealed. The fall had mainly wounded his pride and the paramedics had already checked out everyone involved declaring only superficial injuries.

Douglas and Jacob exited into the parking lot and the father let his son have a few minutes to volunteer his version of events. By the time both of them had buckled their seatbelts and Doug had piloted the Corvette onto the road, Jake still had not spoken.

"So, are you going to tell me what happened?" He lowered the radio volume to a barely perceptible level as to not interfere with the conversation.

Jake shrugged. "It happened just like I said back there."

Douglas laughed. "My nickname is 'Einstein'. Give me some credit. I understand how physics works. First of all, the way the kid fell implied a strong force pushing him back. If his feet really came out from under him while stepping forward to hit you, he would have fallen forward due to the inertia of his body. Also, he didn't just fall backward, he flew." He eyed the boy, trying to urge a confession out of him. "You used your powers, didn't you?"

In a plaintive tone, Jacob cried out. "I didn't mean to. It was a reflex."

"You're not in trouble." Doug exasperatedly stated. "But you have to be more careful. I thought you practiced controlling them the whole time you were at grandma and grandpa's."

"I did practice, all the time. I got really good at moving stuff but someone trying to hit me is a different thing. My body takes over." He leaned back in his seat. "I just wanted to talk to a hot girl. I can't even do that without hurting people."

"Hey, stop that right now." Douglas sharply commanded. "That boy deserved it. The only time that triggers is when people want to hurt you. It's their fault, not yours."

Jacob looked out the passenger window. "Yeah, I guess." He did not sound convinced.

Chapter: The Case

Clarence Sudduth, a heavy set black man, walked through the front door of Caffeine Nation and looked around for his contact. He spotted Mr. Lawson sitting with his adopted son. Everyone else bustled around buying coffee and heading to the exits. Those two were the only ones killing time. Douglas Lawson peered into the screen of a small laptop and clicked a button as Jacob flipped through a guitar magazine. He looked like the "cat that swallowed the canary" as Clarence's mother used to say.

"Mr. Lawson." Clarence gave a terse greeting.

Doug stood up and after briefly shaking the policeman's hand, moved to the other side of the table with Jacob. "Have a seat, Detective. I just bought the coolest new walking cane; it's electric, one million volts of stopping power."

"A cane that doubles as a cattleprod?" Clarence smirked. "You and your spy toys..."

"Yep, so what brings you to my neck of the woods?"

Clarence set a manila folder on the table within arm's reach of Douglas. "I don't really know where to begin."

Douglas pulled a composition book from under the table and handed it to Jacob, who closed his magazine with excitement. "Would you be kind enough to take notes? Remember, no detail is small enough to exclude." He turned his attention to the detective. "The beginning would be a good place to start."

As soon as Clarence started to speak, the sound of a Jake's pen scratching on notebook paper commenced in the background. "I was called well after the death of a military officer named Martin Ramsey. Some kids out on a date called in a wreck. They said they saw a flipped car and a body at the bottom of a ravine off of the road. The first officer on the scene thought it was a traffic accident. The rain was still coming down and it seemed logical that the driver lost control and rolled down there. After waiting a few minutes for an ambulance to get there, he started to notice some irregularities. The body was found a good distance from the car, with drag marks like he survived the crash and was crawling for help. When he looked over the body, the skull was completely caved in and he couldn't have crawled any-where if a head injury that severe occurred during the crash."

He showed Douglas a picture of the body. The photograph gave Doug a jolt. The skull looked like a crater, destroyed to the point that he had trouble identifying it.

Sudduth continued. "Then the officer noticed an additional set of footprints in the fresh mud. These feet turned out to be size four-teens. This officer was a size eleven and the victim was a size nine. So they didn't belong to him. He called back to report the oddities. The lab rats showed up and they found extensive blood spatter outside near the body. I guess there was so much that the rain didn't wash it all away yet. After some more digging, the department discovered traces of black paint from another vehicle and tire tracks right off the pavement up the hill. We took casts and determined the tire model was E70-14. It's a vintage tire, usually purchased for antique muscle cars. I did not get to interview the victim's wife. Shortly after we identified the body, the military stepped in."

Douglas looked through the documents provided by Detective Sudduth. He had already seen the crushed head. The next photo of muddy ground with the imprint of tire tread meant nothing to him. The last sheet was a list of surviving family, complete with names and addresses. He slid it over to Jake and said, "Copy this sheet, please." The boy raced into the office to comply, leaving the two men alone at the table.

The detective looked hopefully at Douglas. "I can't bear to let this go. The military came in claiming that it was their investigation since the victim was an active duty soldier. Even if I fight it, getting through the red tape will take forever. I have been told to lay off but if you were to investigate on your own..." He hinted. "In my line of work, you have to accept that not every case gets solved. I'm too old to fall for the clichés about justice getting served but I'm also too burned out to care about the rules any more. I've given you all that I was able to gather. Do you think that's enough to get started?"

Douglas took the notebook from Jacob and read through the writings. "There's not a lot to go on. We've got a person with big feet and drives an old car. Will I be able to utilize some of your resources? The police department has a little fancier equipment than I can afford."

Clarence looked at him sympathetically. "I'll have to be very discrete. If you need anything, ask and I'll tell you if I can go that far or not."

Jacob returned and put the original sheet back in the envelope and handed the copy to his father.

"Fair enough." Douglas nodded while folding up the list of contacts. "In the meantime, I'll go to Martin Ramsey's house and talk to his wife. We'll leave you now. If there is any additional information, please let us know and we'll keep you posted too. Go up to the register and tell them the owner said that you could have a free cup of coffee." Then he extended his hand.

Detective Sudduth shook it and watched the father and son leave.

Penelope saw Samantha in one of the many hallways of Bryers Hospital and changed direction to pull alongside her. "Hey there, Dr. Nichols."

"Hi, Penny." Samantha replied.

"You remembered this time!" She exclaimed. "How did your lunch go?"

"And you forgot that I asked you to call me 'Sam'." The doctor smiled at her. "It went well. I feel free. Douglas didn't look so good when he left though." She did not add that some of that may have been over his son getting into some kind of trouble.

"So you sent him packing?" Penelope marvelled at her new hero. "I've never been able to do that to a guy. I'm always the one getting dumped."

Samantha corrected her. "I didn't dump him. He already had a girlfriend."

"Still..." An awed Penelope left the word hanging.

"It's really not that big of a deal. Besides, even without the emotional aspect, he's too dangerous to spend a lot of time around." Samantha dismissively stated.

Penny looked at her in surprise. "Dangerous? He didn't seem dangerous."

Dr. Nichols shook her head. "He's not dangerous. He seems to attract it, though."

"I still don't see it. Who'd want to hurt him? He seems nice." The nurse realized she did not know Mr. Lawson that well but felt pretty sure of her first impression.

"He thinks he's a crime fighter." Samantha complained.

"Is that why he was in here, someone beat him up?" Penny asked.

Samantha nodded. "He was assaulted by the terrorists that threatened the whole city a while back."

Penny's eyes widened. "Wow."

"Not 'wow', scary. He chased down extremely dangerous men and paid the price for it. He has to use a cane to get around." Samantha finished sadly.

Penelope shook her head. "That's still amazing. Does Gaston help him?"

Samantha sensed a little too much admiration. "I don't know. He has a whole little group of enablers."

"I've had a lot of experience sewing clothes. Do you think they'd let me make some costumes for them?" She ignored the doctor's plaintive tone and continued on with her own ideas. "I could totally do it."

"They are all crazy. You shouldn't do anything to encourage them." Samantha's voice grew firm.

"But they stopped the terrorists, right? We haven't had any more buildings collapse or any more public threats." Penelope argued.

Dr. Nichols rubbed her temples. "Penelope, that's not the point. If he keeps participating in that kind of behavior, he will get hurt worse or killed. If people actively encourage him, it will be harder for him to see reason. I've washed my hands of him, but I can still hope he realizes those things on his own."

The nurse glared at the doctor. "Washed your hands of him?" She huffed and turned away. As a parting shot, she muttered, "I wish it were that easy for me to give up on people."

The words hurt Samantha more than Penelope realized. When Douglas was confined to a hospital bed, he had accused her of giving up on him too easily. Only a few months had passed but the verbal barb still stung like she had just heard it. No one understood how she just needed to be free of him, of the worry that she would have to witness his downfall.

A voice spoke in her ear. "Nurses, they can be so judgemental of the decisions doctors must make."

Samantha jumped. Turning to see who had managed to sneak up on her, she smiled. "You startled me, Dr. Straub."

The middle-aged man laughed. "Sorry, I wasn't trying to and please call me Stuart." His manner was gracious and warm. "I assume you were discussing a particularly pig-headed patient with your friend?"

Samantha quickly lied. "Yes a patient." Feeling that she owed her senior colleague an explanation, she continued. "Just someone that disregards all my advice and does what he's going to do anyway."

"All doctors suffer in that regard." Stuart Straub marvelled. "Lose weight, stop smoking. Can you guess what happens the next time they come in to the office? Ten pounds heavier and a lung full of tar. Apparently, we speak just to hear ourselves talk."

Dr. Nichols nodded. "I just can't believe how far people are willing to go sometimes, even when they know that it will hurt them."

Dr. Straub placed a lingering hand on her upper arm. "People will not change until they want to. It's good to have some empathy, but if you can't emotionally separate yourself from your patients you won't make it. When you lose one, it's going to hurt so badly that you won't be able to help the next one. You have to stay detached enough to move on without it impacting your work."

"I know. Just easier said than done." Samantha felt a stab of guilt. Stuart had taken her under his wing ever since she had begged him to perform Douglas' initial check-up after the bridge. She felt like she was taking advantage of his kindness and his willingness to mentor her in the ways of a large hospital. She should have already found her feet in this environment, but he still regularly checked on her and occasionally came to her rescue.

Dr. Straub nodded. "Well, if you need to discuss anything, I will make myself available." He walked down the hall to where ever he had been headed before Penny and Samantha's conversation caught his interest.

Samantha felt a little relief. Stuart had confirmed to her that she made the right move with Douglas. She was spinning her wheels trying to help him when he so obviously did not want to change. She was saving herself from the heartache of watching a patient stumble and fall.

Chapter: The Widow

D ouglas stopped the Corvette on the street in front of the Ramsey residence. It was a two story house (not counting the attic) with a well landscaped lawn. Flowerbeds sat under the first floor windows. The lawn was short with no weeds marring the view. A stone path led from the road to the front porch steps. Douglas looked around and noticed that both neighbors had tall privacy fences. The entire street contained nice homes and yards. He imagined that a crew came through on a regular basis to touch everything up.

Doug looked at Jacob. "We're going to go in but I want to talk to Ms. Ramsey alone. If she feels like she's on display for a bunch of people, she's less likely to be honest."

Jake's face twisted in disapproval but he did not argue. "I can look for clues outside."

"Good idea." Mr. Lawson smiled at the way his son still tried to turn it into an opportunity to assist. "I don't know how long it'll take."

"No problem, I'll find something to do." Jake looked around for something to involve him.

Father and son exited the car and slammed the doors, almost in unison. Douglas walked up the stone path while Jacob looked around the yard for anything out of the ordinary. As Doug reached the door, Jake slipped around the side of the house to investigate the back yard. Douglas lifted his hand and executed a series of rapid knocks. Then, he waited for someone to answer the door. There was a long silence until a small speaker beside the door crackled to life.

"Who is it?"

Douglas pushed the button and tried to distinctly speak into the mounted intercom. "My name is Douglas Lawson. I wanted to talk to you about your husband."

After a short pause, a tired voice came back. "Are you a reporter?"

"Nothing so ghoulish, ma'am. I am an investigator." Douglas hoped that she wanted to talk.

"Come in. The door is unlocked."

Now, as he opened the door, he met the widow. Priscilla Ramsey struck him as a full figured but elegant woman used to putting on a social event or entertaining guests for dinner. Now, her eyes stared blankly at the floor and were puffy from crying. As she found Doug standing in the doorway, Priscilla looked surprised but too distraught to care who he was.

"I am sorry to bother you, Mrs. Ramsey. I just have a few questions. What have you been told about your husband's death?" He stepped inside and sat in a plush armchair perpendicular to the couch on which she sat.

Priscilla's lips quivered. "His car crashed last night in the rain." She sobbed once but quickly regained her composure.

"Mrs. Ramsey, a detective was brought in to investigate your husband's death because it looked like murder. But the military warned him off of the case." He blurted before taking another look around.

At the news that her husband's death may not have been accidental, she raised a hand to her mouth. "Tobias."

Douglas looked back and saw the significance of the name in her reaction. "Who's Tobias?"

"Tobias Richmond was my tennis instructor at The Meadows country club." She tried to hide her face behind her hands.

"Why did you say his name?" Doug almost shouted due to the tension within his chest.

"He saw me outside of the club. He was so young and fit and interested in me. I let my guard down." Her eyes pleaded with him to understand. "It was so exciting. Then he started to ask me to leave

Martin. I didn't think he would be the type to..." She burst into tears again.

Douglas prayed the noise would not bring anyone upstairs. "How long has the affair gone on?"

"Three months." She choked out the words between wails of anguish.

"Did you see Mr. Richmond last night?" Douglas asked.

Priscilla only nodded in response.

"What time did he leave you?"

Priscilla tried to speak. "I-i-i-i think i-i-i-it was a-a-a-around Eight last night."

"Did your husband have anyone that you would consider an enemy?"

She shook her head, still crying.

"What cases was he currently working on?"

"I don't know. He never discussed his job with me." She wiped her eyes with the heel of her palm.

Douglas was at a loss. She was devastated, despite her infidelity. Could her lover have murdered Mr. Ramsey? Could it have been a soldier that Martin had prosecuted? "How about in his past? Did anyone he prosecuted make threats against him or you?"

"No, I can't think of anyone."

Douglas took a shot in the dark. "Was your husband into muscle cars or friends with anyone that was?"

Priscilla shook her head. "Why do you ask?"

"Another set of tire tracks at the scene of the accident." Doug offhandedly commented. He was getting nowhere except for the fact Mrs. Ramsey had a lover. Mr. Lawson made a mental note to check the timeframes and see if Tobias Richmond could have been at the scene in quickly enough.

"What does Mr. Richmond drive?"

"A little two-seater Mazda." Priscilla hesitantly answered.

Douglas reached into his wallet and pulled out a business card. "If you have anything else that comes to mind, I can be easily reached at this number. It's for a coffee shop but trust me, they know how to get ahold of me." He paused. "And I am very sorry for your loss. If there is anything to the claims that this was murder, I will do everything in my power to see that the perpetrator is caught."

Emotionally drained, Priscilla nodded and spoke a quiet "thank you".

Letting himself out, Douglas stood by the Corvette and waited for Jacob to return. The boy had gotten bored looking around the backyard and wandered up the street. Jake slowly walked back to the car, and seeing his father, quickened his pace. Reaching the passenger door, he asked, "Did you find out anything useful?"

Douglas slipped into the car. "I have a starting point. How about you?"

Jacob shook his head. "Nothing. It was a long shot that there would be incriminating evidence just sitting out in the middle of the yard though."

"Don't be so sure. You'd be surprised what breaks cases wide open sometimes." Douglas tried to reassure the boy that his time had not been wasted. He turned the key and started moving forward.

Scott Edwards looked in the mirror and smiled. Straight, white teeth gleamed in the bathroom light. He checked his eyes for bags hanging under them. He applied a moisturizer to his face, rubbing the lotion in small circles with his hands. As his skin absorbed the various vitamins, he did not kid himself that he suddenly looked younger. True, he was still attractive, but time took its toll, regardless. His evening routine tried to stay the inevitable aging process, or at least disguise it, but he had to wonder how long he could keep up being the face-man of the organization.

Scott felt nervous that he was last year's model. Even his newest assignment had been to seduce a middle-aged housewife. Raven no longer gave him challenges. He wanted to take an oak and make it bend. That was how he felt powerful, in control. He wanted to be the center. The world only made sense if people were serving him: favors, gifts, or sex.

He left the bathroom, flicking off the light as he exited. In his bedroom, he opened the door to his walk in closet and began the lengthy process of selecting his eveningwear. Should he go formal or a slutty casual look? Maybe he could mix it up. Brand names worn in a haphazardly manner would convince people that he knew style but possessed enough self-confidence to not care.

As Mr. Edwards systematically scanned through his shirts, the prepaid cell phone Valerie had given him to use as Tobias began ringing. It was the mark, Priscilla Ramsey. Annoyed at the need to provide her attention, he grudgingly slipped into character. "Hello my darling, I was just thinking about you." His voice flowed like honey, sweet and slow.

"Tobias," her voice shook. "An investigator came by asking questions about my husband. He said that he thinks it was murder."

Scott mentally cursed, but the words he spoke hid his frustration. "Oh my God, your husband is dead?" He added a liberal amount of astonishment to his voice.

"I thought you knew. I left you several voice mails." Truthfully, he had ignored her messages. She had tried to call him and he refused to pick up. He wanted as much plausible deniability as possible, in addition to loathing the woman.

"I'm sorry. I've been out and forgot my cell. I just got home." He spit out the first lie that came into his head. "What happened?"

"He had a car crash while it was raining the last night we were together. Now someone is saying it wasn't an accident but murder. He has your name. You may be a suspect." She nervously warned.

Inwardly, he fumed. Outwardly, he kept a naïve demeanor. "But I was with you. I couldn't have done it." He let the silence hang for a moment to let his words stick. "I wanted him gone for our sake, but not like this. You know I had nothing to do with it, right?"

Thinking over the timeline of the evening, Priscilla found herself agreeing. "I remember you left later than normal."

"See? I'm innocent. The only thing I'm guilty of is being in love with you." The character of Tobias had fully taken over.

"Stop. Please stop. I can't take this right now. I still loved my husband." Priscilla tried to explain. "When you say that to me, I feel responsible, like my secret wishes caused this."

"You were unhappy. There's nothing wrong with wanting to find joy in life again." Scott consoled her. "You did nothing wrong."

"Oh, Tobias, it's not that simple." Priscilla felt her arguments drying up. She felt terrible but her lover had a way of muddling her mind. She could not think straight while he whispered his syrupy words in her ear.

"It is very simple. Your husband was a good man but he stopped making you feel fulfilled. Then we connected. Our love should not be punished because of the randomness of the world around us. Do you want me to come over?" Scott took a calculated risk. He did not want to go over there but wanted her to believe the depth of his love. To his relief, she declined.

"I don't think it's a good idea right now. I hope you understand." Priscilla Ramsey thought of the scandal of being caught with a man so soon after Martin's passing.

Scott pretended to feel unyielding disappointment. "I don't like it, but I'll stay away for now. Let me know when I can bask in your presence again." He smiled at how he could lay it on so thick for her.

"I will and I do love you, Tobias." Her voice strained, about to crack.

Still smiling, Scott replied. "I love you, too." He heard her hang up and his hand dropped to his side. "Damn that woman."

Scott Edwards walked over to his nightstand and picked up a different phone. After waiting for someone to answer, he heard a click. "This is Valentine. I've got a problem."

Raven's voice replied, "Yes?"

"The mark gave my name to an investigator." Scott elaborated.

"The local police were chased off the case. Who's investigating?" Valerie demanded.

"She didn't name anyone. It could be army."

"I have assurances that no one in the military is pursuing this case." Ms. Gossard responded.

"Maybe it's your boyfriend." Scott snidely responded.

"If it is, I will distract him. Continue as planned." The line went dead.

Scott glared at the phone before putting it back on the nightstand. "Continue as planned?" He was not going to jail for anyone. He knew how his boss handled people who were caught. After the bridge fiasco, she had Valentine and a corrupt cop personally deliver a tainted meal to that electronics geek, Greg Phillips. If the investigator got too close, Scott Edwards would end up dead or with no recollection of who he was.

He pondered the best way to go to sleep tonight: pill, drink, or dalliance? Drinks would take too long and too much. Scott may even have to run out and buy another bottle. He could not remember how much liquor was in his freezer. He could also call one of the men or women in his little black book. Not feeling the energy to sweet talk anyone tonight, he opened a prescription bottle and dry swallowed a zolpidem tablet.

Chapter: Time to Quit

Valerie Gossard tapped her fingers on the small writing desk in her apartment. Valentine's assertion that her "boyfriend" went to Ms. Ramsey asking questions agitated her. She had underestimated Douglas once before and her crew witnessed the entire affair. She could not let him get the best of her again. It would sow the seeds of mutiny. *Bestia* already accused her of being soft where Mr. Lawson was concerned. Valentine was a coward at heart but would stab her in the back if it meant saving himself. Devildriver was looking for an excuse to kill anybody. Luckily, she had an ace up her sleeve when it came to controlling her pet psychopath.

Regardless, she needed to confirm the identity of the investigator. She grabbed her cell phone and dialed one of her contacts within the Kios Police Department.

A husky voice answered. "Yeah?"

"In your last communication, you reported on the Ramsey case being dropped due to a jurisdiction fight with the armed forces. Is that still the case?" Valerie asked with no urgency or tension in her voice.

"Yeah, it was assigned to a guy named Clarence Sudduth but he let it go. He's been around for years and doesn't rock the boat." The voice quickly whispered.

"Verify that. I've heard that someone went around to the widow's house and interviewed her."

Exasperated, the voice spoke. "Sure, but did you ever think that it was someone with the Army? One of their own died."

"That had crossed my mind, but I will handle that. You just make sure Sudduth isn't looking into the matter any further." Raven's voice grew threatening.

"Jesus Christ, I said I would. Anything else, your majesty?"

"Not for now, serf." A trace of vitriol slipped into her reply. She hung up and stared at the phone for a moment before calling someone else. Her military contact would not be available at the moment. She could go ahead and talk to Douglas. Maybe she could maneuver the conversation on to the subject without arousing suspicion.

When he answered his cell, she greeted him enthusiastically. "Hey sweetie, I am back from my business trip."

"That's great. It's only been two days but I still missed you." Lawson responded with sincerity.

"What did you do while I was gone?" She conversationally asked.

"Not too much, I took Jake to the mall so he could hang out with kids his own age and he ended up getting into a fight, sort of." Douglas explained.

"Sort of?" Curiosity temporarily derailed her objective. Besides, she could not drive to the point of her call right away without raising some concern.

"Some punk accused Jake of hitting on his girlfriend. The kid fell down trying to hit Jake and Jake panicked. A security guard chased after him when he ran."

"Oh, poor boy. Is everything okay?" Valerie tried to imagine the situation and stifled a laugh.

"Yeah, bruised egos are the worst thing to come out of it."

"Did you get up to anything else? That couldn't have taken your whole Friday and Saturday." She prompted.

"Well, I started a new case. It's interesting, a traffic accident that is really a murder, some JAG officer." Douglas relayed the gist of the investigation to her.

Valerie's heart dropped and she thought to herself, "Damn it, Douglas! How do you get in my affairs so often?" Instead of voicing those thoughts, she showed a vague interest. "What evidence have you gathered?"

"I don't want to bore you with it. I'm sure you get enough of law and order dealing with clients. Besides, there's not really anything to go on so far." Douglas' tone changed to a jokingly seductive one. "I'm more interested in talking about you and me right now. What do you say we meet up for some mattress dancing?"

Valerie could not help but laugh. "Your euphemisms are remarkably subtle."

"What do you say? I'll give you a good night's sleep, y'know, after the staying up part."

Raven pondered whether or not she should meet him. "I'm exhausted from my trip and don't feel like getting out again." That part was true. Traveling with *Bestia* had worn her out. "If you come to me, we can spend the night together." She heard silence on the other end.

Finally, his throat cleared. "Yeah, no problem. Give me a few hours to get some work done and Jake a place to stay for the night."

Valerie sat on the edge of her bed. "I am looking forward to it." Despite the inevitable hardship of dealing with Douglas professionally, she did want a warm body beside her tonight. As she hung up the phone, she spread out on the bed and thought about how to handle him.

Valerie Gossard cursed Arturo for being right about Douglas. It could not continue this way. The question was who should be the one to remove Mr. Lawson as an obstacle. Deep down, Valerie knew it should be her but Devildriver and Arturo would be more than willing to do the deed. Of course, she did not trust Devil to make it painless. She still had trouble imagining the sadism required to torture a man named Dwayne Kimble. It was the kind of sick, ritualistic technique of the most horrifying serial killer. She shuddered, remembering the grisly details.

No, it was something that she needed to do herself. She would not trust it to her subordinates. Valerie prided herself on cleaning up her own messes

Douglas had just finished speaking with his girlfriend and dialed Clarence Sudduth to update him on his progress. "Detective, it's Einstein."

The deep voice on the other end chuckled. "You and your code names…"

"What time did you say the wreck occurred?"

Caught off guard by the way Douglas jumped right to business, Clarence did not answer immediately. "Uh, it was around 7:45. Kids called it in just a few minutes after that."

Douglas hissed between his teeth. Priscilla said her lover left her place around eight. He quickly decided to keep the information about Tobias Richmond to himself for now. Lovers were always high on the list of suspects but the timeframe did not seem feasible. How could Tobias leave Mrs. Ramsey and have time to run Martin off the road miles away, unless she lied to cover for Tobias?

"You mentioned a tire model that was not the most common. Can you look up other crimes in the area with that some track left at the scene? Maybe we'll get lucky." Douglas hoped that Mr. Richmond would prove to be a good lead.

Detective Sudduth agreed. "It sounds like a plan."

"One more thing that struck me as odd: Ms. Ramsey had not been interviewed by an investigator from the army and had not been told her husband's death was suspicious at all. From what you told me, it'd take a blind man to miss all those clues."

"Yeah, that is unusual. I've seen a thing like that happen within the department and it usually involves some cops that are rumored to be dirty." Clarence confided.

"So, we're talking cover-up?" Doug asked.

"Well, let's not jump to conspiracy theories yet. Maybe, they are giving her a little time to grieve before questioning her." Sudduth hopefully voiced the possibility.

"Maybe. Anyway, I'll keep working my end. Let me know when you get the tire stuff back."

"Will do."

Douglas hung up and looked at the mounted clock on his coffee shop wall. He had enough time to drive to his Brazilian Jujitsu class and cancel his membership. With his bum leg, he did not feel like it would be useful to take it any longer. Also, it did not seem to do him any good when he was in a real fight. *Bestia* made short work of him on the bridge.

Mr. Lawson looked at Cindy. "I'm heading out. Gaston is going to take Jake tonight. You can close up whenever business drops after 10PM."

Cindy nodded. "Have fun."

"I will." He mirthfully replied. Talking to his instructor would be difficult but seeing Valerie would more than make up for it. He stepped out into the night with his cane gripped tightly in his hand and hobbled to his car.

After a quick drive, he pulled up outside of a nondescript gym in the heart of the city. Like the rest of the neighborhood, the building showed signs of age. As Douglas entered, he breathed in and caught the musty smell of sweat, canvas, and medicated ointments. On the mats, students were taking turns practicing side control positions. The instructor walked around pointing out small corrections to the students' techniques. When he saw Douglas watching, he tapped one of the students with a darker colored belt and asked him to take over.

Douglas watched the teacher walk toward him. Carl Stovall stopped in front of him and extended his hand. "Welcome back. Val told me you were going to be out for a while. That must have been some accident."

Douglas shifted uncomfortably. "Yeah, the doctors say I'll never have full use of the leg again but I can move around okay." He looked at the instructor with a sense of envy. The man had a muscular build and a broad chest. His face sported uniform stubble that Douglas never seemed to be able to grow.

"So, how is Valerie? When your attendance dropped, hers did too. Is she alright?" Carl crossed his arms and raised an eyebrow.

"She's fine, just working a lot." Doug answered, hoping the small talk would soften the blow when he quit the school. "I actually came up here to talk about my membership."

"Hey, you're all paid up. Change into your clothes and we'll work you in to the beginner class to ease you back in." Carl slapped him on the shoulder. "Use it or you lose it."

Mr. Lawson sighed. "I came up here to let you know I'm not returning. With this leg..." He lifted the cane a few inches and wiggled it around. "...it's just not something I can do anymore."

Carl Stovall leaned in close. "Doug, who told you that you couldn't do this?"

Douglas leaned away from the instructor. "No one told me, but seriously, how much good is it going to do me with a bum leg? I wasn't that great when I had two good legs."

Carl shook his head. "You weren't the best, but you came to class. You listened when I gave you advice. You were a consistent student and that is more important than natural talent."

"You can't be for real. I suck." Douglas exasperatedly declared.

"Guys with natural talent don't want to listen when you try to get them to tweak something they're doing. They also don't learn to handle setbacks well. The first big loss and they either crash or they mature and get serious. But you already know about incremental improvement. You've had to do it since day one." Stovall put his hand on the student's shoulder. "I've seen you out there. You try hard and you are a pleasure to train. That leg is not a barrier. There is no handicap preventing you from learning submissions, joint-locks, or chokeholds other than the ones you have created in your mind."

"Of course you don't want me to quit. I'm paying to be here." Douglas could not stop himself from making the accusation.

Carl stepped back with a look of shock on his face. "You think this is about money?" He motioned to the students grappling on the floor. Then he pointed to a pair of fighters sparring in the ring stationed deeper into the gym. "I've got plenty of people paying me to be here. I am talking to you right now because I don't want to see that leg that you keep mentioning stop you from doing the things you want to do. It's tempting when you have such a ready excuse but it's a slippery slope. One day you could wake up realizing that you've used that excuse to keep you from taking any risks at all."

Carl entreated Douglas. "Give me three months. If you really think it's about money, I won't charge you. That's a quarter of the year for free. If you don't think that this class has helped you with your confidence, stamina, technique, or anything else; I won't press it any further. Just give yourself a chance to realize you are stronger than you think you are."

Douglas smiled. "That's a good speech. It makes it very hard for me to walk out now." Shaking his head, he laughed. "Okay, I don't have my *gi* with me but I've got some gym clothes in the car. Give me a second."

Carl nodded. "You'll thank me."

Valerie heard a knock on the door. Looking at her simple but elegant watch, she expected her caller to be Douglas. Cracking open the door, she saw him across the threshold. His hair looked wet and she could smell the aroma of dried sweat on him. "My God, what did you do before coming over here?"

Grinning, Douglas stepped inside. "I went back to our Brazilian Jiu-Jitsu class."

Valerie watched him slowly limp into her apartment. Should she discourage him from taking a martial art? Arturo had easily bested Mr. Lawson but she did not want any challenges to her organization's supremacy. Besides, what were the odds that he would develop enough skill to adequately defend himself?

Unable to resist, she spoke. "Are you sure you should do that with that leg?"

Douglas excitedly relayed his story to her. "That's the thing, I was talking to Carl and he convinced me to give it another shot. I can't let this lame leg become a crutch that stops me from doing all the things that I still want to do. It's like a virus. If I say that I can't take the class because of my leg, it will be easy to say I can't do something else because of it. Before you know it, I'll use it as an excuse for everything and turn into some kind of crazy hermit."

"That sounds like a stretch." Valerie rolled her eyes. "He just doesn't want to lose revenue from students leaving his academy."

"Not true." Doug quickly retorted. "He's waiving three months of tuition as a trial period."

"Oh, Douglas, he's trying to guilt you into staying." Valerie spoke with a world-weary confidence.

"What is this? I thought you'd be happy for me. I'm still fighting the good fight. I'm not letting some bad luck bring me down or prevent me from honing some tools for my mission. I'm getting my confidence back after weeks of feeling down and worthless." Douglas gripped his cane until his knuckles turned white. "Come on, you are supposed to be supportive. You're my girl."

Valerie changed her tone to one of concern. "I just don't want you to set yourself up for failure. You may become over-confident if you keep taking the class. You need to know your limitations."

Douglas groaned as he walked forward and tossed himself on her couch. "You sure know how to get me in the mood. Insult me and take away my buzz. Can't you just let me have this moment?"

With a remorseful countenance, she slipped onto the cushions beside him. "I'm sorry. I'm just trying to look out for…ugh, you need a shower before we go to bed." She waved her hand in front of her nose to waft away the scent.

Douglas smiled. "Sure thing, but you may have to help me up." Suddenly remembering his discussion from the gym, he asked, "How come you haven't been going to class?"

"I've already learned everything Stovall could teach me." Valerie commented with no trace of humor.

"Jesus, you accused me of over-confidence?" Doug laughed.

"Get in the shower. I'm tired of waiting." Valerie playfully pushed him.

"Man, I must be great in bed to make you this impatient." Doug winked as he painfully stood up.

"Don't flatter yourself. I do most of the work." Valerie stood and followed him to the bathroom.

"Only while you're on top." Douglas defended.

Chapter: The Bulwark

Jacob and Gaston stood inside a run-down building in the industrial district of Kios. Douglas had cheaply purchased the dilapidated property immediately after the bridge incident. He began converting it into a crime fighting headquarters. To save money, Gaston had moved in. The old plant had shower facilities and a small kitchen that used to serve the different shifts on their lunch breaks. Gaston was not sure what the building manufactured as the industry specific equipment had been liquidated long ago.

Douglas had quietly made the purchase and started stocking the building with things he thought they needed. He set up a gun range and had a hat rack his father, Cliff, had built holding ear protection. Next to that, he had a metal rack with sparring gear and a section of the floor covered with old gym mats he bought off of a school that had been blessed with a donation of new equipment. There were uneven bars for gymnastics, a small section of rock wall, and a variety of free weights.

Large delivery doors allowed them to pull their vehicles inside. Douglas had seen fit to provide a large board with pegs holding a variety of wrenches. There was an upright toolbox about four feet tall containing some of the larger tools. An air compressor rested by that. Douglas wanted this building to handle the majority of the maintenance and conditioning for the Sentinels.

Gaston had volunteered to move in, though he complained about living in a factory to no end. He also enjoyed when Jacob stayed with him. After leaving France, he spent most of his time alone. Now that he had friends, he found himself growing used to the company of others again. The sleeping arrangements were sparse but comfortable. The manager's office held a twin bed, as did the old payroll office.

Jacob spent so much time at "The Bulwark", as Douglas called it, that he had started moving some of his possessions out of the apartment above the coffee shop. Doug approved of the move since some dangerous men knew where he lived. If Jake stayed in a building that only The Sentinels knew about, he would be safe.

Gaston set three aluminum soda cans on the edge of a table and walked ten yards to stand beside Jacob. The Frenchman turned to face the cans and told the boy, "Whenever you are ready."

Jacob looked at the cans with concentration. He raised his finger as if it were a gun and pretended to shoot. The can on the far left flew off the table and clattered to the floor, sending echoes off the tall empty walls. Jacob opened his hand and pretended to crush the second can in his grip. On the table, the second can's sides caved. The sounds of bending metal reached their ears as the cylinder deformed into a twisted aluminum ball.

Jake laughed. "What should I do to the last one?"

Gaston shivered. "No matter how many times I see you do this, I cannot grow used to it." He looked at the last can and shrugged. "Make it float."

Jacob opened his hand, palm up, and acted as if he were lifting an invisible object. His eyes followed the can as it gently levitated off of the tabletop. After letting the empty soda hang for a moment, Jacob flung his hand high above his head. The can emulated the motion and shot high into the rafters. Silence followed as the object fell back to the floor and a clang erupted when it hit the concrete several feet away.

Gaston jumped at the noise and, awestruck, inquired about the nuances. "Must you perform the hand motions to manipulate the items from a distance?"

Jacob shook his head. "No, it just helps me visualize the outcome a little better. If try it without the (what did Dad call it) pantomime, it takes a little longer to warm up."

Gaston nodded, despite having no idea how Jake did the thing he did. Truthfully, Gaston was not even sure how he used his own power. It seemed to be on all the time. The only exception was the few times he had become enraged and thought about hurting someone. Then the power still functioned, but the flow reversed. Instead of absorbing the pain of others, he sent it flowing into them.

"You are improving. Did your grandparents ever catch you practicing?" Gaston wondered about the boy's time in Clearwater Springs while Douglas recovered in a hospital bed.

Jacob shook his head. "Grandma and grandpa encouraged me to walk in the woods, since I'm from the city. I would practice out there where no one could see me. I would work with rocks, branches, and pine cones. I did scare some squirrels." His youthful face broke out in a boyish grin.

Gaston sagely nodded. "I wish I could control my abilities."

Jake sensed an opening to talk to a kindred spirit. "When did you know you were different?"

The Frenchman shrugged. "When I was a teenager, it was part of the reason that I went into the priesthood." Gaston suddenly quit talking, realizing he had segued into his carefully guarded past.

"Yeah?" Jacob prompted.

"*Oui.*" Gaston flatly replied.

"C'mon, it's me. Tell me what happened." Jake pleaded.

Gaston pulled more empty cans from a plastic recycling bin and walked back to the table in silence. He set up three more and faced the boy. "Show me some more of your tricks."

Jacob crossed his arms. "Why don't you talk about it?"

"Because it is painful. Do you enjoy reliving the worst parts of your life?" Gaston stared daggers.

"Jesus, I'm sorry. I thought you'd want to get if off your chest." Jacob felt wounded by the man's refusal to trust him.

"I will make you a deal. I will tell you soon. Just let me think about how I want to say it. In the meantime, we can discuss other matters." Gaston promised.

Jake nodded. "I can live with that." He left a pregnant pause and then asked another question that had been on his mind. "Is Desiree going to come back?"

Gaston perked up. "Why do you ask?"

"I'm just curious. Dad doesn't like to talk about her leaving. We haven't heard from her. I don't understand how she could follow my father and then suddenly cut herself off from him. I thought she believed in him." Jacob looked with downcast eyes.

Gaston walked back and gave a sad smile. "I don't know if she's coming back, but Douglas wants her to."

"How do you know?" Jacob looked up at him with hope.

"He installed the gymnast bars. He can't use them. You haven't started learning and he hasn't suggested it. I have no use for such skills. The only one of us that would use them is Desiree. He's waiting for her to come back." Gaston confirmed the idea to himself as much as to the boy.

"I hope you're right. If those bad guys come back…" Jacob turned and focused on the cans again. "I don't know if I can do this when it counts."

Gaston assured him. "Just keep practicing. I have faith in you."

"You were a priest. It's easy for you to have faith." Jake remarked.

"If only you knew…" Gaston let the subject drop, but glanced back at the acrobatic equipment.

Two men milled about outside an alley door. They did not have guns in hand but were armed. The tall black woman sauntered up wearing knee high boots and a short skirt. A fur-lined denim jacket covered her torso, hiding what was underneath. In the dim light of the alley, neither man could make out her expression.

"Hey boys, I'm supposed to be the entertainment." Her voice was husky for a woman's.

The closer man shook his head. "No one ordered a girl."

The woman tapped her foot impatiently. "I was booked for to-night. There's a card game going on in there, right?"

"Girls and cards don't mix. Whether you're a stripper or a pro, you're not going in. No one told me about this and you'll just distract them from the game." He sternly stated. "Now hit the road."

"Okay, okay." She knelt down. "Shit, my boot came unlaced." Her fingers slid into the top of her footwear and she sprang up with a knife in hand. The blade penetrated the closest man's thigh, severing the femoral artery. The second guard started to react but the woman was faster. She lunged forward and shoved the blade into his chest. It pierced his lung which quickly collapsed after she pulled the knife out. She spun around to the man gripping the spurting wound on his thigh and plunged the weapon into the base of his skull. He fell to the ground with a thump and the woman wiped the blade clean on his shirt.

With the two guards down, Desiree pulled her ski mask over her face and took a deep breath to steady herself. She had caught wind of an illegal card game run by a loan shark as a side business. She had staked out the event and snapped pictures of the attendees as they entered. They all had rumors of organized crime swirling around them. She had a golden opportunity to wipe out five scumbags plus their guards in one well-executed hit. All she had to do was move in for the kill.

Desiree waited with attentive ears for any indication the tussle with the guards had given her presence away. Erupting laughter from inside told her that she had passed undetected. Desiree rushed forward with her .38 drawn, using a two handed grip to ensure her shots were accurate. She would have the advantage of surprise but would also face multiple targets. Each shot had to count.

Flinging open the door, her eyes quickly appraised her victims. The card table sat in the center of a restaurant's staging area. Pallets of unloaded dry goods lined the wall where room was made for the game. Of the five players, the one directly in front of her had his back turned and was struggling to turn and see who had entered. He would be shot last.

In a controlled manner, she swung the gun around to the player on her left and fired. She hit him center mass and cards tumbled from his hand as he instinctively reached for the wound. Without hesitation, the barrel pointed at the next target and she pulled the trigger. Another center mass hit, but at this range, she would have been disappointed if she had missed. One of the gamblers snapped out of his daze and reached under the table. Before he could draw his weapon, Desiree had fired into him as well. After dispatching the fourth person, she placed the hard steel barrel against the man with his back to her.

"I need names. Who's next up the ladder?"

"You're not getting anything out of me. This was just a friendly game." He snarled like a caged beast, harmless but posturing nonetheless.

"I don't have time to torture you; so have it your way." She fired and watched him slump over the table. She was too close and a little spatter hit her clothes. "Damn." Fortunately, the dark colored jacket would hide the blood from a cursory glance. She scooped up the cash and walked out. Robbery had not been the motive but the stakes they had been playing for would cover rent for at least the month.

Chapter: Examining the Evidence

Detective Clarence Sudduth looked over the cases involving an uncommon tire size (E70-14). The tracks in question matched up with a few other crime scenes. If they were related, the cases represented an inconsistent and violent individual. The three instances he found each involved a different type of murder weapon and one of them was a robbery gone wrong. The others appeared as random murders. With a laptop in the seat beside him, Clarence stopped the car in a parking spot in front of Caffeine Nation. The amateur, Douglas Lawson, needed to see what the professional detective had found.

Clarence stepped out with the computer in hand and walked into the shop. A *ding* announced his entry and Cindy waved at him. He gave the cute college student a nod and continued to a table in the corner where Douglas waited.

"Good afternoon, *detective*." The owner greeted him.

"Lawson." Clarence responded concisely but not without warmth. "Your boy's not with you today?"

Douglas shook his head. "He's in class. I've gotta make sure he gets his education."

"Brass tacks." Clarence sat down and opened the laptop, spinning it so that Douglas could see the screen.

"Three recent crimes with matching tire size and tread pattern. Chronologically, the first was three teenage boys murdered with a large caliber handgun. They were joyriding and we had gotten some reports of them harassing people. We're not sure what happened next, but it appears that someone with E70-14 tires ran them off the road and executed the survivors."

Douglas looked at the pictures on the display. "Jesus, they were just kids."

Clarence solemnly nodded. "The last one is the one you are currently investigating. No new info on my end. Here's where things go bonkers.

"A pharmacy delivery vehicle was robbed and the driver killed with a shotgun blast to the stomach. The perpetrators tried to avoid security cameras and were mostly successful but one of them caught them carrying a tote full of drugs. We followed their general direction and found the same tire tracks in a nearby parking lot." Clarence took the laptop back and quickly pulled up grainy black and white footage.

Douglas' face drained of color. "You have to be freakin' kidding me."

The screen showed two men dressed in dark clothes with ski masks over their faces. The taller one wore a trench coat but it was obvious he was very thin. The second man stood a head shorter but even with the darkness, appeared very muscular.

Clarence resumed speaking. "They didn't go after the normal junkie fare or anything with a real street value."

Douglas finished for him. "They were stealing ingredients for Bernard Miller, our resident mad scientist. That connection, plus the distinctive body types, means the two men on camera are *Bestia* and Devil."

Clarence smiled. "Congratulations. It looks like you may get another crack at them."

"Or they'll get another crack at me. I'll never walk normally again." Doug spat with bitterness in his voice.

Detective Sudduth shook his head. "You've got the deck stacked in your favor this time. You've got your Sentinels and you've got a cop that believes you."

Douglas laughed. "Desiree left. She is no longer in my employ and she was the only one that could hold her own in a fight."

Clarence nodded. "We'll just have to bring you up to speed on kicking ass. Do you have a conceal and carry license?"

Doug nodded. "Desiree convinced me to do the paper work and a class but I've never gotten around to buying a gun."

"Okay, find a shooting range and I'll teach you and any of your friends that want to learn. Also, any other self-defense measures you can take, go for it."

"Will do." Doug shifted in his seat. The time had come to lay all his cards on the table. He had to come clean about the uncovered infidelity. "I have a lead from the wife's end, but I don't see how it factors in with Devil and *Bestia*."

Clarence perked up. "Tell me something good."

"Priscilla Ramsey was having an affair, some tennis instructor from her country club." Douglas flashed a smile. "I know you've got evidence that our friends from the bridge killed Martin, but that's a pretty big coincidence. I'm going to check out this Tobias Richmond guy, if anything, just to cross him off the list."

Sudduth nodded. "Follow up all possible angles and don't leave anything to chance. You know, you wouldn't make a half-bad detective."

Doug could not conceal the pleasure of being complimented. A dopey grin spread from ear to ear.

"Calm down Einstein, I didn't say you'd make a good one." He laughed.

Douglas joined him with a chuckle. "Watch out, we might actually become friends one day."

When Clarence left, Mr. Lawson called Gaston. The Frenchman picked up the phone and heard his boss inquire, "How would you like to visit a country club?"

Gaston sighed into the phone. "What are you up to?"

Douglas continued. "You'll need a really nice suit. Do you own one? We can get you fitted for a rushed job if you don't."

"No, I do not have a suit. Why do I need to go to a country club?"

"I'll explain on the way to the tailor." Douglas promised. "I'll be by to pick you up."

Gaston muttered as Douglas hung up the phone.

Chapter: Happy Hour

D r. Samantha Nichols had her purse slung over her shoulder and walked out of Bryers Hospital. The heat radiating off of the asphalt caught her by surprise after spending twelve hours in air conditioning. She stopped wondering what she would do the next day. She did not have to come to work and without something to occupy her mind, she worried about going stir-crazy. She could read a novel, but had already finished every book in her apartment. She thought about catching a movie but felt weird going alone. Plus, none of the current cinema offerings appealed to her. She almost wanted to walk inside and volunteer for another shift to avoid another day to herself.

A voice caught her ear. "Good evening, Dr. Nichols."

She turned to see Dr. Straub walking toward her.

The middle-aged man spoke with a casual confidence. "I was ending my shift too, and had the crazy idea of grabbing a drink."

Samantha was taken aback. It was not unusual for a few of the staff to get together after work sometimes, but Samantha had never been invited. Furthermore, Dr. Straub rarely socialized. "Oh, I don't know. I haven't been much of a drinker since college."

Stuart chortled. "I'm not talking about getting wasted. I'm talking about sipping a drink and having a nice conversation." His face betrayed amusement with her. "If you decide to join me, there is only one rule: No shop talk. If you don't leave your work at work, you will drive yourself crazy."

Samantha looked at her mentor's earnest face and made her decision. "Okay, where are the good watering holes?"

This time, Stuart guffawed. "Watering hole? Are we in the old west? Let me hitch my horse to the post."

"Are you making fun of me?" Samantha felt like an embarrassed schoolgirl for a moment.

"I meant no offense. My dear, you have to lighten up. Else, you'll put yourself in an early grave." Dr. Straub's soft eyes pleaded with her to not hold anything against him. "I'll show you a great place. It's quiet, stately, and reasonably priced."

"It sounds too good to be true." Samantha gave him a suspicious look.

"Okay, so the drinks aren't that reasonable." He smiled and offered his arm to her.

A short drive later, Samantha found herself in a hotel bar. The floor was carpeted with plush seats around small four person tables. Against the back wall, well stocked shelves towered over a long ornate wooden bar. Dim recessed lighting gave all the glassware a gleam that accented rather than distracted. As she walked up to a stool with Stuart beside her, a pretty woman in her late thirties greeted them. "Good afternoon, Doctor Straub. Brought a friend today?"

"I finally decided that I needed help holding down this bar. We can't let it float away now, can we?" Stuart tapped the counter top. "A dry martini, if you don't mind."

Samantha noticed how easily Stuart had made the bartender light up when he entered. She wondered if he had that effect on everyone. She had never heard a complaint about his bedside manner at the hospital. Lost in thought, Sam heard the bartender clear her throat and realized everyone had been waiting for her to order.

"I'll have rum and diet cola."

"Do you want the well or something else?" The lady behind the bar had already quickly assembled Dr. Straub's drink.

"Well is fine." The words felt awkward in her mouth.

Stuart began speaking. "I've been watching you and your work."

Samantha felt a sudden fear shoot through her. "What do you mean?"

"It's nothing sinister. I'm just worried." He gestured toward the newly appeared napkin and glass by Samantha's hand and did not resume until she picked it up and took a sip. "You are focused and that is commendable."

"But?" Samantha waited.

Stuart gave a soft chuckle and continued. "But you are burning yourself out. I don't think you have an outlet. When you are not at the hospital, what do you do?"

Samantha's look grew flinty. "I thought you said no shop talk."

Stuart's smile faded. "This isn't about shop. This is about getting you out of the shop more often. Now answer me, how do you spend your days off?"

Samantha took a long sip to buy a few more seconds to formulate her answer. Put on the spot, nothing came into her mind.

Tired of waiting for her silence to end, the elder doctor continued. "That's what I thought." He looked down at his drink and suddenly looked much older when he stopped smiling. When he looked up, his jovial expression had returned. "Let's do something together tomorrow. You need to get out of your rut."

Samantha took another long pull from her glass and realized there was nothing left but ice. Where had her drink gone? "I don't know. There's lots of TV to watch."

Stuart shook his head. "Ready with weak excuses? That's a disappointment."

Dr. Nichols motioned for the bartender and pointed at her empty glass.

"Have you even seen this city you live in? Kios has the botanical gardens, a zoo, parks, historic buildings, clubs, bars, museums... Surely, something here is worth going out for." His voice became more impassioned.

Samantha suddenly felt resentment toward Dr. Straub. She thought, "Who the hell does he think he is? I am fine on my own and he shoves his nose into my life without asking." She grabbed her new rum and coke and slung it back, taking a huge gulp.

Stuart reached out and slid the glass away from her. "You've downed two drinks in a matter of minutes. I think you should give them a chance to metabolize."

Dr. Nichols fumed. "I am a grown woman."

"Yes, but you should probably not drink like an inexperienced student. I invited you out because I thought you needed to cut loose but this may have been a mistake." Straub sounded disappointed.

"Don't you condescend to me." Samantha suddenly heard Douglas' words in her voice. Was that how Douglas had felt every time she attempted to help him? She stopped, dead in her tracks. The effects of alcohol had snuck up on her. One minute she was sober and the next, her head seemed to bob on an uncertain sea.

"I am so sorry, Dr. Straub. This isn't me." Samantha tried to apologize but the rum hindered her ability to elaborate.

Stuart nodded. "I know." She wondered how he really could, but he continued talking. "You have a fan in the hospital, a gossipy little nurse."

Samantha rolled her eyes. "Penelope?"

"I believe she prefers Penny." The older man corrected. "She said you were having trouble with an ex-boyfriend. Tell me about him."

"This is a bad idea. I need to think about him less, not more." Samantha looked down at the bar and wondered if it really moved or she just could not hold her head steady.

"If you truly could forget about him, it would be great. Most likely, you will bury thoughts of him without resolving anything. Then, those feelings will rise up to haunt you again when something reminds you of him. You are a psychiatrist. I shouldn't have to explain the need for closure to you."

"Dr. Straub, he is a conflicted individual. I thought I loved him but he wasn't stable enough for me. He also resented any attempt to help him. He has a new girlfriend but recently started calling me for help. I basically told him that it was too little too late. I'm not sitting around waiting for whenever he needs me." Her tone shifted to anger as she spoke.

Stuart nodded with understanding but countered her argument. "You say you offered to help him repeatedly in the past. When he finally realizes that he needs help, you would naturally be the first person that he thinks to contact. He probably never imagined that an offer of help would be rescinded, especially from someone in the mental health field."

Samantha glared at him. "You're saying I'm wrong?"

"No, I'm saying that you feel like he's using you, and that may be partially true, but he also sees you as someone that wants to help. He sees you that way because of your past behavior. Your refusal probably came as a shock." The doctor sipped at his drink and continued. "I don't think either of you is totally right or totally wrong and I'm not telling you how to handle him. I just want you to look at it from his point of view."

"God, why are you so smart?" Samantha put her hands in her hair and gave a tug. "You've probably written me off as a psychiatrist."

"Of course not." He laughed. "We're the most blind when looking at our own problems." He put a hand on her shoulder. "I hope you'll think of me when you need someone to talk to. I've been around a while and have a lot of experience to pull from. I want to see you succeed, Samantha. Now let's change subjects while you sober up a little."

After an hour of sitting at the bar, Dr. Nichols caught a ride back to the hospital parking lot and drove herself home. The whole ride, she thought about Dr. Straub. Patient, wise, charismatic; was there a virtue that he did not possess? She smiled at the thought of such a man looking out for her. He certainly forced her to have an epiphany.

Ruminating over his words, she decided to do something new on her day off. The Botanical Gardens of Kios sounded nice.

Chapter: Return to the Fold

Having come from the Bulwark, Jacob walked into Caffeine Nation with Gaston. Douglas greeted them with an excited shout across the shop. "Come over and look at this! It finally arrived!"

Jacob smiled at his father's child-like enthusiasm as Douglas waved around a sleek black walking stick with ergonomic handle. "Is that the self-defense cane?"

Mr. Lawson nodded. "Should I name it Zeus or Thor?" He thought for a moment and then spoke again. "I guess Vulcan is the one that actually creates the lightning for Zeus. Well, Hephaestus is the Greek equivalent of Vulcan but it doesn't have the same ring. I don't know; what do you think?"

Gaston apathetically replied "Zeus" at the same moment that Jacob yelled "Thor!"

Douglas tapped the end of the cane on the ground. "I need to charge this thing for eight hours before I can use it." Sighing, he changed subjects. "We need Desiree back. I think I can get her on-board if I could just talk to her. I've received new information that could appeal to her sense of vengeance. Which one of you thinks you could convince her to meet me on the rooftop?"

Gaston raised an eyebrow. "Why the rooftop?"

Douglas laughed. "I've always wanted a rooftop meeting between crime fighters. This will be just like one of those team-up issues where the two heroes decide to put aside their differences to take on a bigger threat."

Jacob jumped up and down. "I need a costume."

Gaston rolled his eyes. "I will speak to Desiree. I know where she's staying. However, you need to give me some information to entice her. I doubt she will be easily convinced."

"Just use your charming personality." Douglas attached the adapter to his new walking stick.

Gaston gave an exaggerated smile for a split second and then sneered at Douglas. "Your sense of humor is too predictable."

"At least I have one." Douglas laughed, oblivious to the ugly looks his friend gave off.

"Really, I need something to pique her interest. She won't be swayed otherwise." Gaston emphatically repeated his request.

"Okay, tell her that she'll have an opportunity for revenge. If she wants to know more, she has to be on the roof."

Gaston nodded. "I will deliver the message."

Jacob watched Douglas stand with the wind whipping around his trench coat. Jake stood against the door to the stairwell trying to keep out the chill. He was cold but enjoying the thrill of being up late and acting like a real comic book character. He wore a black hooded sweatshirt, pretending that it was his cape and cowl. He had spent the evening drawing sketches of his future costume.

A figure moved in the shadows of the roof across from Douglas' shop. The lean, black-clad vigilante flung herself over the narrow alley and landed with a soft thump. She stood to her full height and coldly nodded to Mr. Lawson.

"I'm glad you could make it." Doug opened the conversation.

"It's nice to see you again." Desiree added a little too formally. "How's your girlfriend?"

"I don't want to talk about that." Doug did not want to go off on a tangent. He was anxious to hear her say she would return but also understood that he needed to establish some common ground again.

"Did I find a sore spot?" She maliciously teased, not knowing the status of his current relationship.

"The news mentioned two dead drug dealers over on the corner of Olive and 14th. Was that you?" Douglas asked with real interest.

"Are you going to turn me in?"

"Of course not." Douglas scoffed as Jacob and Gaston breathed twin sighs of relief. "I may not agree with the methods but I think your intentions are noble."

"Yeah, it was me." Desiree quickly changed the subject. "That's a nice looking cane."

Douglas held it up for her to examine. "Look at the handle."

"Is that an input for an AC adapter?" Desiree's eyes intently studied the device.

"Yeah, and there's a button on the handle that discharges the electricity. This bad boy is a giant cattle prod." He reminded her of a big kid. "It's so fun to see it in use."

"So, what did you want to meet about?" Desiree cut to the chase.

"Join us. The Sentinels need you." Douglas stated with conviction and enthusiasm.

"Can I kill?"

"No." Doug did not hesitate.

"Then I'm going." She turned to leave.

Gaston stepped forward. "Wait. Douglas misses you." He paused and added with a voice full of sorrow. "We all miss you."

Desiree turned back to face him. "Gaston, Douglas' rules are holding us back."

"He hasn't told you why he really wanted you to meet us." Gaston tried to change the subject.

"And why is that?" Desiree watched for any signs of deception.

Douglas took over again. "I have a lead on Devil and *Bestia*. They are up to something and we can square off against them again."

Desiree shifted her gaze from face to face. Jacob appeared youthful and exuberant. The boy carried himself with more self-assurance ever since the fight on the bridge. Gaston eyed her with longing and melancholia. Douglas looked at her with hope and trepidation, but something in his eyes filled her with confidence that they could decisively win this time.

He held out his hand, begging her to take it. "We can be heroes."

Desiree smiled and shook her head as her resolve crumbled. "I will help you as long as we are going after Devil and *Bestia*, but once they are captured, I'm gone."

Gaston's expression soured but Jacob cheered. "We're a team again, sort of!"

Desiree laughed. "It's nice to see you, too."

The boy stepped closer and pulled a fluorescent yellow tennis ball from his hoodie pocket. "I've learned a few new tricks since you left."

Douglas mirthfully added, "He likes to show off."

Jake tossed the ball to Desiree. She had no trouble catching it. She examined the sphere, looking for anything unusual. "It's just a normal tennis ball."

Jake made a flicking motion with his hand and the ball sailed out of her hand and into the black night sky. With an equally quick movement, he clenched his fist and the ball stopped, frozen above them like an unnaturally colored moon. He gritted his teeth in effort and the ball collapsed. The air rushed out as an invisible force punctured the felt and rubber. As the boy opened his hand, a mangled mess of fabric and curved sections of a hard yet ductile compound plummeted to Earth.

Desiree muttered, "Holy shit."

"Yes." Gaston agreed, dryly.

"Hey, virgin ears." Douglas chastised.

Jacob laughed. "I've heard that word before."

Douglas shrivered. "Okay, let's go inside. I think late night crime-fighting rendezvous should be done in the summer." He opened the door and let everyone follow him inside.

Once downstairs, Desiree asked to be briefed on the state of things. Relishing the moment, Douglas mentioned the Bulwark. "We have a new base of operations since this one has been compromised. Gaston will meet you tomorrow and show you the location of our secret lair. After that, we're going to follow up on a lead. Priscilla Ramsey had a lover and I happen to know where he works." He wore a self-satisfied smile as he outlined the rest of the plan.

"You are Louis Cherieffe and I am your business partner that injured himself on a ski trip with you to the French Alps. My name will be Robert Paulson. You will insist on a tour of the club and I will complain that my leg hurts so that I can break away and get some intel on Tobias Richmond. Got it?"

"Could you have had you're accident in *Haute-Savoie?*" Gaston asked.

"What does it matter?" Douglas asked.

"I've always wanted to visit but never went."

"Fine. We went to the alps." Douglas conceded.

"*Oui.* I shall be the elegant and sophisticated French business man and you will be the clumsy American." Gaston spoke with condescension.

"Great!" Douglas acted as if he did not understand the insult. Turning his attention to Desiree, he continued. "If we find Tobias on site, I want you standing by to follow him to his residence, wherever that may be. You'll need a very vanilla vehicle to follow him as to not attract attention. Gaston's Honda is boring." Doug flashed a joking smile at the Frenchman.

Jacob interrupted. "What about me?"

"You can ride with Desiree. A second set of eyes would be good. Keep her in line, okay?"

Jacob emphatically nodded.

Chapter: The Meadows

Tobias Richmond left his Mazda Miata parked with the top down in the employee lot of The Meadows. No one would take anything from the open cockpit. Truthfully, the tennis instructor had no items to steal. He walked past a manned guardhouse waving and smiling politely as he entered the grounds. He carried his racket, carefully protected in its case, and thought about the wasted trip. Priscilla would not join him for her noon appointment and one o' clock lunch date. After all, her husband had just died. Still, he did have quite a hold on her. She may have fallen so far out of love with Martin that she would come to see him today anyway. One could never tell with women. Regardless, he had to keep up appearances. Any deviations from his routine could be interpreted as suspicious.

Gaston walked beside the official from the membership office. Doug staggered along behind them. Originally, he acted like his crippled leg slowed him down, but only a few minutes into the hoax, he realized that he did not have to act. The cane helped but the country club grounds were too expansive. His ankle, knee, and hip started to ache deep in his bones. Ahead of him, Gaston and the administrator discussed the merits of the farmland in *Cote d'Or* until Douglas interrupted

"Louis, I am afraid that I will have to sit down. The weight on my hurt leg is unbearable. Monsieur," he looked at the Country Club employee. "Is there a lounge where I could rest for a few moments?"

"Of course," The tour guide pointed to a pair of double doors leading into a building designed to resemble a log cabin. "The lounge has a full service kitchen and bar. I'm sure you will find our bartenders mix the best martini in the city."

Douglas gave a weak smile. "Thank you." Then he looked at Gaston. "Louis, I defer judgment to you. If you would like to join this establishment, I would like to as well. I will re-join you as soon as I am sufficiently refreshed."

Gaston nodded at him. As soon as Douglas hobbled away, he heard derisive laughter after a few whispered words.

Douglas ignored the slings and arrows and worked his way into The Meadows lounge. No one sat at the bar. So, Douglas limped up to a stool and sat down.

The bartender sauntered over. "What can I get for you, sir?"

Douglas started conversationally. "I've heard that you make a mean martini. Is that true?"

"That's what most people order. I think I make a better Manhattan."

Douglas nodded. "Well, I trust you more than that douche bag giving the tour. He looks like he drinks lemon juice straight out of the bottle."

The bartender laughed. "One Manhattan, do you prefer yours wetter or dryer?"

"You're the expert. Make it like you would drink it." Douglas continued. "You seem like the honest sort. I've heard about a tennis teacher here named Tobias Richmond. Is he any good?"

The bartender conspiratorially leaned in as he mixed the drink. "I've seen much better come through." He poured two ounces of blended whiskey. "He's passable but not up to the caliber you'd expect in a place like this." He added half an ounce of sweet vermouth followed by the same quantity of dry. "He was hired by reputation alone."

"Well, that's interesting. I'd heard pretty good things about him." Douglas prompted.

The bartender threw in a dash of bitters. "Most of the guy's students dropped out or found another instructor. We keep three on staff." He swirled the mixture with ice. "I've overheard them say he was kind of aloof." He filled a clear cocktail glass and tossed in a maraschino cherry. "The only student he's kept is Priscilla Ramsey. Boy, he sure acts differently when she shows up. They even have lunch in here after her lesson. Get this; she picks up the check for both of them. I tell ya' they have the rumors flyin'." The bartender punctuated the last remark by setting the glass on a white square napkin in front of Douglas.

Einstein took a big gulp and smiled. "That is a damn fine drink. How much do I owe you?"

Bartender shook his head. "Fifteen. It's sad, 'cause there's only about four dollar of liquor in there."

Douglas handed him a twenty and displayed an extra ten. "Could you look at a picture and tell me if you recognize someone?"

The bartender looked at the tip and nodded. "Sure thing."

Douglas unfolded the printed picture of Tobias Richmond from Phoenix, Arizona and handed it to the bartender.

"Sorry, never seen him before." He handed it back. "He's a stranger to me."

Douglas showed it to him again. "This isn't Tobias?"

The bartender closely looked at it a second time. "The hair's the same but they look different. Chin, cheekbones, eyes."

"Really? Could you point him out?"

The bartender looked concerned. "Sorry, I'm not supposed to come out from behind the bar, even if the place is burning down, but if you go to that window," he pointed to a wide pane of glass overlooking the green and white tennis courts. "You could see him."

Douglas handed him the ten dollar bill. "Thanks, buddy." He pulled out his cell phone and limped toward the window. He dialed Desiree and waited for her to pick up.

"Yes, sir?"

"I am looking at Tobias Richmond and he doesn't look anything like his picture. Does that seem odd to you?"

"It does." Douglas could visualize her waiting with disciplined patience.

"Sandy blond hair, athletic build. I think we should end our tour and stake out the employee parking. We need to follow him at a distance, find out where he lives." Douglas rattled off the plan and waited for confirmation.

"I'm on it."

Douglas looked over the tennis courts again but did not see the possibly fake Tobias. The instructor had slipped away. He hopped to the door, hoping to find the suspect outside. It looked like the man had just vanished.

"Someone matching that description is getting into a Mazda Miata, kind of a teal color." Desiree quickly asked, "Do you want the boy to go with me or stay behind?"

"Take him. Let him see how boring a stakeout is. If you get a chance, try to lift Mr. Richmond's finger prints. I'm not sure if our police contact can do anything with them but we should try." Douglas paused. "Be careful. This guy is not who he's pretending to be. He could be dangerous."

"People who use false identities usually aren't the most open of people. I'll be careful and I'll keep the boy safe too."

"Have fun." Douglas mockingly spoke and then pushed the end-call button.

Chapter: Penny

Penelope entered Caffeine Nation swiveling her head, looking for any sign of Douglas Lawson or Gaston De Paul. She liked the ambiance of the shop. It did not resemble a franchise in the slightest. The whole place felt lived in and personal. She could picture regular customers being greeted by name as they walked through the door.

A young girl wearing a name tag inscribed with "Cindy" spoke up. "Good afternoon, can I get you anything?"

Penelope suddenly felt self-conscious. "Um, I was looking for Mr. Lawson."

"Oh, he stepped out. I'm not sure when he'll be back." Cindy followed up with suggestive selling. "You could have a drink and wait for him. I make a delicious Mocha Latte."

Penny ignored the offer and leaned in conspiratorially. "Are you part of his crime-fighting team?"

Cindy started giggling. "Crime-fighting team? I'm just a college student."

Penelope leaned toward her and whispered. "Is that code for something?"

"Uh, no. It means I go to school." She eyed the strange woman warily. "How do you know Mr. Lawson?"

"I'm a friend of his ex-girlfriend." Penny tried to sound nonchalant.

"Are you referring to Samantha?" Cindy asked, suddenly interested.

"Yeah, we work together at the hospital." Penny smiled.

Cindy nodded. "Does she ever talk about Mr. Lawson?"

"All the time, mostly about how she's over him." They both laughed.

Cindy nodded. "I told Douglas she was in love with him and he didn't believe me."

Penelope looked up at the menu as she replied. "Yeah, there's some drama there. Apparently, he has a girlfriend. Can I get a pumpkin spiced latte?"

"That's more of a seasonal item. I don't have all of the ingredients right now." Cindy shrugged.

"Okay, give me that mocha latte you mentioned." She fumbled with her purse and handed a debit card to the cashier. "So, back to our gossip, do you think they'll hook up?"

"I'd like to see it happen." Cindy swiped the card and handed it back. "I don't really care for his girlfriend. She seems kind of cold sometimes."

"Is she a crime-fighter?" Penny asked.

Cindy paused to give the customer a suspicious look. "Where did you get the idea that Mr. Lawson is some kind of vigilante? He plays chess and reads books. Besides, he's one of the sweetest people I know."

Penelope did not know why she expected everyone to readily admit to Douglas' peccadillo. She needed to earn the girl's trust. "I know he needs to keep his identity a secret but it's okay. I want to help. I can sew and patch the uniforms or costumes or whatever he calls them."

Cindy grew nervous; her hands visibly shook as she handed the drink to the customer. "I don't know where you get your information from, but Mr. Lawson doesn't have costumes or stay out all night leaping across rooftops. He has to have a cane just to walk."

The nurse thought for a moment. What could she say or do to convince Douglas' employee that she was serious? "Tell him I'll be back with some costume samples. I'm quite the seamstress."

Cindy warily replied. "I'm sure you are. Listen, come to think of it, I have no idea when Mr. Lawson will be back. It'd be a waste of time to wait for him, but I can pass along your message."

That seemed to mollify Penny. "Okay, I'll go home and get to work. It was nice meeting you, Cindy." She lifted the drink and added, "This is a really good latte."

Cindy sheepishly waved goodbye and shook her head when the strange woman exited. "Mr. Lawson sure does attract some eccentric people."

Nurse Penny's home was a cramped apartment close to the hospital. A 21 inch television provided background noise with basic cable programs that she did not watch. A small laptop with external speakers sometimes provided music. Her neighbor shared his wifi with her, probably in the hope that she would sleep with him (which never happened). The kitchen and bedroom blended into the living room as was common in budget rentals. Dishes peeked over the lip of the sink. A disposable coffee cup for Caffeine Nation sat on the counter. Her scrubs were tossed haphazardly on to an unmade bed only ten feet away from the refrigerator.

Dolls took the focus from everything else though. Particle board shelves lined the walls and each one held tens of displayed dolls with different outfits. None of the miniature clothes were purchased. Penny had sewn each article based on patterns before she graduated to playing fashion mogul and creating her own styles for each doll.

The practice had started when she was younger and she could not afford the accessories for her toys. The mocking of other children served to remind her how low her station in life really was. Rather than give in to the japes and sneers from the wealthier girls, she had resolved to have her own despite her parents' lack of income. Her first attempts only brought more heckling as her skill could not match her ambition. The clumsy outfits barely fit her curvaceous plastic women, but later dresses incrementally improved until she had developed a reputation for quality work. Of course, that did not happen until years later and the other girls had outgrown dolls. Penny held onto her hobby almost out of spite.

Then, the same scenario played out with clothes in high school.

Penelope had learned though. She scaled the clothes up to her size and continued working diligently at her sewing, crocheting, needlework, embroidery. As a new style spread through the halls, she would observe and replicate in her bedroom. Within weeks, she would catch up on the latest fashions. Despite her efforts, the popular girls never seemed to accept her, even after she had sewn in counterfeit tags of the name brands. In the end, it did not matter. They could sense that she was not one of them.

But those thoughts left her as Penelope sat on her couch with a sketchbook on the coffee table in front of her. She sat hunched over drawing different designs. She needed something that would make Douglas Lawson bring her on board as his costume maker. The clothing needed to be strikingly bold. She did not know his measurements. So, her plan was to make something for herself and model it. "This is what I can do." She'd unveil the piece for him, twirling around so he could see the craftsmanship that went into every aspect of it. Of course, he would want her to help after seeing her work.

The only problem was finding a design with which she wanted to move forward. Several false starts bore angry scribbling to obliterate any evidence of their previous existence. Then she smiled. An idea had occurred to her and she started drawing in hurried strokes. It was a rough draft but she wanted the image committed to paper before it slipped away. The concept had popped into her nearly fully formed. She set down her trusty No. 2 and picked up her colored pencils. She grabbed purple and red. Her pulse quickened. Gaston and Douglas would marvel at her work, she just knew it.

Chapter: Playing Personnel

Douglas paced around the Bulwark while Gaston sat in front of the PC monitor. Both felt a worry gnawing at their entrails. Gaston glanced at the computer screen. "We should call them. Maybe the matter could be easily clarified?"

Douglas nodded. "Tobias Richmond made it home without issue and Desiree is watching him. Still, this doesn't make sense. The time Mrs. Ramsey gave me and the time her husband's body was discovered make this imposter unlikely to be the killer. He couldn't have made it to the murder scene in time, but this is too big of a coincidence." He held up a finger to represent his first point. "He drives away all his students except for Priscilla Ramsey." He extended the next finger. "He starts an affair with her." Three fingers. "He is using a stolen identity the whole time." Now, four fingers sprayed out. "The husband is murdered and it is made to look like an accident."

Gaston impatiently gestured toward the phone. "*Je suis d'accord avec toi.* Please call his former employer already."

Douglas put the phone to his ear after dialing. While waiting for someone to pick up, he asked Gaston, "How is that list of cars with that model tire coming?"

"*Ça ne sert à rien!* That tire is used on everything from Pontiac to Dodge and everywhere in-between."

Someone on the other end answered. Douglas quickly introduced himself. "Yes, may I speak to the personnel manager?" He waited as his call was transferred.

"Hello, this is Marcus."

"Hello, Marcus. I am looking to hire a tennis instructor and had an applicant named Tobias Richmond. I understand that he worked for you previously. Could you tell me anything that would help me with this hiring decision?" Doug tried his best in impersonate a human resources manager.

"Tobias, huh? Yeah, he was a phenomenal player and instructor with a very good rapport with students. The only black mark against him was the way he left."

"Oh, how's that?" Douglas tried to keep his tone subdued.

"Well, he didn't give us any notice. He just didn't come in one day. We received a letter from Kios asking that his final check be forwarded to his new address. He didn't even come in and say goodbye." Marcus held a tone of disappointment in his voice.

"Well, that doesn't sound very professional." Douglas tried to lead the conversation further.

"It was very out of character." Marcus sighed.

"Thank you for your time. I think I have all that I need." Doug hung up the phone with a heavy heart. He looked at Gaston with genuine worry in his eyes. "This guy is more dangerous than I first thought. I am sure the real Tobias Richmond is dead."

Gaston nodded, unsurprised. "According to your detective friend, the tire tracks incriminate *Bestia* and Devil. Where does the *faux* Tobias come in?"

Desiree walked in through the large garage door proudly holding a meticulously preserved aluminum soda can in a clear baggy. "Our mystery man threw this into the trash on his way into the apartment building."

Jacob trailed in behind her hopping with excitement. "We have his fingerprints!"

Doug clapped. "Yes! We can have Detective Sudduth see if this guy is connected to any other crimes." Looking at Desiree, he ordered. "Go ahead and pull the car in. We have time to kill before we'll have an answer on these fingerprints."

Gaston handed the phone to Doug. "*Excusez-moi*, the sooner we get the drink can to the officer, the sooner we know if the gentleman has a violent past."

Douglas silently dialed. "Yes, Detective Sudduth, please. This is Douglas Lawson." He paused, waiting for the investigator. "Hello, Clarence. If I had an item with fingerprints on it, could you lift the prints and get an ID? Uh-huh. Well, you're in luck. We've got a soda can in our possession that a person of interest just handled. Can you meet me at the coffee shop and I'll fill you in? Alright, see you in a few."

Doug hung up. "Gaston, can you continue looking at the list of cars for that model tire. I know we discussed the usefulness of it but if these prints come back as Tobias Richmond, we've wasted time that could have been spent following up other leads."

Gaston nodded.

"Desiree, could you drive me to the shop? My leg is aching and I may have trouble driving the Vette."

She nodded also.

"So Jake, how was your first stakeout?" Doug asked.

"Boring." Jacob honestly answered.

"Good." Douglas thought. "Maybe that'll keep you from wanting to accompany us on more dangerous missions."

He tapped his cane on the hard floor, letting the sound echo off the walls. "Okay team, let's go."

In Caffeine Nation, Detective Clarence Sudduth waited with a comic book opened in front of him. He occasionally flipped a page and sipped on his coffee. He preferred a medium roast with a little cream and sugar. He found that society had progressed to the point where he could not order a regular coffee. There were too many varieties available. Even in a gas station, they had four or five options. Cindy, the cashier, seemed unable to assist him until he named a specific type of coffee. "Whatever happened to just regular and decaf?" He asked her.

The young girl shrugged. "We're a coffee shop. We've got a lot of coffee."

Grimacing, he had handed her cash and briefly entertained the idea of writing a check just to see if she would know what it was.

As he waited on Douglas Lawson, he looked at the brightly colored pages of a superhero battling another strangely costumed man. In the pages, every man had chiseled features and a well-defined physique and every female had curves that would be proportionally absurd on a real woman.

Douglas entered with his son, Jacob. Both of them looked pleased with themselves. The young boy held a plastic bag containing an aluminum can. The cane acted as a surrogate for his bum leg, bearing most of Doug's body weight every other step.

Mr. Lawson laughed and pointed the sleek black walking stick at the comic book. "Interesting reading material. Feeling a little whimsical, Detective?"

"I'm just trying to get into your head. I figured stuff like this had a hand in your little hobby." He handed the comic to Jake. "Here you go, kid. I don't think it's for me."

Jacob excitedly snatched the thin bundle of pages and immediately started reading. Douglas cleared his throat. "Jake, what do you say when someone gives you a gift?"

Sheepishly, Jacob looked up from his comic. "Thank you, Mr. Sudduth."

"You're welcome." Clarence grinned at the many hats Douglas wore: father, businessman, and vigilante. "So, why are you lugging around an empty can? Could that have a certain boy-toy's finger prints on it?"

Douglas nodded. "Yep, special delivery of our illicit lover's prints. None of my people touched it." Douglas shifted from foot to foot. "So, if the fingerprints come back as someone other than Tobias Richmond, what's the next step?"

The detective leaned back, pensively looking at the ceiling. "I'm not even supposed to be investigating Martin Ramsey's death. If he has identification with the false identity, we can book him for that. Maybe we can get him for fraud considering he's entered into some business transactions under a presumed identity."

"And we still don't know if he had a hand in Officer Ramsey's death." Douglas chimed in.

"Regardless, I'll see what comes back. It could take a while, and if he has no prior record, we might not get a hit." Sudduth warned them. Jacob did not hear, too immersed in his new comic book, but Douglas nodded with no hint of levity.

Clarence found himself wondering how the man's mind worked. One moment, he was smiles and jokes. The next, he was as serious as a heart attack and it did not take more than an instant for the transformation. "Another thing," the policeman added. "Do you still feel like you need the patrol cars checking in at night? Nothing has happened in months."

Douglas' dismissed the question with a wave. "They're just biding their time. There is no way they'll let me go unpunished. I ruined their hold on the city and was responsible for getting their tech-guy arrested."

Clarence sighed. "It just seems like they would have acted by now."

"Revenge is a dish best served coldly." Douglas reminded him.

Clarence stood up and gathered his things, including the evidence from Tobias Richmond. "Clichés notwithstanding, the beat cops feel like it's a waste to check on a coffee shop that's not even opened."

"It won't be a waste when someone tries to kill me." Doug did not crack a smile.

"It comes with the territory. If you want to play with dangerous criminals, you have to expect that you're a target." Clarence's voice held very little sympathy. "Anyway, I need to head out if I'm going to drop this by the lab. I've got a date and don't need to be late for it."

"Oh really, getting back out into the dating scene after your divorce?" Doug asked.

"You're slipping, Lawson. I've been wearing my ring for weeks. The wife and I are going to give it another shot." Detective Sudduth held up his left hand. Sure enough, a gold band encircled his ring finger.

"Congratulations." He gave a sincere smile to the detective. "Since love is involved, I won't keep you."

Clarence left in a jovial mood. In addition to his marital reconciliation, the cop had to admit that meeting up with Douglas had added excitement back into his life. Spit-balling theories with Mr. Lawson proved to be one of the high points of his day. Douglas filled out no paper work and worked the cases that he wanted to work. The detective felt a pang of jealousy for his amateurish friend.

Chapter: A New Development

Dr. Samantha Nichols walked through the halls feeling a little more at ease. She had listened to Dr. Straub's advice and went out exploring. She had rented a paddleboat at the lake in the park. It would have been nicer with someone to share it, but regardless, she found that drifting on the lackadaisical waves soothed her. It had been quiet except for the occasional chirping of birds and the slap of water against the bottom of her boat. She lost track of time and may have even fallen asleep amidst gentle rocking. The day before that, she visited the botanical gardens and breathed in the scents of different flowers. She stood on a small red bridge and stared at the koi lazily swishing its tail. That had been a great day as well.

Now, in the hospital, she felt refreshed and ready to dive in to her charts with enthusiasm. She poked around in the rooms, observing that the hospital had continued to function without her. Her patients remained where she had left them. She spent an hour updating her cases and walked the floor again. Smiling and giving gracious hand waves, she greeted the staff and made small-talk with anyone that showed an interest. After socializing, she delved back into her work. While checking on Sean McGuire, she bumped into Penelope.

The waifish nurse excitedly ran up to her. "I've been looking for you! I've got such great news."

Samantha stepped back, afraid she would be tackled as the excited Penny sprinted to her. "It's nice to be back." Dr. Nichols meekly stated.

Penny stopped short of running the woman over. "I went to Caffeine Nation."

Samantha shook her head in disappointment. "Please don't tell me you spoke to Douglas."

The nurse shrugged. "He wasn't there, but I spoke to a girl running the register. Would you believe she tried to convince me that Mr. Lawson is not a crime fighter?"

Samantha shrugged. "I'd believe it. Why would she admit that to a stranger?"

Penelope whined. "But it's me!"

"And how does she know you?" Sam pointed out.

"Well, I have a trustworthy face." Penny lamely replied. "Anyway, I decided to make an outfit for myself. I'm almost done and it's stylish and sexy."

"And where will you wear this outfit?" Samantha's voice became concerned.

"I'm going to model it for Mr. Lawson to show him that I can make quality costumes for him." Penny's face radiated excitement.

"Oh Penelope…" Dr. Nichols sighed. "Didn't we discuss how you shouldn't exacerbate Douglas' delusions?"

"You told me not to but I don't recall agreeing with you." Penelope grew defensive. "I'm designing clothes. How dangerous can that be?"

"You are sewing clothes for a vigilante." Samantha corrected.

"It makes me feel good to help. Besides, it'd be a good excuse to take Gaston's measurements." Penny gave a sly smile.

"Do you even know him? How can you be so infatuated? I've spent time around him and he's a jerk." Samantha countered.

"He can't be that bad. He checks on Mr. McGuire all the time. He was here every day for Mr. Lawson's recovery. Why shouldn't I want someone to dote over me like that?"

"I think you are fixated on him because you need someone to validate you." Samantha impatiently explained. Before Penny could respond, Samantha rolled the conversation forward. "Have you been doing your self-esteem exercises?"

"Yes, but they make me feel stupid. I'm talking to a mirror." Penelope complained.

"Has it helped at all?" Samantha pressed her.

"Not really." Penny looked down at her feet to hide the failure plastered across her face.

"Keep at it. Eventually you will be comfortable enough with your-self to find someone when you are ready for a relationship." Samantha spoke to her like a child.

"I'm ready now! I've spent so much time alone; I just want some-body!" Penelope suddenly shouted.

"That's exactly why you don't need to search for someone at the moment. You are vulnerable and will be easy prey for a man that takes advantage of codependent women." The doctor's detached, clinical voice cut like a knife.

"You think I'm codependent? It must be nice to be such an expert on human nature." Penny turned around and walked away, shaking her head with disgust.

Samantha let her leave and thought, "That'll put a damper on the rest of my day." She thought about what she had said. Had she been too hard on the poor girl? On one hand, she felt that she was correct in her assessment. Penelope demonstrated concerning signs of a lack of socialization. On the other hand, the girl already suffered from a diminished self-worth. "You could have been more tactful." Samantha said to herself.

The doctor entered Sean McGuire's room to check on the patient, as if there would be any change. The probability of recovery plummet-ed the longer someone stayed in a vegetative state and Mr. McGuire had been unconscious in a hospital bed for years. Douglas and Gaston kept using the term coma incorrectly in reference to the man they had somehow sent to the hospital, but Samantha did not judge them for not knowing the nuances of "disorders of consciousness".

Dr. Nichols entered Sean's room and found everything as she had left it. The patient exhibited no change. She sighed. "If you were awake, I could ask you some questions. How did you end up here? Was it the shock of seeing your brother hit by a car or was it Gaston's magical powers?" The thought made her want to laugh. The priest's serious demeanor had almost convinced her but then she remembered that he was covering for Douglas, trying to stop her from pushing for institutionalization. She felt such relief that Mr. Lawson's drama resided only in her past.

Samantha did not want to visit those memories but they tumbled through her mind, dominoes one after another. She remembered the excitement in his voice as he pieced together the puzzle left by an insane doctor, Bernard Miller. She found herself caught up in it too, until Douglas was taken in for questioning. A building collapse and an amnesiac Dr. Miller made Mr. Lawson look guilty of something, even though no one really knew what. She remembered the night that she kissed him after he shared a painful memory. "What was I thinking?" It was such a stupid move on her part. Luckily, Douglas had fled from the apartment. She was angry at the time but it worked out for the best. She needed to find balance in her life and Douglas would never provide it. She would discover it for herself.

Dr. Straub entered the room and cleared his throat behind her. "Dr. Nichols, how were your days off?"

"Very pleasant, thanks." She tucked loose strands of blonde hair behind her ear as she turned to face him. "You dispensed sound advice." Her voice seemed too formal in her ears.

"I'm glad. Hopefully you are rejuvenated; it's going to be a long week. We have inspections Thursday." He tried to act positively. "It's a formality. We know that we are a great hospital."

Samantha nodded in agreement.

"Oh, this came to the hospital, addressed to you." He handed an envelope to her. Not knowing the nature of the package, Stuart Straub left the room and let her open it in without an audience.

Samantha ripped the envelope, pulling the paper out and reading it to herself. She let the paper fall from her hands and thought "I have to call Douglas."

Chapter: Under Observation

Detective Clarence Sudduth strolled with confidence into Caffeine Nation. His sport coat hung open and he looked like he had put in a full shift at work, but his expression conveyed joy. He nodded to Cindy, behind the counter. "Is Douglas here? I've got some news for him."

Cindy nodded. "Let me call upstairs."

"If he's busy, I can leave a note in his office." Clarence offered.

"It's no trouble. He's spending quality time with Jake. I think he's teaching him about video games."

Clarence laughed. "Who's teaching who?"

"Mr. Lawson is teaching Jake." Cindy joined in his mirth. "You've been in a better mood the last few times I've seen you. You look better without a scowl."

Clarence blushed but Cindy did not notice due to his dark skin. "Well, getting my wife back left me less to complain about."

"Awww. I love a good romance." She picked up the phone and dialed. "You'll have to fill me in after you get done talking to – Hello Mr. Lawson, Detective Sudduth is downstairs. He says he has some news…and he's smiling." She paused. "Yes, that is unusual." Then she winked at Clarence. "Okay, bye."

She set the phone back on its cradle and faced him. "He'll be right down."

Clarence nodded but before he could speak, a door marked "Private" swung open. Douglas stepped through with Jacob in tow. "Hello, Detective."

"Hey, Einstein." The cop smirked.

"News and a smile, I hope they are related." Douglas joked.

"Oh they are. Tobias Richmond is a fake. The fingerprints belong to a conman named Scott Edwards. He has a few minor charges for fraud. He seems to specialize in romancing lonely women out of their savings. Nothing violent in his record but he still could've graduated to murder."

"Where is he now?" Douglas asked with excitement in his voice.

"Don't know. I sent a car to pick him up but he wasn't home. We have his apartment under observation. When he shows, we'll move in for the kill."

Doug clapped. "I still think it was *Bestia* and Devil, but I won't complain about another criminal off the streets."

Jacob looked displeased. "We didn't see any action."

Mr. Lawson turned to his ward and clasped his shoulder. "We don't want to see action. Diligence and observation are our tools."

Clarence looked the boy in the eyes. "Listen to Douglas. The cops that try to emulate action movies wash out fast. The majority of crime is solved with evidence and paperwork, not guns or chases."

"I need to watch him, officer. I think he may have the tell-tale signs of an adrenaline junkie." Douglas adopted a mockingly serious voice.

"Can I at least see the guy you caught? Can we watch you interrogate him?" Jake blurted.

Lawson leaned in to the detective and whispered, "Honestly, I'd like to sit in on that. Maybe he has some information related to Ramsey's death that would help me."

Clarence looked exasperated but still in a good-humor. "Give you an inch and you take a mile. I'll see what I can do." He turned and addressed the entire room. "I'll leave you to your gourmet coffees and what-not. Have a good night."

Chapter: A Lonely Valentine

Arturo Gomez threw his gym clothes into his bag and walked out of the locker room. His black hair still glistened with water from the shower he had taken to purge the stink of sweat from his body. He felt elated after his fitness routine. His upper body was fatigued but in a satisfying way; he had accomplished something with his effort. As he walked through the weight room, rows of mirrors reflected his thick arms back at him. He smiled, not out of vanity regarding his appearance, but because he knew those muscles' capabilities. When standard pull-ups had quit making him feel a delicious burn in his arms, he had started strapping a weighted belt to his body to increase the intensity. When he performed squats, he lifted the equivalent of a couple of people with his trunk-like legs. If Raven ever let him loose to go to war, he would be ready to show the world what kind of beast he really was.

He passed the front desk and gave a perfunctory wave to the polo clad manager. "Have a good night." He stepped into the electric lights of a dark city and took a deep breath. The cool air filled his lungs and made him feel invigorated. As he walked through the empty rows toward his Hummer, one of his two cell phones began to vibrate. He had a personal phone and then the pre-paid phone Valerie had provided for business. As he pulled the mobile device from his pocket, he realized the call was arriving on the work phone.

"Hello?" He tentatively greeted.

"Hey, I'm in a little trouble and need you to pick me up and settle my tab." The words came out slowly and slurred.

"Valentine?" Arturo could not believe the amateurish behavior of his co-worker. "You're drunk at a bar?"

"Of course, where else am I going to get drunk?" Scott tittered. "Come on, man. Help me out. I'm in a jam. I'll explain when you get here."

Arturo cursed in Spanish before addressing Valentine again. "Where are you?"

"At The Cosmo. It's near the college." Scott made an effort to speak clearly.

"Isn't that a..."

"Yeah, it's a gay bar. Just help me out, please." Scott's voice lost its mirth. He suddenly sounded old and tired.

Arturo closed his eyes and tried to steel himself. "*Jesus Christo*, I'll be there shortly." He shoved the phone back in his pocket and jumped in his truck. As he navigated the large vehicle through crowded city streets, he wondered what the hell Scott Edwards had managed to botch.

Arturo had to pay for parking in a private lot and scanned the rows of bars for The Cosmo. The unassuming blue neon sign contained no warning that it catered to homosexuals. Arturo could imagine people wandering in by mistake, but knowing Valentine's bisexuality, he doubted that Scott had gone in blind. Arturo walked over and stepped inside. His skin crawled as he entered. Gooseflesh rose as a shudder ran the length of his entire body. He just wanted to grab Valentine and leave, but first he had to find the screw-up.

Arturo stepped around two men having a conversation in the empty dance floor. The music had fallen in volume and a few patrons stood up from their tables and left cash under empty glasses. He caught snatches of conversation, a little bit of laughter, and a voice softly singing along to the song that had just started up. Arturo had not known what to expect but the normalcy of it made him feel even more confused. Nothing seemed overtly gay, the scene was just a bunch of guys having drinks.

Finally, he spied Scott seated at the bar with his head in his hands. Arturo walked directly over and sat on a stool beside him. "Why am I here again?" He growled at the drunken man.

Scott looked up with red eyes. "I need a ride home and enough cash to pay my tab."

Arturo's mouth twisted into a frown. "You called me on the work phone for that?"

Scott shook his head. "I used up my cash taking a cab over here. I figured I could get a ride home with someone." His face momentarily flushed red. "It didn't work out. When I went to pay, my card was declined, well, Tobias Richmond's card."

Arturo leaned in and whispered. "You couldn't get one of your fag friends to cover you? You're supposed to be our con-man."

"I had too much, too fast. I'm having trouble thinking straight." Scott complained as he tilted an empty glass and peered at the sip of brown liquid at the bottom. "Besides, I have no friends."

"Spare me the pity party." Arturo chastised him. "Do you realize how much you are putting the rest of us at risk? What if you let something slip while you're drunk? Right now, you are supposed to be a tennis instructor in love with a middle-aged woman."

Scott threw his head back and laughed. "Oh please, a quarter of the guys in here are wearing wedding bands."

"I don't care what they are doing. I want to know that a member of my team isn't going to sink us because he can't hold his liquor and feels guilty." Arturo wanted to shout but kept his voice down to a throaty whisper.

Scott hissed back. "You think I feel guilty about Priscilla? I don't give a shit what happens to some spoiled, bored housewife."

"Then what is wrong? You sit there sulking like a bitch for a reason." Then Arturo looked up and saw the bartender waiting expectantly.

"Are you going to carry your friend home?" The man asked with mild annoyance.

Valentine interrupted. "You'll have to literally carry me. I need to sober up a little more before I can walk."

Arturo sighed. "Give me a beer. I'll get him out of here when I finish."

The bartender nodded. "What'll you have? We've got..."

"Just give me a beer." *Bestia* rudely cut him off. When the bartender stepped away to fill up a pint, the Mexican continued. "So, what is it that's got you down in the dumps?" His tone softened and a nearly-full beer slid down the bar. Arturo reached out and stopped it, causing some of the head to slosh out and spill on his hand. He grabbed a couple of napkins and wiped off the wasted drink.

Scott obliviously continued complaining. "I didn't set out to be your face man. I never even set out to be on the wrong side of the law."

Arturo nodded in agreement. "Few people wake up and say 'I want to be a career criminal'."

"It crept up on me. I was dating a girl and everything was going fine. I had a bit of financial trouble and needed help fast. I conned my girlfriend out of some money to make ends meet and the next time I found myself living beyond my means, it was a little easier to repeat with the next girl. Before I knew it, I couldn't have a relationship because I would inevitably rip them off." He placed his head on the bar and forlornly looked at the shelf of bottles. "I'm just an actor that has to be satisfied with the role rather than being a real person."

"If you hate it so much, why don't you just stop? Quit the business. Make a new life." Arturo already knew the answer. It was the same reason that he could never stop.

Valentine sat up. "I don't know how. Even if I could, Raven would never let me go. I know too much about her, about the operations."

Arturo awkwardly patted him on the back, wanting to minimize the duration of contact. "Feeling sobered up yet?"

"I think I can walk." Valentine stood on shaking legs. He wobbled for a moment but reached out and caught Arturo's arm.

The Mexican pulled out two twenties and left them on the bar. "Keep the change."

As they crossed the empty dance floor, Arturo chuckled. "So, your first con was a girl?"

Scott stumbled but steadied himself by clinging to his co-worker's right arm. "I prefer girls. I think I'm about 70/30."

Arturo shook his head. "I'm never going to understand that." He reached out with his left hand and pushed open the exit door. Outside, he became highly self-conscious of the fact he had just exited a gay bar with a man holding his arm. No one else seemed to give him a second glance but Arturo still felt eyes upon him.

"You know I'm going to have to tell Raven about this. She needs to know if you're going soft." Arturo warned to distract himself from the feeling of being watched.

Valentine sniggered. "I'm not going soft. I don't care about the people I con. I've been doing this too long for that. I'm scared because I realized that I can't do this forever. I'll get older; my looks will fade. What am I going to do when I can't charm people with my smile?"

Bestia callously replied, "Develop a personality."

"I love you, too." Scott stumbled after his droll retort.

Arturo caught the inebriated man and stood him up. "Watch it." The Mexican gave a quick look around to ensure no one saw him. Many of the other pedestrians were college students out for the night and were too plastered to notice. "We're almost there. I parked right across this street."

On the sidewalk, Arturo could move as slow as he needed to keep pace with Scott, but while crossing the street, he was acutely aware of how sluggishly he crept as each headlight shone like a spotlight on him. The traffic light turned before he finished his journey and car horns honked trying to hurry him. Impatiently, he moved faster, dragging a shuffling Valentine behind him.

Once in the vehicle, Arturo felt relieved. The tinted windows prevented people from seeing the occupants. Looking out the windshield, he watched a few college kids pass by his SUV as he tried to back out of his parking space. "Do the frat boys ever try to pick on your people?"

Valentine looked at him with bleary eyes. "My people? I just told you I prefer women."

"It doesn't matter. One time and you're gay for life." Arturo felt like he added enough of a light tone to indicate he was joking but Scott did not smile.

"As long as we're stereotyping people, you can swim back across the *Rio Grande*." Valentine sulked, looking out the passenger window.

"Come on, I was joking." Arturo felt unusually apologetic toward Scott. He'd never seen the con-man so distraught. "I want to know, does anyone mess with you out here?"

Scott Edwards gave his designated driver a searching look. Assuming his co-worker's sincerity, he answered. "Sometimes, but everyone in that bar is pretty smart about leaving in groups. Gay-bashers are usually cowards. It's always some drunk guy wanting to prove his manhood by beating up some sissies. They back down when we're in groups because they can't stand the thought of losing a fight to 'the gays'." He chuckled. "I knew no one would mess with us tonight because you're a scary bastard."

"Thanks." Arturo smiled at the thought that he could intimidate so easily. Much of the drive passed in silence and each man became lost in his own thoughts. Arturo glanced over at Scott and realized that the alcohol had caught up with his passenger. With eyes closed and his head resting against the window, Valentine slept. His chest rose and fell in a steady, deep rhythm.

Arturo knew where Valentine lived because he had trouble trusting people. When Raven had first assembled them as a unit, *Bestia* had spied on each of his new team mates. Valerie Gossard had caught him at it. Instead of being angry, she complimented his healthy dose of paranoia. Valentine and Devildriver had no idea how much he knew about their lifestyles. Of course in Devil's case, there was nothing to know. The man worked on his car and waited until Raven summoned him. He thought briefly about a new associate that did not last named Greg Phillips. The electronics expert had built a device with which they could hold the city hostage but he had been captured during the execution of their plan. Now, he sat in a mental hospital with no memory thanks to Raven's order and Valentine's poisoning. It was just another reminder of how, in the end, they are all expendable. Mistakes were costly and that made Scott Edwards' indiscretion tonight all the worse. Raven would punish Valentine for sure.

Arturo stopped in front of the apartment complex. "Wake up. You're home."

Scott rubbed his eyes and blinked the drowsiness away. He almost appeared sober. "That was fast."

"You dozed off." Arturo informed him. "Can you make it the rest of the way on your own?"

Valentine winked at him. "You don't want to tuck me in?"

Arturo sneered. "You're treading on thin ice as much as you've already inconvenienced me."

The passenger door swung open, and (unused to such a tall vehicle) Scott fell onto the sidewalk. "Son of a bitch!" He looked at his fleshy part of his palm and admired the scrapped skin. He reached out and grabbed a parking meter, using it to pull himself to his feet. Turning to face his driver, Valentine smiled. "Thanks for being a friend."

Arturo started to open his mouth, but just curtly nodded. As the door closed, the Hummer pulled away. Neither man noticed the nondescript car sitting across the street with the driver discretely watching the building. As soon as Scott Edwards disappeared in the front door, the man lifted a radio and spoke. Unbeknownst to Valentine, a net was closing in fast.

Chapter: Alone Together

Desiree felt the passing air against her face as she sprang forward, gripping the bar and swinging her legs out to generate momentum. Her fingers slipped from the metal and she tucked her knees in and her head down. Leaving the gymnastic bars, the mercenary spun in a tight ball until she unrolled, landing firmly on her feet. She smiled. Douglas had outfitted "The Bulwark" nicely. She had even fired on his homemade gun range. The only portion of the headquarters she left untested was the sparring pads and the wrestling mat. She had wanted to but none of the Sentinels would act as a training partner. "Einstein" never graced them with his presence unless it was at the coffee shop, Jacob was frightened of being beaten by a girl, and Gaston seemed oddly distant since her return (as if she made him nervous).

Desiree glanced over at him and wondered what had changed. There he sat, clad in a black button up shirt, hunched over a computer looking at cars on the monitor. "Gaston, are you thinking of replacing your Honda?"

The Frenchman replied with annoyance. "Douglas asked me to compile a list…"

"I know. I was trying to be humorous and get a conversation going. You don't speak to me anymore. Have I offended you somehow?" Desiree watched as he slowly turned to face her.

"I am not offended. I am not angry. Do not worry about me." His short tone indicated that no reply would be necessary.

"You sound angry." She probed.

"I am annoyed because you are interrupting my work." Gaston's shoulders visibly tensed.

"That's not all. You've been freezing me out for days." Desiree closed the distance between them and looked over his shoulder at the screen. "You've never been chatty, but now you might as well be a mute."

"Did you ever consider that I have said everything that I needed to say on that rooftop?" Gaston icily replied.

"What are we talking about? I'm lost." Desiree tried to remember back to the conversation and decipher her friend's issue but was having trouble. Douglas had mainly spoken. The only thing Gaston had said was "We all missed you." Then it hit her: taciturn Gaston had confessed to her under the guise of his statement on behalf of the group. Then she had announced her intention to leave after this mission, unknowingly trampling his feelings. Desiree put her hand on his shoulder. Her fingers came dangerously close to touching the skin of his neck and he jerked away, jumping to his feet.

"Please, don't do that." Gaston firmly requested.

"Can't you control your power? Maybe turn it off for a moment?" Desiree stepped forward.

Gaston stepped back, keeping the distance between them constant. "The only time I can touch someone without suffering is when I am pushing the pain into them. If I want to touch someone, I have to make a choice. Which one of us will be the one to hurt?"

Desiree stepped closer. This time, Gaston backed into the desk where he had been researching tires for the Ramsey case. The mercenary reached out, her calloused hands inches from caressing his cheek. "Is there someone that you want to touch?"

He swallowed; his mouth dried out. "Desperately," he croaked. Her fingertips were close enough that he could feel her body heat radiating off of them. Dread of her proximity spread across his face.

"I've been hurt enough to know how to cope with pain." She offered. "If you wanted, I could let you touch me and you wouldn't have to hurt."

Gaston's eyes widened in alarm. "I could never do that to you."

"Just concentrate. Focus on diminishing the flow, like turning a faucet." Desiree urged as the pads of her fingers brushed his skin.

Gaston hissed as if he had been burned, but he did not move. "It's not working."

Desiree commanded him. "Channel it into me. I don't feel a thing, yet."

Gaston's eyes shut tight and his eyelashes trapped small beads of salty water as he strained. He visualized a flow of energy into her but his concentration was broken when he heard her gasp. Opening his eyes, he saw that Desiree had stepped away from him.

Apologetically, she explained. "I'm sorry. It surprised me. Let's try it again." Before Gaston could protest, her hands were already cupping his face. He channeled the pain into her, but kept the idea of a faucet firmly at the front of his mind. Eyes closed, he could see his fingers easing the handle on a faucet, until trickle of water fell. Gaston tried to scale it back but every time the dripping liquid stopped, the pain would return to him. It required focus that he could not keep up for long and jerked his face away, breaking contact with her.

Desiree asked, "What's wrong? I thought it was working."

Gaston wiped the moisture off away from his eyes with the back of his hands and tried to steady himself. "How badly did it hurt?"

"The first time shocked me. The second attempt fluctuated, but was just a mild discomfort. It's nothing that I can't handle." She carefully watched him for any signs of deceit. "Now tell me why you quit." Her voice left no room for argument.

Gaston sat down at the desk and looked up at the woman towering over him. "It was like flexing a muscle. I can't keep it up for long. It's exhausting." He closed his eyes for a moment and took several deep breaths. When he had regained his composure, he inquired, "Why are you helping me? You already stated that you aren't staying once we catch Devil and *Bestia*."

Desiree smiled and knelt in front of him. Their faces were almost even, his just slightly elevated. "Maybe you should give me a reason to stay." Her hand clasped his knee and she steadily leaned forward.

Gaston, speechless, let her lips brush his. The warmth felt so welcomed that he could temporarily ignore the sudden burst of anguish. She kissed him harder and felt him responding, but in a reserved distracted way.

Suddenly, he pulled back. "Please stop. I...I don't want to hurt you, but it's too much. Whatever you've been through is too much for me to absorb."

Desiree looked into his eyes. "We'll keep practicing. You said it's like flexing a muscle. We'll just keep building up your muscles then."

Gaston picked up a pair of gloves from the computer desk and slipped them over his hands. He had taken them off to type and had need of them again. Deliberately, he reached up, his skin now covered, and stroked her face. "I would like that." Then they both broke out into self-conscious grins.

Chapter: The Cure

Samantha Nichols watched television in her apartment. The distracting sound of a laughing studio audience kept her from really buying into the sitcom. Every time she started to immerse herself in the character's world, a burst of exaggerated guffaws pulled her out of it. Her eyes scanned the screen for actors and actresses that she could recognize but keeping up with pop culture had never been her strong point. A familiar book was a far better companion than the handsome or beautiful flavor of the month that Hollywood spat out.

Of course, her eyes kept returning to the envelope on her coffee table. She had taken it home from the office. She kept telling herself it was so she could read it verbatim to Douglas since she did not call him from the hospital. However, she postponed the call again once she arrived home. She could not bring herself to dial his number. Part of her wanted to share the news, but another part feared...what exactly? She could not even articulate why she would not pick up the phone.

A large Freeman Pharmaceuticals logo at the top of the paper loomed over the text below. As soon as she saw that corporate symbol, she knew it had to do with Dr. Bernard Miller, currently one of her patients. He had been fired from Freeman for an inappropriate relationship with a subordinate. He had reproduced an experimental formula for blocking the recall of long term memories and tested it on random people. Three victims and two criminals (one being the doctor himself) lived in Bryers' hospital with blank slates for histories.

The document she received served as a harbinger. Change was coming. Freeman Pharm had developed a medication that targets the protein blocker Dr. Miller had developed. The three test subjects could be cured. The mad scientist Bernard Miller and the terrorist Gregory Phillips could finally be put on trial for their crimes. She knew that Douglas would want to know. Several of Mr. Phillips' accomplices, the men responsible for Doug's injuries, had escaped.

Samantha Nichols came to a decision. She would contact the police department and have them on hand for the administering of the cure. If Doug's friends inside the station wanted to alert him, they could be the point of contact.

She briefly wondered what Stuart would say to her hesitance to communicate with Douglas. Would her newfound mentor support the decision as a clean break or would he push her to talk to Doug herself as proof that she was truly over him? "I could call." She spoke out loud. It never hurt to listen to a peer's opinion.

She grabbed the remote and turned down the volume on her uninteresting sitcom. When the television was a barely perceptible whisper, she tossed the controller on the cushion beside her and plucked her cell phone off of the end table. She scrolled through her pitifully short contacts list and stopped at Stuart Straub. She tapped on the name and put the phone to her ear.

"Samantha, this is an unexpected surprise." His voiced carried a subdued elation. "To what do I owe the pleasure?"

"Just bored." She replied. "I wanted to talk to someone."

"Well, I'm flattered that you thought of me. I will have to take a rain check though. My children are here and we have just sat down for dinner." His enthusiasm waned as he explained that he had guests. "They are going back to their mother's tomorrow. How about we go out to dinner after they leave? I promise to give you my full attention and the best conversation my feeble mind can muster." Dr. Straub laughed at his own admission.

"You are one of the sharpest men I've met." She contradicted him.

"We'll settle it tomorrow, agreed?" He pressed.

"Okay, but I won't get off of work until eight." She warned.

"Excellent, that is a great time for me. Okay, I'll try to get us a table at Angelus for 8:30. I will see you tomorrow evening."

Samantha sat mutely allowing him to hang up with no farewell. The mention of Angelus had surprised her. The last person to suggest eating there was Douglas Lawson on the night that she dumped him. He had tried to reserve a table at one of the most prestigious restaurants in the city in an effort to rescue their relationship. It was a noble effort but a poor college student with no famous last name had no pull in this town.

Samantha could not tell if Stuart had been serious or not. He was affable but not prone to throw away statements when it came to making plans. She set the phone down and realized that she had forgotten to ask his opinion of her predicament. Shrugging, she decided it could wait until tomorrow.

Valerie Gossard picked up her work phone and put it to her ear. Her contact in the police station hurriedly whispered. "One of your people is in the station. He's being booked under the name Scott Edwards."

Valerie's stomach dropped but she maintained her composure. "What is happening?"

"He's in a holding cell. Apparently, Sudduth in homicide had a hot tip that his guy was a con-artist and put the fraud guys on to it."

"Sudduth? The one that was investigating the Ramsey car crash?" Valerie suddenly felt nervous. This had Douglas' stink all over it. Valentine should have never been fingerprinted. The military should have put the city cops off of the case before it reached that point. Doug had been digging into the case. Of course he would follow up the lead of the illicit affair!

Valerie swore into the phone and the crooked officer responded. "Sorry honey-cakes, what do you want me to do?"

"Shut him up. I don't care if he's breathing or not by the end. Just make sure he can't talk." Valerie growled. After stating it, she realized she had just consigned Valentine to death. It could not be helped though. Unless... "Wait, stall them. We will handle this like we did with Phillips."

"Sure thing, but it's going to look kind of odd if I start throwing up roadblocks and sticking my nose in a case that's not mine. It'll also look odd if yet another prisoner loses his memory while in custody."

Annoyed, Valerie snapped at him. "It will just have to look odd then. Get it done."

Hanging up, she paced around her apartment. *Bestia* would throw this incident in her face as well. If only she had killed Douglas earlier, she would not have the headaches that plagued her today.

She needed a way to kill her lover that would not look suspicious. It also needed to be soon, before he did any more damage to her enterprise. Under normal circumstances, she would do the job herself. "I clean up my rubbish." Unfortunately, their relationship being common knowledge to friends and family meant she would face scrutiny as a suspect. If any forensic evidence linked her to the crime, she would face a lengthy trial (at minimum). As much as it pained her, she needed another hand to do the deed.

Valerie Gossard, aka Raven, dialed her favorite subordinate. "Hello, you can target Lawson. I don't care how. Just make it quick and relatively painless." After a verbal confirmation of her orders, she set the phone down.

She stared blankly at her apartment feeling like the world had dropped out from under her. She had effectively lost Scott and Douglas in the same night. Her feet carried her into the kitchen. As if in a dream, she suddenly realized she was in a different room and did not remember walking there. She opened a cabinet and grabbed a glass. Then she pulled out a dusty bottle of 16 year old scotch, which she reserved for special occasions. "This is a special one, for sure." She laughed bitterly. She filled her glass with a double shot and slung it back like it was cheap rot gut whiskey. She could not enjoy the flavor at the moment. Looking at the empty glass, she poured another.

Chapter: New Toys

Penelope Daniels, registered nurse, picked up a wooden box from the counter top. She opened it and marveled at what was inside. She snapped the lid shut and looked at the man anxiously awaiting her reaction. "It's beautiful." She truthfully told him. "It's just like I imagined it."

The heavy set man smiled as he stroked a short beard. "It was a pleasure to work on, a fun project." His long, salt and pepper hair fell into his eyes as he glanced down at the display box that he included with the purchase. Rarely did a customer come in with such an interesting custom order. Ms. Daniels had even provided some very well drawn sketches, complete with measurements. "If you don't mind me asking, what're you going to do with it? Display it in some art exhibit; put it on the wall in your home?"

Penny gingerly tucked the box under her arm. "It's an accessory. I'm going to wear it."

The man's eyes popped open. "You're not going to use it are you?"

Stifling a short giggle, she assured him. "It's for appearances only. It's part of a costume."

"Hell, it must be some costume to spend that much on an accessory." He said, visibly relieved.

"Oh it's worth it. Haven't you heard? Accessories make the outfit." She giggled and playfully waved goodbye with her free hand. She simultaneously felt lighter than air and stronger. Something about her costume imparted a confidence that she felt she had always lacked. When she looked at herself in the mirror, she had shed the skin that was Penelope Daniels, the woman who still played with dolls. In her costume, she was something dangerous and sexy. The feeling, being new to her, filled her with the urge to show someone but she had to stay her hand. It needed to be perfect when she revealed it to Mr. Lawson. He would have no choice but to accept her help.

As she walked down the street to the bus stop, she thought about Gaston's physique. What design would complement his natural body shape? There was also the attitude to consider. Gaston treated people curtly and seemed to constantly brood. Maybe he would be a dark avenger…a muted, color palette consisting of mainly of black and shades of gray, maybe a brown. She decided that he definitely needed shoulder pads to make him look bigger than he was.

Douglas was easier. He already had a type of theme. Fancying himself as a mastermind and wielding a cane, he came across as an aloof genius. The long, black coat he normally draped over his shoulders made an excellent stand in for a cape. She would not have to do much with him to complete the image of a comic book character.

Penny's stop came up and she realized that she had spent the entire trip home lost in her own thoughts. Hurriedly, she stood and exited a bus for which she did not remember boarding and paying. Stepping out on to the sidewalk in front of her apartment, she felt the weight of the wooden box and smiled to herself. This was the last detail. Tomorrow, she would find Douglas Lawson and reveal her talents to him.

Jacob Lawson sat in Caffeine Nation holding an acoustic guitar. He knew Douglas had purchased it out of guilt for making him stay at the Bulwark instead of the upstairs apartment. Despite understanding the danger of villains knowing where he lived, Jake could not help but feel rejection. Douglas tried to see him but between running a coffee shop, his martial arts classes, cold cases, and girlfriend; there just were not enough hours in the day.

Jake absentmindedly plucked at the strings while trying not to be jaded by his adopted father's shortcomings. When he had finished a meandering series of arpeggios, he heard sparse clapping from the customers. Suddenly reminded of the presence of other people, he blushed. Jacob had just been practicing, not performing. Now that they were watching him, he cursed only studying hard rock and heavy metal. He knew no songs that belonged in an acoustic set in a coffee house.

A customer with a foam cup and multiple paper sleeves asked, "Do you take requests?"

Nervously, Jake shook his head. "I'm just learning. I don't know many songs yet."

The customer shrugged and took a sip of his coffee. "What you were just playing sounded like a song to me."

"Thanks." Jacob felt his lips twitch at the corners, threatening to expose his inward joy. After a moment of gathering his thoughts, he started fingerpicking a common chord progression and saw people take notice. Since he consciously crafted instead of aimlessly shuffling about the fret board, he could tell a difference in the customers. They actively listened as he contorted his fingers into unfamiliar shapes. He had developed some muscle memory, but not enough to effortlessly flow. He still had to will his digits into the correct configuration. He stumbled a few times but the patrons seemed not to notice. This time when he stopped playing, the applause was louder.

He grinned and formed a power chord. He strummed the strings harder and faster, improvising a punk rock song. His hand flailed sloppily above the strings; the pick imprecisely hitting its targets. Without the benefit of distortion, the accidentally muted strings and pick scrapes jarred the customers out of enjoying the music.

The one patron that had struck up the conversation with him winced. "Stick to the softer stuff, kid."

Jacob nodded but inwardly fumed. He thought, "I want to rock." Instead of continuing, he hopped off of his seat and started walking toward the back.

Cindy stopped him. "Hey Jake. Don't let it bother you. Practice the music you want to practice."

He dismissed her comment with a sigh and kept moving. As he walked up the stairs, he had a funny thought. Could he become a better lead player if he used his powers to hit some of the notes? He laughed out loud, caught off-guard by the insanity of it. He could manipulate objects easier but there was no way he could concentrate hard enough to play the guitar that way. However, he did realize that he had not used enough imagination in utilizing his telekinesis thus far. He needed something more unique than crushing soda cans.

Resolving to put his guitar up, he was going to spend the rest of the night coming up with more ways to use his special ability. Excited by the prospect, he started taking the steps two at a time.

Chapter: Lockup

Valentine sat in lock up. Through the bars, he could see police officers striding past, some with purpose and some just in a hurry to avoid the smell of vomit where a drunk driver finally lost his lunch. Someone had promised that it would be cleaned up soon but no one had shown. The drunk could not do it himself as he started snoring seconds after he released his stomach's contents.

Scott Edwards felt half-mad. The mixture of fear and inactivity chipped away at his nerves until he wanted to scream. Of course, he had called a lawyer (not Valerie Gossard) and tapped his foot, hoping the man would arrive soon. He needed to get out and speak to Raven. She had to understand that this was not his fault. He had not spoken a word about the job. He had not slipped up and mentioned anything in his lovers' beds. He had been on his best behavior except for calling *Bestia* for a ride home.

He sighed, knowing that his innocence meant nothing to Raven. She would punish him regardless. She valued her safety above all, and regardless of who was to blame for the unmasking of Tobias Richmond as a phony, she would still sever all ties back to her. Basically, Scott Edwards was a dead man and if not dead, then a memory wiped blank slate like the poor bastard Gregory Phillips. The nerd had designed a weapon that could shake a building to pieces but was dosed with Dr. Miller's miracle drug just because he had the misfortune of being caught at the bridge.

Greg was a new member of the team and that could have explained the ease with which Valerie let him go, but Valentine's years of service would not save him. No goodwill had been stockpiled in Miss Gossard's heart. She had no soft spot for anyone, except Douglas

Lawson. Scott impotently stamped his foot on the hard floor of the jail. "She'd bring the hammer down on anyone except him." He cursed the man and his uncanny ability to get in their business.

The arresting officer had not told him anything more than "fraud" when he had clasped handcuffs on Mr. Edwards. Even at the station, no one seemed to be in a hurry to inform him on any aspect of the charges. Hours had slipped by in lockup. Where was his lawyer? If he could get out on bail, where would he go? Would Raven turn a blind eye to this misfortune if he could convince her it was not his fault?

The myriad of questions had to wait. A man in plain clothes walked up to the door and called out, "Edwards!"

Scott looked up and raised his hand as if he were a child in grade school.

"Put that hand down and get over here." An electronic lock turned and the door swung open. Scott walked through trying to keep a stiff upper lip, but his legs shook. He had a record. They knew he was a con-artist, but how much else did they know?

"Is my lawyer here, yet?" He asked affecting an air of indifference.

"How the hell should I know?" The cop grumbled.

Moments later, Scott sat in an interrogation room alone. The overhead lights were on but it was not the blinding single bulb surrounded by darkness he pictured from films. Standard fluorescent tubes bathed the entire room in artificial light. The noise of an operating police station diminished as the door closed when two detectives entered.

The men flanked him and one started talking while the other stood over the seated prisoner. "You know that we know your real name." The speaker unceremoniously began. "I'm not going to insult your intelligence by making you play a game of how much we know. The truth is we have more important things to do than chase after a womanizing con-artist. If you ask me, they had it coming for falling for your particular brand of lies." He paused as if he suddenly remembered something. "Can I get you a water or coffee?"

Scott blinked in confusion. "Uh, water would be nice."

The silent companion slipped out the door, creating a brief swell in the noise level. He returned just as quickly with a paper cup filled to the brim. The detective resumed. "You are a small fish, or we thought you were at least." With a dramatic flourish, he pulled a small vial of clear liquid sealed in an evidence bag out of his jacket pocket and gently set it on the table in front of Mr. Edwards. "Internal Affairs had been watching another cop for a while. They caught a phone conversation between him and someone providing him with a little supplementary income. It was a woman's voice and she said to kill you."

Scott eyed the innocuous looking vial with fear.

"Then she changed her mind and said to handle you like 'Phillips'. Does that mean anything to you?"

Valentine did not respond though he knew what it meant. It also meant that if he did not have his memory erased, he would be killed. Whoever stopped the crooked cop had effectively signed his death warrant.

"Playing the silent game? Okay, let me spell it out for you. We've got a corrupt police officer in custody and a mystery fluid you were supposed to be poisoned with. Gregory Phillips was caught at the scene of a terrorist attack, and a short while later, he was drugged and doesn't know who he is. So, it stands to reason that you are connected to the group responsible for the bridge attack a few months ago."

Scott spoke up. "I didn't have anything to do with that!" Truly, he had not been included in that part of the plan and did not know it was even happening. He was already intensely training for his new role as a tennis instructor. However, the outburst only reinforced the image of guilt.

"You're in with them enough that our mystery woman tried to have you taken out. Since the drug failed to make it to you, you're probably just going to be murdered." The detective leaned in to make eye contact. "We can help you. We can make a deal. You'll be protected, charges dropped. Just give us everything you know about the crew at the bridge: names, faces, organizational structure."

Scott swallowed. Raven would kill him if he talked. He stifled a laugh. "She's going to kill me anyway." He thought. Throwing himself on the mercy of Valerie would be tantamount to suicide.

"Okay, I'm in, but she's dangerous. She'll do anything to shut me up if she even suspects that I've flipped." Scott felt his heart constrict as he verbally betrayed his co-workers.

"You have my word." The cop solemnly stated.

"She goes by Raven and she has multiple teams that are semi-autonomous cells. They are capable of independent action but still check in with her for missions and guidance. They aren't terrorists like the modern term is used. They are more like extortionists. They don't have a political agenda. They just want money; it's all about the bottom line. There is no robbery, bombing, or murder unless it helps them get richer."

"So, what was your job?" The cop interrupted.

"Reconnaissance, I gathered information, usually through pillow talk. I would also form relationships with marks to convince them to betray an employer." Scott felt a kind of relief as the words flowed out of him.

"How many people work for Raven?"

Scott shrugged. "I really have no idea. Like I said 'semi-autonomous cells'. I was a member of a three man team."

"Uh-huh, who else was in your cell?" The cop closely watched the suspect's face for any signs of deception.

"We all went by code names: Devildriver and *Bestia*."

The cop thought for a moment. "Raven, Devildriver, and *Bestia*... what did they call you?"

For a brief moment, Scott smiled. "They called me Valentine on account of how I could make anyone fall in love."

"Are you proud of that?" The cop asked with a trace of anger.

"It's a solid trade. I make someone feel special; I get to live beyond my means." Edwards mused almost forgetting the detective was there. "I made people happy, even if it was just for a little while."

Disgust skittered across the cop's face, quickly disappearing. "Where do we find your boss?"

"I don't know. We always met at safe houses." Truthfully, he knew Arturo's name and where he lived but didn't want to play all his cards immediately. He had not signed any papers yet and did not entirely trust the officer's promise.

The cop seemed to believe it and continued with the questioning. "You had face to face meetings. Can you give us a description of each player?"

Feeling a little more in control, Scott sat up straighter. "Sure but I'm a little hungry. Could I get something to eat? It's been a while and I could use some doughnuts." He flashed a confident smile at his interrogator.

Chapter: The Fashion Show

Douglas sat down in his coffee shop and wiped the salt from his evaporated sweat from his brow. His fingers caught the coarse texture and he marvelled at how exhausted he felt. He drove straight over from his Brazilian Jujitsu class to sit down with his girlfriend and have a relaxing cup of tea.

Valerie sauntered in, giving a smile and a nod to Cindy behind the counter. As the attorney neared her boyfriend, she waved her hand in front of her nose. "You've been working out."

Doug laughed. "I have. I'm sculpting this body for you."

Valerie sat across from him. Her lips formed a smile but there was something in her eyes that betrayed her mood. The deep blue pools behind her glasses told of sadness. "Are you ready for our date? I haven't seen you in forever."

"I'm really tired." He complained. "I've missed you but I can barely keep my eyes open."

Valerie coyly asked, "Are you trying to take me straight to bed?"

"Seriously, I don't know if I can get up. My legs were shaking when I walked in here." Parts of his hair glistened with sweat while drier parts became unruly, strands akimbo.

"I have a very special night planned and you will not refuse me." Her eyes grew flinty. "No one will interrupt us. Promise me that."

Douglas raised his right hand as if taking a pledge. "Unless Jake has an emergency, I am all yours." He quickly dropped it back to the table top.

"Good, I have dinner reservations at Angelus. After dinner, dessert, and cocktails, I have a penthouse rented. We can spend the night in each other's arms without anyone knowing where we are." She reached out and clasped his fingers with hers.

"Why should we be worried about someone knowing where we are?" Douglas looked at her with a flare of suspicion, but his over-taxed body did not have the energy required to dwell on the question.

"I just want you all to myself. Tonight needs to be our night." She thought of Arturo and knew he would waste no time in eliminating Mr. Lawson once he was given permission. This evening could be her last date with Douglas. Despite knowing he was a dead man, she would miss him and wanted one last day of having him treat her like a queen. "No one will be able to find us." She emphasised to herself.

Doug smirked. "Okay but I didn't budget for Angelus."

"It's my treat. Don't worry about a thing. Tonight is totally on me. Consider it a thank you for the time you've given me." Ms. Gossard spoke with an earnestness that surprised her.

"I wish I had more to give." He playfully lifted her hand to his lips and kissed the pads of her fingers.

"Oh, I wish you did too." She sadly mused. "Speaking of time, you need to shower and change quickly if we are going to make it."

"Fine, I'm moving, I'm moving." He jokingly acted as if she were a nagging wife. He grabbed his cane and braced himself for the effort it took to stand. After a grunt and a push, he hobbled toward the stairs to his apartment. Pausing, he turned back and searched her eyes. "Thank you for the surprise. A night away is just what I needed. Truthfully, I have trouble sleeping here knowing that bad people can find where I live."

Valerie shooed him away. "We're going to be late."

Douglas made it to the top floor and searched his closet for his proper clothes. He shrugged and picked the same suit that he wore to the country club. As he changed, he glanced at a mirror and stopped. He felt a sudden shock at his appearance. A wave of disgust washed over him as he looked at the shirt hanging open, revealing his stomach. Doug had always been a little heavy and had slimmed during college but still had a few pounds too many. His jawline was nothing to write home about. His hair just parted on the side in one of the most boring haircuts possible. How could he snag a cutie like Valerie? He wanted to ask the reflection, demand an answer. Instead, he stayed silent and went back to changing. As he buttoned up the dress shirt, he started to feel more like his old self. The pale flesh of his torso no longer taunted him. As he slid the dark suit coat over his shoulders, he thought "I'm okay looking when I dress up. If I were a girl, I'd hit that." He cracked a smile and fumbled with a pair of cufflinks he had picked up cheap from a pawn shop.

As he walked down stairs feeling like James Bond entering the villain's favorite casino, Valerie cleared her throat in annoyance. "A lady friend stopped by."

A jolt of fear froze him in place. Had Samantha walked in at the worst possible moment? He knew that Valerie hated her and that in turn Samantha was afraid of Doug's girlfriend. "I'm not expecting anyone." He explained in a bewildered tone.

Cindy interrupted. "It's a lady that came in here a while back. She wants to design superhero costumes for you."

"What?" Doug laughed. He was simultaneously flattered and confused. "We don't need costumes. I don't want to be recognized. Recognition is bad."

Cindy shook her head sadly. "She's in the restroom changing into her outfit. She said she made it so you could see the quality of her work."

Ms. Gossard condescendingly added, "The seamstress is desperate for your attention, Mr. Lawson."

He knew the disapproving tone and sensed an undercurrent of jealousy. "Listen, I didn't ask her here. I'm not even sure who this is."

As if on cue, the ladies' room door swung open. The entire establishment grew quiet. Nurse Penelope Daniels stepped out with a flush of confidence. She wore black steel toed boots and white stockings which disappeared under her skirt. An off-white corset wrapped around her waist and pushed up her breasts. She wore a leather belt slung across her hips with a large scabbard for a knife. Her face sported a uniform layer of powder, a touch of rouge on each cheek, and a single beauty mark just above the right side of her mouth. Her face was framed by large curls spilling down from her pinned up hair. She looked like a Victorian lady crossed with a slasher movie villain.

"It's not just stylish; it's practical." She twirled to show off the entire ensemble. "The boots have steel toes for kicking and protection from falling objects. Nothing interferes with a night of crime fighting like a broken toe." She stuck out her foot and motioned toward the footwear. Seductively running her hands up her leg, she tugged on the skirt. "This is short to decrease excess fabric and make running easier."

Penny pulled the knife out of its sheath and held it out for all to see. The handle resembled the handle of a pair of scissors. A loop existed for the thumb and a separate ergonomic loop for her four fingers. The double-edged blade had a line running down the length to simulate the appearance that it could come apart. Instead of a hilt, the weapon had a non-functioning bolt running through. The overall effect was a pair of scissors, but it was also one solid piece to be used for slashing or stabbing.

"The name of the ensemble is Penny Dreadful. I've even named the weapon after one of the most popular penny dreadful characters of all time." She motioned to an engraving on the handle. "Mr. Todd, as in Sweeney. I can put the same level of craft and creativity to work for you and your group."

Douglas let out an impressed whistle and started clapping. "Ms. Dreadful, that is an impressive outfit." He paused and thought about how to proceed. "The thing is..."

Her face fell as he spoke.

"We don't use costumes. They make us too conspicuous. I like to fly under the radar. We all do." Douglas did not want to hurt the girl's feelings but did not see a way that he could use her services. Then, he had an idea. "Well, there is one of us that would use a costume..."

Penny's eyes lit up. "Who?" Excitement positively crackled around her.

"His name is Jacob, but he likes to go by Cataclysm." Doug smiled.

"Ooo, that's a good name." Penny nodded.

Doug grinned back at her and excused himself. "Come by tomorrow and we'll get his measurements. Forgive me, but I am late for a very important date." He made a show of offering the crook of his arm to Valerie. "M'lady, are you ready to depart?" He feigned a British accent.

Ms. Gossard entwined her appendage with Mr. Lawson's. "Of course, my good sir." The two made it out the door and into the night. "I hope we can still make it."

Douglas searched the street for her car. "If you drove, we would probably get there quicker. I'm having trouble working the clutch, gas, and brake with a faulty leg."

She leaned in and kissed him on the cheek. "I'll drive. You just relax." As he lowered himself into her luxury coupe, she spoke again. "You are going to let that crazy lady make a costume for Jake?"

"I think he'd love his own superhero outfit. Besides, I meant what I said about her doing impressive work. Also, I don't think she's that crazy. She wants a challenging sewing project and to help out the neighborhood crime fighters." Douglas watched her get in and start the car as he explained.

"I would be afraid to let her around my son." Valerie shrugged as the vehicle pulled out into traffic.

"Jake will be okay. I will be there the whole time."

Glancing briefly at her boyfriend, she curiously asked, "What if you're not there one day? I mean, let's say that these men from the bridge find you. What happens to Jacob if you die?"

Douglas looked out the window, thinking. "I have no plan. I just kind of assumed I'd be around for a while."

Valerie stared straight ahead, keeping her eyes on the brake lights in front of her. "I would give it some thought. You never know what tomorrow holds."

Chapter: Angelus

S amantha Nichols sat across from Dr. Stuart Straub, her colleague and mentor. She had never before dined at Angelus and could not focus on the conversation due to the opulence of her surroundings. The dim interior and accent lighting caused the crystal of glasses to throw out a prismatic flare when positioned at the correct angle. Her hands absently fondled the thick burgundy table cloth. With a name like Angelus, she had expected the interior to be bright lights and gleaming whites, but the décor shared a color scheme with angels of the fallen variety. Cherry wood and deep reds were everywhere.

Every time Samantha tried to speak to Stuart, she felt as if the waiter was eavesdropping. He hovered around, anticipating their needs so consistently that Dr. Nichols had started to feel paranoid. She opened her mouth to speak only to see her servant swoop in and pour fresh water into her drained glass. She waited until he had retreated back into the shadows before speaking.

"I don't think I can get used to being waited on hand and foot." She grabbed her drink by the stem and took a sip, trying not to leave a lipstick stain on the pristine rim.

Stuart laughed. "There's no need to be so nervous. Treat it like any other sit down restaurant. You'll make a bigger fool of yourself if you try to act proper."

Samantha blushed. "Easy for you to say. You blend in." She pointed at his well-tailored dark gray suit.

Dr. Straub smiled as he nodded. "I'll admit that this is a very nice suit, but it is also the only one I own. It's worth too much to wear regularly so I only break it out for special occasions."

Momentarily confused, Dr. Nichols pointedly asked him "Why is tonight special?"

He paused for a sip of ice water before answering. "It's a congratulatory dinner."

"For?" She impatiently prompted him.

"You are getting some interns. We feel like you are mature and skilled enough to teach medical students from the college." He lifted his glass as a salute. "Let's toast to Dr. Samantha Nichols, the shaper of young minds."

Her face soured. "I don't want to toast."

"Of course, water isn't appropriate." He hastily set down his glass. "Give me a moment to order a bottle of wine."

"No, I mean babysitting a bunch of snotty college brats is not my idea of a promotion. It's more of a punishment." Samantha levied a charge against him. "The veteran staff doesn't want to be bothered with it. So they dump it on the new faces."

Sighing, Stuart leaned in and lowered his voice. "I'm going to be frank with you. Yes, shit rolls downhill, but be grateful that you aren't one of the screw-ups that couldn't even be trusted with this task. Are the interns obnoxious? Of course. But pay your dues and do the job right and you'll move up. Don't take it seriously and you get put in the 'competent doctor but no ambition' group where you will stay for the rest of your career." He leaned back and raised an eyebrow in a fashion that reminded Samantha of Douglas Lawson. "What will it be?"

Swallowing her pride, she picked up her water glass and gave a hollow smile. "I suppose a toast is in order. Here's to promotions."

Dr. Straub dutifully clinked his water against hers. "To promotions." He took a gulp and set his drink down. "So now that the business is out of the way, on to more leisurely topics."

Samantha shook her head. "I'm afraid that I have a little more shop talk in me. Well, it intersects with my personal life too."

"Oh?" Stuart's interest piqued.

"Freeman pharm sent me some information about a potential cure for their experimental drug that Bernard Miller was using on people. The clinical tests have shown a complete recovery in non-human test subjects. They want to begin testing it on Miller and some of his victims." She slowly explained.

"I see. That's excellent news." Straub waited for her to reach the issue.

"Well, two of the victims are unfit to stand trial until the cure is administered and proven to work. So, there will be some police involvement. The real reason I'm bringing it up is that Douglas was directly involved and I feel that he has a right to know, but I also do not want to reopen communication with him." Samantha watched her mentor's eyes for understanding.

"If a patient came to you with a similar issue, how would you advise them?" The elder doctor inquired.

"I can't be objective; even pretending the advice was for a patient. There is too much history involved between us. I need someone impartial to put things in perspective."

Stuart nodded. "If you are worried about having to speak with him, send him a text message or an email."

"There's the danger of him messaging me back."

"Ignore him. If you don't feel like you could, just let the police contact him. He will get the information he needs and you will avoid dredging up old emotions." Straub tapped on his menu. "Now that we have settled that, can we concentrate on having a nice dinner?"

Samantha's face drained of color and her jaw slackened in surprise. Stuart followed her eyes in an attempt to determine what had caught her so off-guard. As he turned his head, he saw Douglas Lawson and a beautiful woman being seated several tables away.

Giving a hollow chuckle, Dr. Straub mused, "Well, speak of the devil."

Douglas sat down across from Valerie. "This place is posh. I didn't think they let people as *gauche* as me in here."

Valerie smiled and nodded. "Their standards have fallen in recent years."

The couple quietly read over the menu for a moment. Douglas broke the silence with a question about the food. "Are the crabcakes good?"

"I don't know. I've never tried that dish. Honestly, I rarely come here."

"What have you had?" Douglas did not look up but kept studying the elegant lettering in his menu.

"I have had the clay baked roast. It is quite large and meant to be shared. They bring it out and still wrapped, and crack it open in front of you. The escaping scents are mouth-watering."

"Did you share this with an old boyfriend or eat it by yourself?" Douglas followed up absent-mindedly.

"It was a business dinner." Ms. Gossard defensively replied.

"Would you like to have it again or try something new?"

"Something new, I don't know when I will be back here." She watched the approaching waiter. "I think we should order a bottle of wine. The hotel is within walking distance. Feel free to indulge without worry."

A muffled buzzing sound emanated from under the table. Embarrassed at the intrusion, Douglas pulled out his phone and looked at the caller. "It's Gaston. Let me just get rid of him." Doug put the phone up to his ear. "Hey, I can't really talk right now...uh huh. Okay, just email it to me. For the rest of the night, I am to only be contacted in case of an emergency. Thanks." He hung up and smiled at Valerie. "That was the only interruption, I swear."

"It better be. I went to great lengths to set up this night alone."

She glanced at the waiter and that fleeting glance held enough sway to send the servant scrambling to their table. "I believe we are ready."

Douglas ordered a rare steak with grilled asparagus. Valerie requested *coq au vin*. "Excellent choices" the waiter remarked and disappeared into the kitchen.

Douglas looked around with wonder at the décor. He remembered his previous attempt to eat here ending before it began. He had the erroneous idea that he could salvage his relationship with Samantha if he took her out to dinner. His younger self had been too cynical to decipher what would really save them as a couple. She had wanted him to control his mood swings, to accept responsibility, to grow up. The fool that he was thought he could spend his way back into her heart.

Oblivious to his demeanor, a self-deprecating grin spread over his face. Valerie cleared her throat. "Is there a reason you are smiling like an idiot?"

Douglas started to laugh. "I've tried to eat here before but could never get in. Apparently, I'm not important enough."

Ms. Gossard lifted her glass. "Then it's fortunate that you are dating me." Under the table, she playfully rubbed her foot up his pants leg.

"This is going to sound really shallow, but do you know one of the things that I like most about you?"

Valerie perked up. "This should be amusing."

"Your sex drive." He stated with remarkable bluntness.

"Am I unusual in that regard?" Her foot fell back to the floor.

Douglas was unsure if he had offended her. "I'm just not use to someone so comfortable with herself. I don't have to question what you want. You let me know. That kind of honesty is refreshing."

"My kind of honesty..." Her tongue played with the syllables, unsure if she liked the way they felt. As her eyes drifted across the tableau in front of her, she stopped. The expression on her face darkened. "Did you tell anyone where we were going?"

Confused, Douglas tried to turn and look behind his chair. "No, why?"

"I see your bitch of an ex." Valerie sneered, eyes locked on Samantha.

Douglas swung around and looked across the dining room. Dr. Nichols seemed to nervously chat with a man. It was difficult to determine his age. He had a handsome face but the gray in his hair made him look much older than her. "Oh, it looks like she's on a date." Pointing out that she was there with a man, Douglas hoped to diffuse the bomb that was about to go off.

"Are you sure you haven't been talking to her? How in God's name would she end up here at the same time as us unless someone told her?"

"Maybe she just wanted a nice dinner with her boyfriend." Doug theorized.

"It figures she couldn't find a younger man." Valerie jabbed.

"What the hell?" Douglas found himself leaping to Samantha's defense. "What does age matter if she's happy with him? Why should you care who she's with?"

"Why are you defending her?"

"Hey, I don't hate her. I want her to find someone. I want her to be happy. I'm not vindictive or bitter about it. And in case I need to remind you, I had a chance with her and I chose you." He positioned his head to block Samantha's view of her perceived rival. "I chose you. You are the one that I want. How many times do I have to show you that?"

Valerie fumed for a moment but began to soften. "Why did you choose me?"

"You are beautiful and intelligent. You take care of yourself. You are self-confident and that is incredibly sexy. What isn't sexy is petty jealousy. You are far more attractive when you are Valerie Gossard, badass lawyer." He reached out and took her hand. "Hating my old girlfriends is beneath you. I know who you are and you are better than that."

Valerie slipped her hand away. "I'm not though. I'm not as good as you think I am."

"Come on. You're seen with me in public. That has to count for something." He comically batted his blue-gray eyes at her. "Don't let this weird coincidence ruin tonight."

"Okay." She looked into his eyes and felt overwhelming lust. "I can't resist your come hither look."

The plates arrived at the table coupled with profuse apologies for the slow service. Valerie realized that she had not even noticed the delay. A slight smile crossing her lips, she started eating.

Chapter: Busted

Jacob stepped out of a taxi several blocks from the Bulwark. Douglas had infected the boy with paranoia and Jake did not want a cabbie knowing the exact destination. As the yellow car pulled away, Jake straightened his backpack and started walking. His keychain was a small bottle of pepper spray which he kept clutched in his hand as he made his way through the abandoned industrial district. Usually deserted, he occasionally saw a junkie or a homeless person. He had never been accosted but he still felt a stab of fear. However, with his unique power, he was probably safer than any other member of the Sentinels.

After an uneventful stroll, he reached the door and sorted through his keys for the correct one. Gaining entry, he stepped inside. The lights, already on, revealed the training equipment but no people. Gaston and Desiree were supposed to be here to babysit him while Douglas wined and dined his girlfriend.

"Hello?" Jake called, hearing his voice echo off the bare walls. He spotted a glowing computer monitor and walked over to the desk. Absently, he glanced over the screen and realized it was a list of vehicles. All of the listed models were from the early seventies. He started reading, trying to find any other patterns within the data.

"*Bonsoir.*" Gaston De Paul stepped through one of the office doorways.

Jacob had never seen his father's friend in such a state. The Frenchman's short curly hair was an unruly mess. The black dress shirt he usually wore was opened down to the naval and the unbuttoned cuffs added to his slovenly appearance. The strangest change was his face. A broad grin replaced his usual Stoic expression. Jake did not know what to think. Gaston looked alien to him.

"What's going on?" The boy asked with unconcealed suspicion in his voice.

"I was just working on a problem for Douglas." Gaston gestured at the computer. "His friends Devil and *Bestia* left tire prints. I am just compiling a list of cars that use that size tire."

"That's not what I meant. You're acting weird." Jake looked at the screen unable to resist assisting on a real case.

"I am in a good mood. That is all." The adult dismissed the child's assertion.

Jacob scanned the list and suddenly stopped. "Hey, there's a car called a Demon."

Gaston nodded. "*Oui.* So?"

"One of the bad guys goes by the name Devil. Isn't that, like, the perfect car for him?"

Desiree's voice surprised them both. She had followed Gaston out a few moments later but during their discussion. "That is a good observation. Has anyone informed Mr. Lawson?"

Gaston shook his head. "He's out on a date and did not want to be disturbed except for emergencies. I am emailing the list. I will highlight the Dodge Demon and give our young detective the credit." Taking the mouse from Jacob, he set to work.

Stepping away from the desk so Gaston could work, Jake turned around and studied Desiree for a moment. She looked different as well, but he could not place what had changed. "Something's going on." He made the statement and carefully watched her reaction. Her eyes flittered over to Gaston and a soft smile played across her lips.

Jacob's mouth dropped open as he intuited the reason for the change in atmosphere. "You guys are doing it!"

Chuckling, Gaston clicked "send" and turned around. "What is it that we are doing?"

"You know...*it*." Jake looked from one to the other waiting for confirmation.

Gaston blushed, but Desiree explained. "Let's not make a big deal out of it."

"Does Dad know?" Jake quickly inquired.

"No, but apparently, it will not take him long to figure it out. I have a terrible Poker face." Gaston dryly replied.

"Are you two in love?" The boy continued with his questions.

Desiree laughed at the naïve child. "Let's drop the subject. It's not polite to ask such personal questions."

The Frenchman gave her a worried look. He caught her evasion. "Jake, why don't you set up some targets? We can exercise your powers."

Sensing he was being intentionally shuffled off, Jacob sighed and walked over to the firing range.

Gaston watched her, waiting for some kind of conversation to begin. Impatiently, he went ahead with an opening statement. "Shouldn't we figure out what we are?"

"I'm a mercenary and you are an ex-priest." Desiree quickly replied.

"I meant our relationship. What is our status?" Gaston plowed ahead, anxious to know.

"It had been a while for me and I made a spur of the moment decision." She shrugged.

"So there is no 'us'?" His soft voice fell.

"I don't know, Gaston. I haven't had time to think about it." Desiree pulled her kinky hair back and wrapped a rubber band around the ponytail to keep it out of her face. "I need to work on some of my combos. Help Jake or hold the pads for me." She walked away without further comment.

Gaston sat in front of the computer feeling lost. Moments earlier, he had been elated, but the uncertainty of the woman's feelings left him adrift. Swallowing his pride and determined to be patient, he stood up and walked over to Jacob.

Jake had not set up cans or tennis balls. He placed twenty-five pound dumbbells on the floor at the end of the gun range. The cast-iron weights sat several feet apart and the boy stared at them in concentration. Slowly, the left dumbbell lifted off the ground, hovered a few inches and then steadily climbed higher. It stopped ascending three feet off the floor and the second weight began to float.

Gaston watched the first weight, expecting it to fall, but it continued to levitate. Astonished, he asked Jacob, "You can simultaneously affect multiple objects?"

"Yes." He muttered and both weights fell with a metallic thud. "Damn it, I got distracted."

"Language." Gaston warned, knowing that Douglas chided the boy over the same thing.

"Sorry. It's just that I keep trying to get better at using my gift but I can't stay focused forever."

Gaston nodded. Earlier that very evening, he had cursed himself for the same reason. "It's just a matter of practice. I am learning the same lesson myself."

Taking a deep breath, Jacob glared at the dumbbells again. Both weights hopped off the ground with more velocity and stopped at eye level. Jake's breathing intensified as he struggled to control them. Slowly, Gaston saw what the boy was attempting. Hanging at the same altitude, both weights began rotating as if invisible fingers spun them. They slowed, stopped, and then floated to the floor. Each one gently touched down without a sound. Gasping with relief, Jacob let himself relax.

"That was hard." His shaking hand wiped sweat from his forehead.

Gaston patted him on the shoulder. "Does the weight make a difference?"

"Not as much as it does physically." Silently, Jacob began his exercises again.

Gaston watched in fascination. Neither of them noticed Desiree slip out into the night.

Arturo Gomez watched the front of Caffeine Nation with rapt interest. Douglas Lawson had not been seen in a few hours. The hour had grown late and there had been no glow of upstairs lights all evening. Lawson's adopted child had left in a taxi and Arturo briefly considered following it but decided to wait. He had employed a junkie to kill Douglas when he tried to leave, but so far, the target failed to show. The assassin sat in a nearby alley, pretending to be homeless. It had been Arturo's idea. Transients blended in to the background. No one really ever saw them. Even the sensitive soul that would stop and give them some spare change never really saw them. The homeless just bled together into one unidentifiable mass. That made it an effective cover.

Arturo scanned over the front of the building again. A taxi slowly rolled down the street until it came to a stop in front of the coffee shop amidst a squeal of worn brake pads. A cute girl locked the front door and stepped out. She quickly entered the cab and the car pulled away.

"Smart girl." Arturo said to himself. She had minimized the time she was exposed on the sidewalk to just a few seconds. If she did not have to lock the door, it would have been an even faster process.

Arturo felt an overwhelming pleasure at seeing the old Raven return. Over the past year, he could feel her growing soft. While the schemes were profitable (with the exception of the bridge incident), Devildriver grew more unstable and Douglas Lawson continued to meddle in their affairs. Valerie scolded the lunatic and kept sleeping with the amateur detective. Arturo bristled at the memory of having to retreat from the approaching police. Through a stroke of genius or dumb luck, the thoroughly unimpressive civilian managed to disrupt their plans and capture one of their team members. Finally, she gave *Bestia* the order he had been looking forward to for months. He could take out her boyfriend. A small smile spread across his face as he contemplated one less obstacle in their way.

He scanned the darkened building and looked for any sign that Lawson was in there. Still nothing. Cursing under his breath, he decided to leave his assassin to do his work. He would quickly know if his druggie turned hired killer succeeded. "*Vaya con Diablo*." He started his SUV and drove off, confident there would be another body in the morgue come morning.

Chapter: Goodnight

Samantha stood on the sidewalk outside her apartment building facing Stuart. The older doctor waited, with patient but amused eyes. Dr. Nichols shooed him away. "I'm not a little girl. I've been living here for years."

Dr. Straub agreed. "Yes, but I'll worry. Let me walk you up."

"You know I survived just fine before you came along." Samantha informed him with false rancor.

"Call it paternal concern."

"Fine, you may escort me to the door, but I'm exhausted and am going straight to bed." Samantha warned him.

"That's fine with me. I've got an early day tomorrow anyway." Stuart walked alongside her into the lobby of her building.

"I cannot believe that his psycho-bitch did not come near our table." Samantha abruptly changed subjects.

"How long have you been biting back that comment?" Stuart started heading for the stairs as she headed in another direction.

"Do you want to take the elevator?" Samantha paused, expecting him to come to her.

"The stairs are better for you." He smiled.

She reversed direction and walked over to the first flight of stairs. "We get plenty of exercise walking around the hospital."

"So, how long?" Stuart firmly continued with his question.

"Since we left the restaurant." She grudgingly admitted.

"Why are you so intent on vilifying her?" He inquired.

"I'm not! She's terrible! She tried to start a fight in the hospital while Douglas sat on the other side of the wall, broken and battered. She did everything except directly threaten me with bodily harm."

Stuart ascended with her and gave his perspective. "I was there that night helping patch up Mr. Lawson. His girlfriend saw him in pain and then saw his ex-girlfriend (with whom he recently shared a kiss) administering to him. How could she not react?" He paused. "I'm not saying you are wrong, but isn't it possible that you want her to be a monster because you still love him?"

Samantha scoffed. "He's out of my system. I'm the one that sent him packing when he kept calling."

"If you were really over him, you would call him and tell him about Freeman Pharm and the cure. Then you would hang up and go back to your life without dwelling on it. You don't want to talk to him because, deep down, you know you will reopen that Pandora's box of emotions." Dr. Straub diagnosed her and left the younger doctor blushing in shame.

"You have me all figured out, don't you?" Her voice contained real venom. "I can call him and it will have no effect on me. I called his girlfriend a bitch earlier because she is. I don't call Doug because he annoys me, as you are starting to." She gave him a confidence wilting glare but the veteran doctor withstood it.

"Make all the declarations you want. I know the symptoms. He glanced up the stairs and looked back at her. "You're a big girl. I think you can make it the rest of the way on your own. I'll see you at the hospital."

Samantha watched her mentor turn and plod down to the first floor as anger seethed within her. She continued to her apartment in a huff. Whenever Dr. Straub spoke with her about Douglas, she tended to react with anger. Couldn't Stuart just leave her be? On top of that, Penelope kept bringing him up at work. It seemed that where ever she looked, people were working to keep her ex-boyfriend in her life.

Once inside she sat down on the couch and pulled out her cell phone. She quickly typed out a simple text. "Have information about a cure for Miller's victims. Call me when you can." After hitting send, she tossed the device onto the coffee table and leaned back, trying to sink into the cushions. She closed her eyes and tried to remember if she had any more wine in the fridge.

Douglas' phone vibrated in his pants pocket but he could not feel it since his pants were on the floor by the king sized bed. Several drinks after dessert and he was walked to his room with Valerie leading him by his tie. "Are you ready for the best night of your life?", she had asked as they tumbled into the room.

Douglas answered with a drunken smile. "That's every night I'm with you."

Valerie took the lead and made love to him with surprising fervor. Sweat made her skin salty and slick as she tried to make the night last. Finally, she rolled off of Douglas and collapsed beside him. She slid her hand on to his chest and felt his heartbeat.

"It's racing." She pressed her body against him and kissed his shoulder.

"You have that effect on me." He yawned. "I had no idea you had that much stamina."

"Yes, you did." She confidently replied. Both of them cuddled in silence as their breathing slowly returned to normal.

Douglas rolled on to his side and let one hand land on her breast. His fingers absently traced circles around her nipple as he started speaking. "I tried to say this once before but the conversation just ended awkwardly."

Valerie shifted closer to him, feeling the heat from his body. "What conversation was that?"

"I tried to tell you how I really felt but you didn't want to go there."

She felt a quick burst of panic but immediately quelled it. She had to maintain that everything was normal. "Douglas, the evening has been so wonderful. Don't make it overly serious."

"But I am in love with you." He forced the dialogue forward any-way. "I don't think I should have to censor myself when I'm trying to express love. If anything, more people need to do that. It makes the world seem less dark when you're reminded that someone loves you ever so often."

Valerie sat up, knocking his hand off of her chest. "You have no idea how dark the world can be and you don't know me well enough to love me."

Douglas repositioned himself so he could face her. "How the hell do I not know you well enough? We've been dating for months. We talk all the time. I share everything with you." His impassioned voice begged her to explain.

"You don't know some of the things that I've done and if you did, you wouldn't love me." It would be easier to reply in kind and affirm his declaration, but Valerie could not bring herself to say it. Maybe it would be best if he hated her.

Douglas took her face in his hands and pleaded. "Tell me what you've done and let me decide whether or not I still love you. You can't make the choice for me and then act like you were right when you've given me no opportunity to prove you wrong."

Valerie felt her resolve harden. "Fine, I am a murderer. I am talk-ing about premeditated murder, not self-defense."

Douglas, normally quick to respond, sat in a gravely silence. Seconds stretched until Raven wanted to scream at him to say any-thing. Just as anticipation of his response broke her will and she opened her mouth, Lawson spoke.

"Explain how that came to pass." He calmly waited for her to begin.

Valerie had expected shock and indignation. She had wanted him to feel a sense of betrayal that would escalate in to a fight. Instead, he made a simple request for more information.

Valerie Gossard knew which story to tell him. There were so

many deaths that she could claim responsibility for, but she would have to tell him about her first one. She had already been punished by the law for it, so Douglas would have nothing legally to hang over her. "I was a girl, barely twelve."

Even in the dark, she could see his eyes widen. Good, it was having the desired effect. He needed to be horrified by her actions. "After my parents moved to the United States, I was enrolled in a private school, very expensive, very prestigious." She shifted her weight and tried to get comfortable. "There was a male teacher who was incredibly handsome, Mr. Mayfield. Many of the girls my class secretly had a crush on him. They would discuss it in their little groups and giggle about their naïve fantasies."

Valerie swallowed. Suddenly her throat felt dry. "As the school year went on, fewer girls participated. It was as if, one by one, something had happened to shatter their illusions of him. Mayfield was still handsome. In class, he had a professional but charming manner to him. Outwardly, nothing had changed, but several of the girls would look ill at the mention of him. Their eyes would follow him with fear as he walked up and down the rows of desks."

Her hands trembled in her lap as she continued the story. Lost in her memories, she stopped watching Douglas and was entirely absorbed by her own recollections. "One day, I went to the lavatory and heard crying. It was a girl from my class curled up in front of a stall. The door was opened and I saw vomit on the rim of toilet. I asked if she was ok and she just started bawling more. Finally, she confided in me."

In the darkness of the hotel room, Douglas waited for her to continue, fearing he already knew where the story headed. Valerie's voice was a whisper. "He had been touching them and making them do things to him. When it was over, he convinced them not to talk."

"How? With multiple girls, surely they could band together and go to someone?" Douglas felt sick at the injustice of it.

Valerie gave a sad laugh. "I wouldn't expect you to know what it's like to be a young girl. If you are the victim, there's a stigma attached to you. People will see you as soiled even if it wasn't your fault. In the backs of their minds, they will wonder if you encouraged it and got what was coming to you. Some will accuse you of lying just to hurt an 'innocent' man. The deck is stacked in the perpetrator's favor."

Douglas waited for her to continue as he realized that he had no idea what life was like for the other gender.

"None of the girls would step forward and he was just going to continue preying on them. I did the only thing I knew to do. I went to the principal. I told him everything." Ms. Gossard stopped. When she continued, disgust dripped from every word. "He wanted to fire the pedophile but not to involve the police. He was afraid that the allegations would hurt the school. Even as young as I was, I knew that meant Mayfield would be free to do the same thing in another school, another town. It wouldn't solve the problem. It would just give him a new crop of girls to begin abusing."

Her voice became iron. "There was only one permanent solution and I was going to implement it. I kept a small nail file in my purse and started sharpening it immediately. I knew I had to act quickly. I could not let the principal let him go. Marching to his classroom, I walked right in. He sat behind his desk grading papers. I walked up to him and grabbed him by his necktie. Feigning that I was going to kiss him, I saw the bastard's eyes light up with lust. Then I shoved the nail file into his throat to the handle. I pulled it out and jammed it in again. Every time his heart would beat, thick jets of blood would spray from the new wounds I had made. I held on to him and continued stabbing until empty eyes stared back at me. Only when I was sure that his soul had left his body did I stop."

Douglas listened to the description and could see how the scene had imbedded itself so vividly in her memory.

"I did not get away with it. I was found in Mayfield's classroom with the weapon still in hand. My pretty little uniform was ruined. Sadly for me, the principal decided to call the authorities on me." She let loose with a bitter laugh. "The police weren't called for a child molester but when I disposed of a piece of refuse, I was promptly arrested."

Her tone resembled steel, the fire within her had burned away the impurities until only the firmest, strongest hate remained. "None of the girls testified to what he had done. The school fabricated a story of a disastrous crush and unrequited love. Apparently, Mayfield's rejection of me caused my murderous actions. I spent my teenage years in a juvenile detention facility. The records of my crimes as a minor were sealed. I emerged back into the world armed with a whole new set of skills learned while incarcerated." Summing up, she shrugged. "That is how I ended up on the path I am on today."

Valerie Gossard, Raven, waited for her boyfriend's recriminations. Instead, Douglas Lawson threw his arms around her and passionately, repeatedly kissed her neck.

"What is wrong with you? I just told you I am a murderer." Valerie felt the barrage of kisses stop.

Douglas continued to hug her and spoke into her ear. A swift and excited cadence entered his voice. "Don't you see? We are more alike than I thought. You fought for justice at a young age and the system let you down. A similar event happened to me, but I let it beat me for years. I stopped fighting the good fight and focused on myself instead of others. However, you didn't let that happen to you. Despite the legal system condemning you, you went on to become a defense lawyer. Your job is to make sure that the accused are properly represented, probably seeing a bit of yourself in every client. While I don't agree with taking a life (even the life of such a terrible person), your admission has only made me love you more."

Valerie sat in shock. What would it take to be knocked off the pedestal upon which he had placed her? She could admit to more unsavory deeds but if she had never been tried in a court of law, she was only giving him ammo with which to send her away.

"Doug, I was sure my confession would drive you away." She blurted with a small amount of awe.

"I guess I love you unconditionally." He held her against him and stroked her back.

"Unconditional love is terrifying when you know it's undeserved." Valerie felt her eyes start to burn.

"Do I have to remind you what 'unconditional' means? I'm going to love you no matter how much or little you feel it's deserved." He whispered the words into her ear and felt her body shiver.

Raven could not turn him against her without incurring more risk. It would be easier to play along until Arturo finished the job. Kissing him on the lips, she finally spoke the words that her boyfriend had wanted to hear. "I love you, too."

Chapter: The Attack

D awn broke and Valentine got to see it. Normally, he slept through such picturesque scenes but worry had robbed him of his beauty rest. After a fitful night of tossing and turning on his bunk, he rose to walk to the barred window and peek out. Surrounding buildings did their best to block out the natural light but they were not tall enough. The sun had technically already risen over the city, but Scott had his personal sunrise as a shaft of light streamed in as the sun crested the facing building.

He felt warmth and closed his eyes to drink in the sensation. He needed some reassurance. He had withheld information about his partners because he needed more bargaining chips for the pigs. They were no longer interested in him, but *Bestia*, Devildriver, and Raven. He had debated telling more but was worried about tipping his hand too soon. If Valerie or Arturo were brought in, how long would it take either of them to send in a hit man. On the other hand, Raven had already lost her cop on the inside. The real question weighing on his mind was which way was he safer?

Ms. Gossard successfully defended a handful of wealthy clients and did so with professionalism and expertise. If she were dragged down to the station in handcuffs, she would quickly be out on the street. Even if charges held up and she went to trial, she could probably beat whatever the prosecutors threw at her. On the other hand, Scott would be in trouble the next time Valerie tried to contact her crooked detective. She would know that he failed to silence Valentine. She would try again, but this time with a weapon of which he was unaware.

He felt the tension in his shoulders as he mulled the problem over in his head. He stepped out of the sun and back into the cool shade of his cell.

Pacing nervously, he muttered "what to do" to himself over and over. As long as he was in a cell in the middle of Kios, he was going to eventually lose. He needed to disappear. With no ideas on how to escape, he'd have to convince the police to move him to a new location. He needed to give up some information worth a transfer to a new facility.

Scott walked over to the bars and peered out. If only he were smart enough to plan an escape, he would not have to sit around waiting for his death. When the time came, there would be no playing off of the sympathies of his crew, regardless of his silver tongue. They were all professionals or psychopaths. Fidgeting, he walked back to his bed and sat down. He gave a mirthless laugh. "At least I don't have to worry about getting older and losing my looks."

Douglas held the phone to his ear. "Hey, sorry to call so early. I'm going to be late opening the shop this morning. Could you run it for a little bit until I get there?"

A sleepy Gaston mumbled an affirmative and hung up.

Lawson stuck the cell back in his pocket and looked at his girlfriend in the driver's seat. "I think last night went well."

Gossard smiled but did not take her eyes from the road. "I'm surprised you woke up this morning. I thought I had worn you out."

"You did. I'm exhausted but I have a business to run. The world needs coffee to kickstart the day."

Valerie smiled. "The caffeine peddler, a hero to millions."

As a faint smile crossed his lips, Douglas watched her. "We had a breakthrough last night. You finally caved and admitted how you feel."

"Ugh, don't remind me. I don't approve of mushy stuff."

"I liked seeing your vulnerable side. It shows that you trust me." Doug reached out and put his hand on her thigh. "Want to tell me any other dark secrets?" He laughed.

She thought, "You are about to die." When she opened her mouth, the only words that came out were "not particularly". In a moment of weakness, she had considered warning him, but the logical part of her brain took over. How would she explain her foreknowledge? She also could not keep him hidden from *Bestia* forever. Her temptation to spare him faded when she realized that she had already set things in motion and stopping them would prove too inconvenient.

The ride had been full of small talk and playful banter but the morning drive came to a close. Valerie stopped the car in front of Caffeine Nation and leaned over. "A goodbye kiss?"

Doug leaned in and playfully bit her bottom lip. When he let go, she grabbed his shirt and pulled him in again. This time, she forced a deeply passionate kiss on him. When she pulled away, she took a moment to softly stroke his cheek. "Goodbye, Douglas." She wanted to say more, but the words stuck in her throat.

"I'll see you later." Douglas Lawson flashed a heart melting smile and stepped out of the car. Elated by the previous night's romp and Valerie's declaration of love, Doug happily tapped his cane against the sidewalk as he walked, stopping in front of the door to Caffeine Nation. Looking around, he spotted Gaston's car but when he looked through the window of the shop, he could not see his friend. "He must be in the back." Doug tried the knob, but it did not turn. Reaching into his pants pocket, he pulled out his key ring. The sound of footsteps made him look up from the lock.

A grizzled man in tattered clothing determinedly walked toward Lawson. Doug assumed the man to be a customer and waved. "I'm a little behind this morning. I'll need a few minutes to get things up and running."

The stranger did not speak but reached under the flap of his stained jacket and pulled out a simple pocket knife. Confidently, he unfolded the weapon and gripped it tightly in his hand. The man did not slow his pace and Douglas realized this encounter had nothing to do with coffee.

Doug dropped his keys and wrapped both hands around the head of his cane. A thumb hovered over the button that would activate the electrical discharge. His opponent smirked at the makeshift weapon and took a testing stab. Douglas backpedalled as fast as he could, but his bum leg refused to move the way his brain ordered it. Doug lost his balance and fell backwards on to his butt. One hand still on cane, he lifted it defensively as his assailant loomed above him.

The attacker's bloodshot eyes locked with Douglas' for a brief moment. Lawson could read the intention in them. As the man stabbed downward, Doug plunged the tip of the cane into the assassin's abdomen. A whoosh of breath escaped him as the knife fell away, clattering harmlessly on the ground. Instinctively, the man grabbed the cane with both hands and Douglas pushed the button, releasing a flood of electricity. The stranger's body turned rigid and he fell to the ground like a statue.

As Doug struggled to stand, he punched numbers on his cell phone. A pleasant voice on the other end asked, "911, what is your emergency?"

"Someone just attacked me with a knife. I am at Caffeine Nation, 412 8th Street. He's still here but incapacitated."

Jacob exited the shop. "Dad, what's going on?"

Douglas motioned to the man on the ground. "That guy tried to knife me as I was opening the door."

Moaning, the would-be assassin stood up and tried to hobble away. Jake narrowed his eyes and pointed at the man's feet. Suddenly, the heels clomped together and the man fell forward, unable to move his feet.

"I can hold him until the police get here as long as no one distracts me." Jacob did not look at his father for confirmation, preferring to stay focused on his target. However, Douglas noted that the boy did not look as strained while using his power.

"Thanks, but I think I have some handcuffs upstairs." Doug

offered. Still focused on the prisoner, Jake shook his head without glancing at his father.

Douglas leaned on his cane and looked at the helpless assassin. "Why'd you attack me?"

The struggling man flung several curses at Lawson. Jacob shouted, "Quit fighting me! Be still or I'm going to hurt you."

Doug patted Jacob on the shoulder. "Squeeze his legs a little tighter. Show him you mean business."

Jake squinted as he tried to focus. A loud snap emanated from the prisoner's shin and he immediately howled in pain.

"You broke my damn leg!"

Jacob's eyes widened in fear and he glanced at his father with a worried expression. Douglas had not intended the injury when he suggested his boy tighten the constraints, but he was willing to roll with it.

"He told you to stop moving. Now, answer me or he'll do worse to you! Why did you attack me?" Doug shouted at the prone junkie.

"I was paid to. I'm not supposed to leave until it's done." The injured man strained to speak through the agony.

"Just injure me or kill me?"

"Kill." The man sobbed.

Jake's brow dripped sweat as he concentrated on keeping the man from moving. He was used to wielding his gift in short bursts, but the prolonged application quickly sapped his strength.

"Who hired you?" Doug commanded an answer.

"I don't know his name."

Lawson took the tip of his cane and gave a sharp prod to the man's broken femur.

"Jesus Christ!" After grunting through a new blast of pain, the assailant answered. "I really don't know his name but he sounded Mexican."

Douglas shared a knowing look with his son. "*Bestia*."

Chapter: Personnel Changes

Valerie Gossard sat down across from Arturo Gomez. Both wore impassive expressions and let the silence hang between them for a moment. Neither rushed to begin. Finally, Arturo conversationally started as he opened a bottle of water. "My guy waited all night for your boyfriend. Apparently, Lawson was out late. Did you have anything to do with that?"

Valerie's face did not twitch. Her stone visage gave no hint as to her internal emotions. "I gave the ill-fated one last happy moment before the inevitable."

"That's sweet." *Bestia* mockingly answered. "I expect you'll get a phone call sometime today notifying you that he's dead."

"I expect I will." Valerie agreed.

"What's our next order of business? I don't like being idle." Arturo finally cracked a smile.

"Valentine." A trace of sadness entered Ms. Gossard's voice. "A little birdy told me that he has been talkative while in lockup. Our attempt to humanely wipe his memory failed and cost me a valuable asset on the inside of the department."

Feeling wary, Arturo hesitantly urged her to continue. "Then the next step is..."

"Valentine has to be permanently retired. The longer he's with them, the bigger a threat he is to us." Valerie's eyes were as hard as the edge in her voice.

"Do we know that he's talking? Do you have another police contact?"

"It doesn't matter if he's talked or not. We can't risk it. He has to be taken out." Valerie continued.

"When it's one of our team members, you have no problem ordering him offed. But when it was poor Dougie, you waited and waited until he was on the verge of sinking us before you lifted a finger." An accusatory tone accompanied his words and *Bestia* felt his temper slipping beyond his control.

"What can I say? I've just been in a killing mood the past few days." Her hand slid under the table, despite the eye contact she kept with her employee.

Arturo knew he had pushed her when he should have backed away. He was certain that she had a pistol pointed at his abdomen. His tone softened. "Hey, I'm just glad things are getting done. It's about time we quit playing cat and mouse. We've always been best when we kept things simple."

"I agree and once Valentine is no longer a threat, we can run like the streamlined team we've always been." Raven stood up, pistol clenched in her hand, and walked away from the table. "I'll leave the details to you. Meeting adjourned."

Penelope Daniels hopped off at the bus stop with her sketch book in hand. Excited, she just finished her shift and took a special trip to Doug Lawson's coffee shop. Anxiously, she hurried to meet the boy for whom she was commissioned to design a costume. She briefly considered calling beforehand but has too afraid that Mr. Lawson would change his mind the next time they spoke. She had also avoided any mention of her plans to Dr. Nichols. She had become irritable whenever anyone mentioned her old boyfriend.

Penny walked a block and turned the corner to see a police car pulling away. She continued closer, realizing that the cruiser had been parked in front of Caffeine Nation. She quickened her pace, curious as to why law enforcement had been present. When she reached the door, she could see a group of strangers gathered around a four person table. The only ones that she recognized were Douglas and Gaston. A tall, black woman sat beside Gaston de Paul. They both wore grim expressions. Across from them, a young boy of twelve or thirteen listened with rapt attention to the discussion of the adults.

Penny set off the bell as she opened the door. Quickly all eyes turned toward her. Douglas showed relief when he recognized her. "Thank God you're not a cop. I don't think I could answer any more questions right now."

"Did something happen?" The young nurse asked with trepidation.

"An enemy tried to have me assassinated. Luckily, he was bad at his job." Douglas motioned to her scrubs. "Did you just leave work?"

Penny nodded. "I thought I would stop by and take some measurements for Cataclysm."

Jacob watched the newcomer with interest. "Are you going to make me a costume?"

"Yes, your father said you needed one." Penelope answered before glancing over at Gaston. The Frenchman occasionally looked her way but seemed more interested in the woman sitting beside him.

Douglas stood up and walked over with Jacob in tow. "Well, let's get started. Get everything you need now because we're going out of town for a little while."

"To hide?" Penny asked.

Doug seemed slightly annoyed at the wording and corrected her. "To keep Jake safe."

She nodded. "How will I let you know when the costume is ready?"

"Just come by the shop. I'm coming back as soon as I drop him off." His comment instantly caused a cacophony of voices. Jacob was the loudest but Desiree and Gaston also voiced their displeasure.

Gaston cried out. "You cannot fight them alone. You were lucky today. Next time, they will not send an emaciated junkie."

Desiree stood up in anger. "You begged me to come back and help you take down these guys and now you want me to babysit your kid while you get yourself killed?"

Jacob grabbed his father's sleeve with a panicked grip. "You can't just abandon me for weeks like you did after the bridge! If it's too dangerous for me, then it's too dangerous for you too. I thought we were a team. If I have to go, we all have to go!"

Lawson looked at each determined set of eyes and sighed. "Just leave word with the Cindy, she has my cell number."

Penny took the opportunity to pry. "Couldn't I just get the number from Samantha? I'm sure she knows how to get in touch with you."

Doug winced. "I suppose you could do that, but she doesn't want to have anything to do with me. Just come by and let Cindy know."

Penny Daniels smiled at Jacob. "Okay, let's get started." She set her sketch book down on the table and pulled a tailor's tape measure from her pocket.

The boy awkwardly stood as she dashed around him getting everything she needed. The flimsy tape stretched from his neck to his shoulder, quickly down the length of his arm, in a flash around his waist, and (causing Jake to jump) a fast ascent up his inseam. When she finished, she jotted the numbers down on a clean page of her book and wrote Cataclysm at the top.

Looking back at the sheepishly grinning child, she asked about his ideas. "What did you have in mind for your uniform?"

Jacob seemed stunned that his opinion was requested. "Hold on, I've got some drawings upstairs." The boy sprinted off and loud clomps echoed through the shop as he bounded to the second floor.

Douglas chuckled. "Can you tell this made his day?"

Gaston bitterly added, "He needed some good news after seeing his father in a life or death struggle."

"I made it through without a scra-." Doug countered.

Desiree cut him off. "You were lucky that junkie couldn't get a hold of a gun."

"Don't worry. I'm on the verge of cracking this case wide open."

Penelope tried not to draw attention to herself, since she desperately wanted to hear more about his life as a crime fighter.

"And how is that?" Gaston challenged.

"The car, I saw the email this morning. Jacob had a good point. Anyone that goes by the handle 'Devil' is probably not big on subtlety. I'm going to call Detective Sudduth and let him know that the vehicle we're looking for is a 72 Dodge Demon. There can't be that many left on the road. The car has to be registered or he'd risk getting pulled over every time he went out. Police follow up and nab him at his home address. Crazy killer off the street."

Desiree crossed her arms. "You're supposed to be 'Einstein'. Did you forget that there's *Bestia* and his boss, Raven? The Latino didn't look like a pushover and his boss is smart enough to still be invisible."

"Scott Edwards or Devil will rat them out."

Desiree scoffed. "I don't think Devil would be intimidated by a couple of cops. That guy seems like he has ice in his veins."

"Edwards?" Douglas seemed less sure of himself.

Gaston volunteered his thoughts. "We don't know enough about the man's personality to predict how he would hold up under questioning. His history paints the picture of a chameleon. We have no idea what his true nature is."

"Okay, okay. Quit ganging up on me. We are all leaving town together while I hand over our newest lead to Sudduth. We'll stay on vacation until he's tracked down Devil."

Jacob appeared behind the counter with a spiral bound notebook. "Sorry, it took me a minute to find it." He ran up to Penelope and opened it to a specific page. "This one is my favorite."

Penelope looked at the crude drawing and smiled. The boy was not an artist but he certainly knew what he wanted. The first thing she noticed was a hood pulled low over the figure's eyes. A cape swirled around the body, which was covered in a skin tight body suit.

Tall boots, gloves, and a utility belt finished off the ensemble. Black dominated the color palate, but each article of clothing was trimmed with flames.

"I like it." Penelope stated and watched an over-eager Jake jump up and down at the praise. "I'll start working on it right away and it'll be done by the time you get back from where ever it is you're going."

Sheepishly, Jacob spoke up. "Could you tear the page out? I've got other drawings and song lyrics in there. They're kind of embarrassing."

Douglas reached out and took the notebook. "I'll make a copy in my office. It won't take but a second."

While they waited, Penny looked at the boy with undisguised interest. "Why the name Cataclysm? It sounds more like a villain than a hero."

Jake shrugged. "I make bad things happen to the people around me. I create disaster."

Nurse Daniels whistled with admiration. "That's a catchphrase for sure."

Jacob grinned at her approval. "I just made that up on the spot."

"I need to pick the materials. Do you have any special requests? Maybe padding or flame retardant fabric?" She had no idea what the young boy would be doing while wearing her creation.

Douglas appeared and handed a photocopied sheet to Penelope. "Flame retardant sounds good."

Jacob cried out. "It's my suit! I get to pick."

"I'm your Dad. I win." Doug turned his attention from the boy to the nurse. "I want him well protected from a variety of threats. Safety is most important."

"I don't need the protection. I have my powers!" Jake argued.

Penny looked at him in surprise. "You have real powers?"

"Of course. I can show you if you want." Jacob offered.

Douglas cleared his throat. "How are you going to keep a secret identity if you go around showing off for every single person you meet?"

"But she's one of us right? She's making costumes for us. You told me she has one of her own. Wouldn't that make her a Sentinel?" Jake's eyes implored his father to agree with him.

Doug looked at Gaston and Desiree, both watching him with curiosity. Turning back to Penelope, he asked, "It's dangerous. Someone tried to kill me just this morning. You can design costumes and help support us as a medic, but there's still a chance our enemies will target you just for being affiliated." He paused. "With that said, Penny Dreadful, do you want to join The Sentinels?"

Penelope Daniels threw her arms around Douglas Lawson's neck. "I thought you'd never ask."

Chapter: Three Phone Calls

Samantha walked through the halls of Bryers Hospital, checking on her patients when her cell phone vibrated in her pocket. Looking at the caller id, she saw the name "Douglas Lawson".

"It's about time." She mumbled and then answered the call. "Hello."

"It's me Doug."

"I know." She dryly replied.

"I was just returning a missed call from you." He fished for the reason she had tried to contact him.

"I felt you deserved to know. Freeman pharm has a possible cure. It's shown promise in the lab and they want to try it on Dr. Miller and his victims. Since you caught him, I thought you'd want to be here." She endeavored to make the call as business like as possible.

"Oh, thanks. That's great. Maybe those people will get their lives back." He paused, remembering that he was going into hiding. "When is this happening?"

"I'm not sure, but I can let you know." She offered despite knowing she'd need to call him again.

"Normally, I wouldn't be as concerned about the schedule but I'm leaving town and don't know how long I'll be away."

"Extended vacation?"

Douglas gave a hollow chuckle. "Something like that. Anyway, you've got my number. Just let me know and I will try to come back for that. If Miller gets his memories back, he may be able to help us capture the rest of the gang."

"Don't worry. I'll let you know." Silence stretched out between them. After too much dead air, Dr. Nichols ended the conversation. "Bye and have a safe trip."

"Thanks again." Samantha heard him say before she hung up. She tapped the phone against her chin. She had successfully talked to her ex-boyfriend without getting personal. She smiled at the thought of how she had finally gotten over him. She waited a moment for her heart to slow down before getting back to work.

Clarence Sudduth had just woken up on the couch with his formerly estranged wife. After a pleasant dinner, they had shared a bottle of wine. Fully expecting things to become physical, they had inched closer to each other with each glass. Eventually, they were side by side, her head on his shoulder. "I've missed this." She quietly whispered into the fabric of his shirt.

Clarence adjusted his arm behind her and replied. "I've missed this, too." An old familiarity returned and comfortable cuddling, they accidentally drifted off to sleep.

Like a shrieking banshee, Sudduth's phone would not give him respite. The sudden explosion of sound sent him bolting upright and his wife sprang away in surprise. "Damn it." He put the phone to his ear. "Yes?"

Lawson's voice came over. "Hey, got some news for you."

Annoyed at the timing, Clarence growled. "I don't think I've been less pleased to hear from you and that includes when I completely hated you."

Momentarily stunned, Douglas could only reply, "Okay…"

"I was taking a nap in the arms of my wife." He explained, realizing that there was no way Doug could have known that.

"Sorry, I just thought you'd want to know we have a pretty good idea of what Devil is driving." Doug proceeded with contrition in his voice. "It's a 1972 Dodge Demon. There are some other possibilities but we feel that's the strongest one."

Clarence tried to clear his head enough to absorb the information.

"Okay, that's good. I've got some information for you too. Um, what was it?" He rubbed his eyes with his free hand. "Oh yeah, Scott Edwards started singing like a canary. He's definitely working with *Bestia*, Devil, and their boss Raven. They were contracted to kill Martin Ramsey because of someone he prosecuted. We don't know who."

"I'll research it and look for some connections." Douglas made a mental note. "Did he say anything else?"

Sudduth tried to remember what he had heard. "The leader is Raven, whoever that is. *Bestia* is the lieutenant. Oh yeah, the name the third guy goes by isn't Devil, but Devildriver. You basically heard them using the nickname."

"I'm pretty sure his birth certificate doesn't say Devildriver. It's more like a nickname of a code name."

Sudduth laughed. "Anyway, Edwards is a small fish. They only use him to get information and then he's left out of the score. Apparently, he's gotten cocky and started demanding more for each tidbit of info. The men handling him are getting really frustrated, but I'll try to see what else I can find out."

"Thanks, I appreciate it. Not to make it all about me, but did you hear that someone tried to kill me this morning?" Doug tried to sound conversational. "Some down and out junkie tried to stab me. He pretty much admitted to being hired over the phone by a guy with a Spanish accent."

"Jesus Christ, are you okay?" Startled, Sudduth sat up.

"Yeah, I managed to subdue him. He didn't provide much information other than the connection to *Bestia*. I was wondering when they would make their move on me. They've known where I live since right before the bridge."

"You can't stay there." Clarence realized that he was frightened for his friend.

"Don't worry. I'm taking a little vacation. I can still do plenty of research as long as I have an internet connection. I'm going to start by combing through Martin Ramsey's cases."

"Good, don't tell anyone where you are going, and I mean anyone. I don't even want to know. They've got people in the department and there's no telling where else they have people planted."

"Don't worry. I'm taking my people with me and that's it. Now that I know they are on the move again, I won't be caught off guard. Oh yeah, Freeman Pharm is planning on curing all the memory loss victims. When they do, I bet that Phillips guy that we caught would have some useful intel."

Clarence smiled. "I'll make sure some officers are there. We can't have a resource like that going to waste."

"Samantha Nichols is a good contact at the hospital. You may not want to mention me though. I've been kind of written out of her life."

Detective Sudduth waited a moment. When no further explanation came, he awkwardly mumbled, "I'm sorry to hear that."

"Regardless, I'm going to let you go and start packing. Stay safe and let me know if anything interesting happens while I'm gone."

"I should be telling you to be careful. No one's tried to assassinate me yet. Be safe. Check in when you can." Clarence felt uneasy as they said their goodbyes. Something gnawed at him but he couldn't articulate it.

Valerie Gossard rolled over on her side and looked at the old fashioned glass half filled with Bourbon. She had plied herself with a few drinks waiting for word from anyone that Lawson had died. As the day slipped away and night descended, she still waited. Now, she was sick of the taste and just wanted to get the job of acting like a distraught girlfriend finished. She had not grown close to any of Douglas' friends. So when she stopped coming around, no one would find her behavior suspicious.

Raven's eyes fixated on the brown liquid and she felt a lethargy creep over her. Why had she kept doing this job? She had money enough to be comfortable. Even if she did not manage her little criminal empire, her fees as a legitimate lawyer would keep her in her current lifestyle. What drove her to continue? The glass of whiskey did not provide any insight. Maybe it was just because she was a monster that knew no other way.

Her personal cell rang. She sat up and scooped it off of the end table and looked at the screen with a sense of shock. A phone icon shook on the display. Beside it, the caller id promised that Douglas Lawson was calling her. Answering with a growing sense of disbelief, she whispered "Hello?"

"Hey, you will not believe the day that I've had." It was indeed Doug. His voice contained a strange mixture of exhaustion and snark. "Someone tried to kill me after you dropped me off. Obviously I'm okay, but wow, it was an intense morning."

Valerie covered her mouth with her free hand to prevent an errant sound from escaping. How the hell had he survived? She did not know Arturo's arrangements but he rarely failed. Finding her voice, she shakily asked, "What happened?"

"Some scuzzy guy with a knife came at me as I was trying to unlock the front door. I managed to subdue him until the police got there." He spoke as if he had completed some banal task.

"You subdued him?" She parroted in disbelief.

"Yeah, I'm making light of it but I was terrified." Valerie could picture him shrugging as he made his admission.

"I'm glad you are okay." She spoke in a flat voice, unsure of whether or not she meant it. If Lawson was still alive, she would have to give the order to try again. She could also do the deed herself. That was ludicrous. Family and significant others were always the first suspects.

"You sound kind of weird. I didn't realize it would shake you up so badly. After the bridge, you weren't near this…"

Valerie cried out. "I'm so happy you're not dead." She felt the last few whiskeys dulling her fine motor skills and slurred her confession.

"Have you been drinking?" Doug asked.

"I've had a long day." She almost laughed. Spending so much time waiting to grieve, she felt relief and rage at his continued survival. Raven had been sent back to square one. "I've been working on a case that just keeps going."

"I'm sorry, but I'm probably not making your night any less stressful. I was calling to update you on today and to tell you that I'm leaving town for a bit."

Valerie immediately cried out. "Don't tell me where you're going!"

Caught off guard, Doug replied "okay".

In a calmer tone, Valerie explained "I have to have plausible deniability. If your enemies try to intimidate me, I can't tell them if I don't know."

Douglas sat in silence for a moment, thinking. "I can't picture anyone intimidating you." He joked but then seriously continued. "Come with me. It will be like a vacation and no one can get to you if you disappear with me."

Raven solemnly responded. "I can't go with you. I have too much going on here."

"Please come with me. I don't know how long I'll have to go without you." Doug's voice carried a quiet desperation.

"I have cases. I can't leave my firm for an undetermined length of time. What if it's not safe for you to return for months?" She argued. "Douglas, this is final. I am not going with you and I don't want to know where you are going."

"I know it's a crazy request but I don't want you left here. What if they try to get to you through me?" Douglas pleaded.

"I can take care of myself. I've been doing it since I was a child." Her manner became stern. "Say goodnight and disappear so that no one can find you. If you continue to try to convince me, our relationship will suffer irreparable damage."

Valerie waited for a response. She could hear barely controlled frustration in the silence on the other end of the call. Finally, a single terse word cracked through the speaker. "Goodnight." He hung up leaving her alone on the couch. Setting her phone down, she picked up the glass of whiskey. Staring deep into the amber color, she wondered what the hell she had just done.

Chapter: Homecoming

Clifford Lawson rode around his property on a brightly colored riding mower. The roaring engine drowned out all other noise and a steady stream of grass clipping fired out from under the blade deck. He owned a large parcel of land but let most of it grow into forest or just tall grass. The only part he mowed was a solid acre around the house.

His wife, Maylene, stepped out of the front door with a tall glass of water in her hand. Cliff killed the engine and swung one leg off the mower. May walked to the edge of the front porch and waited for him. He could see the condensation on the outside of the glass and licked his lips. He forgot what thirsty work maintaining the yard could be.

"Thanks, hon." He took the offered glass and gulped down a huge swallow. It felt so refreshing that he tilted it back again and drained the rest of the water. "You knew just when I needed that."

She smiled and took the empty glass back. "Randall called and said he saw your old Corvette driving through town."

Clifford looked confused. "Dougie has it in Kios. He must have been mistaken."

May shook her head. "He seemed pretty sure of himself, blue and white. He said she couldn't see the driver, but there was a kid in the car."

Cliff looked at the unfinished yard. "You don't think Dougie would show up unannounced, do you? He hasn't been out here in forever except to drop off Jake."

May nodded. "He hasn't called and it's unlike him to just stop by, but just in case, I'll brew some more sweet tea."

As Maylene walked inside, Cliff jumped back on his riding mower. After cranking it and engaging the blade, he took his foot off the brake and lurched forward. Whittling down the unruly grass, he had almost finished when he saw two cars turning on to his driveway. The first one was indeed the Corvette. An old Honda Civic trailed behind.

As the cars rolled to a stop, doors swung opened and Jacob hopped out. He had a backpack slung over one shoulder and ran towards his grandfather. Clifford climbed out of his seat again and felt embarrassed by the sour sweat smell that clung to him. The boy threw his arms around Cliff and immediately recoiled.

"Ew, you're wet." Jake wiped his hands and forearms on his shirt.

"I've been working outside." The old firefighter defended.

Douglas had exited the vehicle and limped over to his father. "I was wondering if you would mind some visitors." Behind him, Desiree and Gaston pulled luggage out of the Honda's hatchback.

"Four of you?" The eldest Lawson raised an eyebrow.

"Yeah, you've met Gaston." Doug pointed at the younger man wearing all black.

"I remember."

"The lady is Desiree." Douglas motioned toward the tall black woman.

"These are your friends?" Cliff looked over the group. Gaston looked sullen and Desiree had coolness in her gaze that indicated not much impressed her. "We weren't expecting guests. We've got Doug's old room, a guest room, and a couch." He pointed respectively at his son and Jacob, Desire, and then Gaston.

Jake spoke up. "It's okay. Desiree and Mr. De Paul can share a room. They're a couple."

Gaston's eyes flicked over to Desiree to gauge her reaction. She gave no indication how she felt. Douglas, on the other hand, demanded answers. "When did this happen?"

Gaston looked at the woman to whom he had made love, hoping

for some kind of direction. She watched him expectantly and he realized she was leaving the handling of the situation to him.

"A few nights ago." He watched Douglas with anticipation. Would he be angry, elated, indifferent? "The relationship was unexpected, but welcomed." Gaston looked at Desiree as he spoke the last two words.

Doug stood in the driveway with his arms crossed in front of his chest. He's face brow furrowed in concentration. After a handful of heartbeats, he broke into a smile. "I should have caught that. I'm really losing my skills. You've been looking at her differently ever since she came back."

Cliff's shoulders tensed as he spoke. "You're not my kids and you're both adults. If you want to share a room, you can."

Desiree nodded. "Thank you, sir, but I can take the couch. I find most beds too soft."

Clifford shrugged. "Let's go inside, out of the heat. We'll see if we have enough of something for six people."

Gaston walked beside Desiree and whispered, "Do you not want to share a bed?"

She slid her arm through the crook of his elbow. "I am the best fighter and a light sleeper. If anyone has followed us, I'm the look out and first line of defense."

Gaston swallowed with relief. "So it's really not about me?"

She kissed him on the cheek. "Not everything is about you."

As she let go of his arm and picked up the luggage, Gaston felt the stinging spot where she kissed him. It had been unexpected and he had not focused fast enough to stem his power. He held on to that pain several minutes before letting it go.

Inside the house, Cliff walked in and loudly announced "Looks like Randall was right. Dougie and Jake showed up and brought some friends."

Maylene poked her head out of the kitchen with a pleasant smile. "Oh, I wish he'd call first. How many friends?"

Cliff held up four fingers. "Including Dougie and Jake." Behind him, the quartet of visitors entered single file.

"Hey, Mom, I wanted to call first but we left in a hurry." Douglas called out, unsure of where she was in the house.

"It's okay. Why don't you come to the kitchen so you're not yelling across the house?"

"Let me get our stuff in my old room and I'll be right there." Doug disappeared down the hall.

Clifford entered the kitchen with Jacob trailing at his heels. "Can I get you a drink, Jake?"

"Could I have some sweet tea? That stuff is so good." Jake grinned at them, basking in the presence of a real family. Even though they were hiding out, he felt lucky to be with his adopted grandparents.

Maylene opened a cabinet and pulled out a tumbler. "A fresh batch is brewing. I'll pour you a glass as soon as it's done."

"Thanks, Ma'am." Jacob replied.

"Oh sweetie, you don't have to call me ma'am. We're family." Maylene assured him.

Clifford interrupted. "Glad to have you, but what made Dougie decide to visit?"

Jake grew nervous. Douglas had kept fighting crime a secret from his own parents and Jacob did not feel it was his place to reveal it. On the other hand, he did not want to lie to his new family.

"Uh, there were multiple reasons." Then he looked through the doorway to the living room. "I'll check on Gaston and Desiree." He quickly left the room.

The wife looked at her husband in confusion. "Who's Desiree?"

"A friend of Doug's. Come out and introduce yourself." Leaving the tea on the stove top, the older couple entered the living room.

Maylene saw the thin Frenchman and warmly greeted him. "Gaston, welcome back. It's been so long." Then she turned and faced a tall black woman. "You must be Desiree. Welcome to our home."

The mercenary started to look uncomfortable, but responded with the required pleasantries. "Thank you for having us. It's a lovely home." In reality, she thought it would be hard to defend in a siege. There were too many windows and the open floor plan did not allow for good choke points.

"How long have you known Doug?" Cliff asked.

"Slightly less time than Gaston, he hired me a few years ago." Desiree's eyes scanned the room for makeshift weapons in case of attack.

Maylene seemed surprised. "You work at the coffee shop?"

Desiree shook her head. "No, I aggressively pursue our target demographic."

"Oh, marketing." The grandmother nodded.

Clifford looked at her with suspicion. "Where did you serve?"

"South and Central Africa."

"Who were you with?"

"Different units." She tersely replied.

"Did you see combat?" His voice sounded conversational but his eyes keenly waited for his guess to be confirmed.

"It's a wild place. Everyone did, whether they wanted to or not."

Douglas entered. "Has everyone gotten to know each other again?"

Clifford glared at his son. "What does she do?"

"Security." Douglas shrugged.

"Coffee has become that popular?"

Gaston nervously laughed. "I see where you get your wit from, Douglas."

An oppressive silence filled the room as everyone stayed focused on the eldest Lawson. "Son, what's really going on?"

Doug gave a fake smile. "What do you mean?"

"Your friends do not seem like coffee shop employees. You show up unannounced. Everyone seems on edge. Last time you were down you dropped off Jacob but wouldn't visit with us."

"I had business to take care of…" Douglas stressed.

"Did this business have anything to do with coffee?" Clifford shot back.

Doug gritted his teeth. "Can't you let me have my secrets?"

"No!" Cliff's voice rose.

"Why not?" Doug shouted back.

"Because you're my son and I worry about you!" His voice roared as he lost his temper.

Doug took a step back, shocked. Gaston reached out a gloved hand and placed it on Douglas' forearm. With a quiet voice, he urged his friend to confess. "Just tell him."

"What do you need to tell me, Chief?" Cliff eyed his son warily.

Douglas sighed. "You may want to sit down. This is a long story."

For the next hour, Douglas explained his crime fighting alias "Einstein" and his group The Sentinels. He told how he found Dr. Miller's hideout. He hesitantly relayed how *Bestia* and Devildriver had tried to drug him for getting too close. He talked about the bridge and how he really hadn't been in an accident. He had taken all of that damage trying to fight a criminal.

His father had tried to interrupt with questions but Maylene shushed him. Doug explained about the lull in activity, discovering the fraudulent Tobias Richmond, and the latest attempt on his life. "And now, we are here until the police catch this guy. Since Edwards is in custody and ratting out his accomplices, it shouldn't take long."

Clifford looked at his son with disbelief. "And this story is true?" His eyes shifted from person to person for confirmation. Cliff ran his fingers through his hair as he exhaled. "Phew, I don't know what the hell to say to that. It's too crazy to be true."

Douglas sat there waiting for more of a response and he got one. His father slammed in hand down on the coffee table. "Are you crazy? You are a single father. What would happen to Jacob if these maniacs had succeeded?"

Douglas sedately replied. "I was coming up here to discuss that with you. I was hoping that you and Mom could take him if I don't make it. You did a good job of raising me and I want him to have that level of quality parenting in his life as well."

Jacob looked around in a panic. "But they're not going to get you! You've already sent three of their men to jail."

"Greg Phillips and Scott Edwards were not fighters and the assassin was a junkie that was being paid with drugs. Next time, they are going to come at me with someone better. I've just been lucky so far." Douglas let fear show in his normally confident eyes. Suddenly, he looked vulnerable to his child.

Jacob countered. "I can protect you! Nothing is going to happen!"

Clifford reached out and put his hand on the boy's shoulder. "Jake, these are dangerous men and you're just a kid."

Jacob recoiled, knocking the comforting hand away. "I'm not just a kid! I have powers. I've been practicing and I can stop them. Just stop treating me like a child!"

Douglas' voice grew firm. "Jake, you are a child and I'm your father. I am not putting you in harm's way. Now when you are speaking to me or your grandfather, you need to be respectful."

Cliff interrupted. "What is he talking about 'powers'?"

Jake launched into an explanation before his father could reply. "I have a superpower. I can move things by thinking about it and I'm getting better every day."

Cliff stood up and pointed at Douglas. "You, come outside with me." The voice left little room to interpret it as anything other than a command.

Huffing like a teenager, Doug stood and followed his father to the front door. Outside in the yard, Cliff whirled around at him shouting. "Are you crazier than a shithouse rat?" Doug had never heard his father swear in such a manner and was stunned into silence. "You run around trying to get yourself killed and know you've brainwashed that poor child into thinking that he's a superhero in training! I had no idea you were this delusional." In a quieter voice, he blamed himself. "I should have listened to your mother. I let you read those stupid comic books."

Douglas paced back and forth with his cane, waiting for an opening to respond. Seizing the momentary silence, he retorted. "Yeah, I read comics and I may have been influenced by them some. But do you know who really drove home the idea that I needed to do this? You did. I grew up under the roof of a well-liked firefighter in a small town. Everywhere I went, people thanked you for saving their homes, their lives. Even when a house burned to the ground, they were grateful to you for running back in and pulling their pets out. It didn't matter how much of a piece of shit they were in daily life, you tried to save them all. How could I not want to do more with my life with a hero as a father?"

Cliff looked at his son with new eyes. In a whisper, he argued. "I never called myself a hero. It was just a job."

"And that made it even more influential. You're humble. You were like a comic book character, not the grim anti-hero, but the Boy Scout type who will always do the right thing. You're like Captain America or Superman to me."

"You've got to stop." Cliff suddenly begged. "You are going to get killed. You don't have any training. If you're serious about helping people, be a firefighter (or a cop even). Just don't run around in tights letting people shoot at you and for God's sake, talk to Jake about this superpower business."

Douglas closed his eyes and breathed deeply. "I can't stop now. I've dealt them a few blows and they're on the run."

"No, they are on the offensive and" Cliff pointed at the cane. "It looks like they dealt a few blows to you too. I'm willing to bet they can hit harder."

Douglas stood impassively. The tip of his cane tapped the ground once, twice and then he spoke again. "Can we stay here for a few days? If you say no, I'm going to have to find another hiding spot and I don't know when you'll see us again."

Clifford stood in the yard glaring at his son. With a huge force of will, he stepped forward and hugged Douglas. "You can stay, Chief, but I'm still ticked off at you."

Chapter: Human Trials

D r. Samantha Nichols walked into the apartment at the periph-
ery of the group. Men in suits were everywhere, watching with
keen interest. Video cameras ran, documenting the proceedings. The
state run nursing home provided Frank Waltrip with a residence that
was not as nice as the home he shared with his wife for so long, but
he had grown to like it there. It was all he had known since a broken
hearted madman robbed him of his memories with a dose of an experimental drug. Samantha had checked in on Mr. Waltrip with regular-
ity. Freeman Pharmaceuticals had followed up on the man less often.
She wanted to hate the company, feeling like they only agreed to help
Miller's victims to avoid lawsuits and bad press, but even she had to
be impressed by the speed at which they moved. The fast tracked antidote flew through a testing procedure that normally took years and
sometimes a full decade.

Samantha leaned against a wall toward the back of the room and
folded her arms across her chest. She had insisted on attending to make
sure they treated Frank like a person. Since entering the medical field,
she had come to loathe Big Pharm. She especially hated the way they
held on to patents, preventing generics from entering the market sooner.
She understood that the companies existed to make a profit but many
of the drugs could have saved lives if poorer people could have afforded
them. Pushing the question of corporate responsibility from her mind
for the moment, she focused on monitoring Mr. Waltrip.

The older man called out, "Where's my normal doctor? I want to
see Sam."

Samantha pushed herself off of the wall and shouldered her way
through the sea of suits. "I'm here Frank."

The old man's face relaxed as he saw her appear by his bedside. "Do we really need all these people here? I feel like I'm a fish in a bowl."

The doctor patted his hand. "Sadly, yes. You know how things get when lawyers get involved, but I'm here and I'm going to make sure they treat you right."

Frank smiled. "Thanks. I'm so glad you're here." He paused for moment and then looked at her with moist eyes. "Am I taking a pill, a needle, what?"

Samantha tried to sound reassuring. "It's just a little shot. They talked about a pill but it will take a while to see if it works and Freeman Pharm is a little impatient."

"Well, I'd hate to inconvenience them while trying to get my life back." He muttered. After a reflective moment, he asked, "Do you think I'm going to be okay? I keep hearing stories about how much pain I was in after losing my wife. If this works, I'm going to still be grieving, aren't I?"

Samantha knelt down beside him so they could be eye level. "It's possible, but don't you want to remember the years of love you had between you, too?"

Mr. Waltrip looked impossibly old as he nodded. Then a curt voice in the crowd called out. "Can we get on with this?"

Samantha stood up with fire in her eyes. "Who said that?" She turned on the crowd with shaking fists of rage. Her eyes scanned faces for a guilty look. No one spoke up and no one moved. She turned back to Mr. Waltrip.

He smiled at her and whispered, "Don't worry about it. I know they don't have time for an old man like me." He looked up as if something had just occurred to him. "Where's the guy that caught the man who did this to me? Douglas something..."

Dr. Nichols gave him a weak smile. "He couldn't be here, but he really wanted to be."

Mr. Waltrip sat back and took a deep breath. "I guess I'm ready." Samantha squeezed his hand and gave him a reassuring smile.

Dr. Stuart Straub waited by Dr. Nichols' car. As she approached, he called out to her. "I heard you did well in there. You didn't even let the Freeman goons push you around. A little birdy told me that someone had to mop up a urine puddle after you snapped."

Samantha gave a patronizing smile. "Thanks so much. I want my reputation to be 'bitch doctor'."

Stuart laughed. "Come on, it's not like they are people." He walked around to her door and looked down at her as she sat behind the wheel. "You don't have to be back at Bryer's until tomorrow. Let's go for a drink. I know you need one."

Samantha pulled the door shut and rolled down the window. "I just want to go home."

"You can't. You'll just sit alone reading." Stuart placed his elbows on the door and leaned in.

"I like reading." She touched the power window button and forced him to jump back and the glass nudged his arms.

"Come on, that man has his life back. Why don't you want to celebrate? Is it because Douglas didn't show up?" Dr. Straub waited for her tirade.

"Why would you say that?" Samantha disappointed him by not starting to hurl insults. Instead, his constant pontificating rubbed her nerves raw.

"This was your last hurrah with him. You cut him off as a friend and he's too much of a boy scout to force himself in your life. Once this case is settled, there will be no other excuse for you to see him." Stuart watched to see if his words had any effect.

Dr. Nichols put the car in reverse but kept her foot on the brake. "Maybe all of that is true, but I'm too hardheaded to tell him I am wrong. The last time I confessed something personal to him, he said that he couldn't get past the fact that I gave up on him years ago. I will not be humiliated like that again."

Samantha lifted her foot and the car began to roll. Stuart stepped back from her vehicle and shrugged. "I'm not telling you what you should do. I'm just trying to make sure you understand your motivations."

Samantha Nichols stuck her head out the window. "I'm getting to hate our profession. We do lots of listening but never commit to an opinion out of fear of alienating the patient with our judgments. If you had any balls, you'd tell me what you think I should do." Feeling a wild streak of rebellion, she raised her middle finger and shoved it out the window as she pulled out of the parking lot.

She glanced down at her cell phone as she drove. Scrolling through the contacts, she found Douglas Lawson. Occasionally peering up at the road, she called him. After several rings, his voice mail picked up. Exasperated, she left him a brief message. "Hey, you need to answer your phone. I just left one of Dr. Miller's victims. The cure is real. If you want to see the people you helped or question Miller or that guy from the bridge, you need to get in touch."

As she hung up, she decided to make an additional call. "Hello, Penelope? It's Dr. Nichols. Would you like to meet for a drink? I need to vent." A surprised and confused Penny readily agreed.

Chapter: A Kidnapping

Scott Edwards sat in the back of the police truck. The stiff suspension caused him to bounce with every minor bump in the road. The constant jostling had settled him in to a meditative state after he finished wondering where he was going. He felt like worrying would be pointless. He was out of his cell and on his way to a new one. Maybe the move would help stave off the assassins that he knew currently stalked him.

After a particularly harsh pothole jarred him from his trance, he looked at the guard and gave a seductive smile. "How long's the ride going to be? If we've got the time, we could get it on. You won't even have to take off the handcuffs."

The corrections officer gave him a bored look. "Hold your horses. There are plenty of willing men where you're going."

"And where is that?" Scott kept his voice from sounding eager for information.

The guard shook his head. "You don't know much about the..."

An explosion ripped through the air and reverberated against the sides of the truck. The guard swiveled his head around trying to determine the direction of the threat. The vehicle had not stopped but a second blast was followed by the sounds of groaning metal. Quickly after, another detonation sounded and the truck impacted something, sending both men flying against the wall.

The vehicle had stopped. "What's going on?" Scott asked, panicked as he picked himself off of the floor.

The guard yelled, "Sit down and stay quiet!"

Valentine complied, but he fearfully looked at the doors. Was he being rescued or executed? He heard the lock turn. As the door cracked open, the guard lifted his shotgun, ready to fire. Scott felt a trickle of sweat slip out of his hair line and run down his face. He could not see anything more than a gloved hand toss a spraying canister of tear gas inside. The guard covered his face with his shirt trying to fight through the discomfort. Scott's eyes watered uncontrollably and his nostrils flared with the sudden onslaught of searing pain. He could not breathe.

Evidently, the make-shift mask did little to protect the guard as well. He suddenly sprinted forward, throwing himself against the door. It swung wide and as the man fell out, gunfire erupted. Muzzle flashes winked in and out of existence through the acrid smoke and a dead man hit the pavement.

Scott staggered forward with his bound hands raised above his head. He coughed as he tried to speak and he had trouble telling where the floor of the truck ended through his bleary vision. Strong hands grabbed him and yanked him off his feet and set him on the ground. A familiar voice greeted him. "*Hola.*"

The details eluded Valentine due to his stinging eyes but the night made the flicking orange of fires stand out. "What the hell did you do?"

"Devildriver was responsible for getting the caravan to stop. He may have overdone it." There was mirth in *Bestia's* voice. He was engaged in battle and could not be happier. "Watch your head." He felt someone pushing at the back of his skull, forcing him to stoop. He fell into the back seat of a car and heard the door slam behind him. Then a door slammed in front as well.

"Devil, get us out of here." The vehicle started moving and Arturo's voice soothingly started questioning him. The tone was soft and conciliatory. "It is very important that you be completely honest with me. When you were in custody, what did you tell them?"

Scott Edwards knew that Raven had additional people on her payroll. This was a question that they already knew the answer to. He was being tested. He shook with the knowledge that his answers determined whether he lived or died.

"I only told them stuff they already knew. I gave them descriptions of you and Devil because they would have already gotten those from Lawson and his crew. I didn't give up anything about real names or where you live." The car made a turn and Scott realized that he had no idea where he was or where he was going. At least in the police vehicle, he knew he was going to another jail. *Bestia* could be taking him to a safe house or an unmarked grave.

"We believe you. Did you tell them anything about Raven?"

"They know she's a woman. They have recordings of her voice. I told them her code name but nothing else." His voice squeaked and cracked. "Her guy on the inside was being watched by internal affairs. I had nothing to do with them finding out about her."

"We know who's to blame." Arturo's words ominously hung in the air.

"It wasn't me! I was careful!" Scott pleaded.

Arturo sucked in a deep breath. "It was Lawson. He figured you out and told the police."

"Damn it! That guy should be dead already." Valentine ranted.

"The *pendejo* has nine lives. We tried again and he fought off the hit-man. I can't fucking believe it." Real anger crept into the Mexican's voice.

Scott hesitantly asked, "Valerie gave the order?"

"*Si*, she said to kill him."

"I thought she'd never..."

The car stopped. "We're here." Arturo opened the passenger door and stepped out.

The snot and tears had dried during the drive and Valentine could see again. His surroundings did not comfort him. There were no city lights and a wall of trees surrounded them. The moon and stars provided just enough illumination to show a black rectangular hole in the ground. He turned and looked at his two teammates. Devildriver stood tall and impassive as a tree. Arturo looked at Valentine with eyes full of pity.

"We've got our orders. It's not personal." The Mexican offered his justification.

Scott threw his hands up. "You know I don't deserve this. You claim that you respect professionalism and results. When have I failed this team? When have I come back empty handed or given less than 100%? When have I let personal feelings stop me from doing what was best for our operation?" He pulled in a lung full of air to continue. "But you know who has failed us? Think about the times that she put us in jeopardy so she could keep her boy toy around a few extra weeks. Lawson should have died before we moved forward with Miller, but he's still alive and kicking."

Arturo shook his head. "You can't talk your way out of this. You're going in that hole, Raven's orders."

Valentine shouted in desperation. "I'm dying for her mistakes! She's failed us. You should be leading us. You were anyway. She gave an objective and you planned out how to do it. You did all the heavy lifting. All she did was pass down orders from on high." Shaking, Valentine clasped his hands together to beg. "You know it's true. She didn't start directly leading us until after the bridge and things did not improve. Lawson is still a thorn in our side and he cost you another member of your team. If you were in charge, would you have hesitated to kill him?"

Arturo glanced back at Devildriver. "Wait in the car."

Silently, Devil cocked an eyebrow but obeyed.

Bestia looked at Scott with pity in his eyes. "She gave the kill order for Lawson. Her head's on straight again. I'll admit you have some points but I can't take over. You're forgetting something about my time in the cartel. I had a group of loyal men and could've taken over, but I don't want to be the top guy. I didn't then and I don't now. I'm made to be a lieutenant and I follow orders."

Arturo pulled out a pistol and aimed it at his former teammate. "You were a professional and even though I never really liked you, I never worried about you getting results. I'm sorry about this."

"Just not in the face." Scott's eyes watered as he tried to compose himself. "I want to go into the ground with my looks."

Arturo nodded.

Valentine stared down the barrel; the black hole looked huge as he lost his resolve and started to sob. "You don't have to do this!"

A loud report echoed though the wilderness, startling the night birds. The only sound was the flapping of feathered wings ascending into the sky.

Chapter: A Girls' Night Out

Samantha sat on Penelope's couch staring at the shelves of ornately dressed dolls. Little else in the apartment provided a distraction as she waited. The television was off and the stereo played the current hits on one of several pop/rock stations based in the area.

With a flourish, Penny leapt through a doorway one arm lifted high above her head and the other hand propped on her hip. "Ta-da! I am Penny Dreadful, defender of the weak and downtrodden."

Samantha's mouth fell open. "What are you wearing?"

Penny motioned to her meticulously crafted costume. "It's my proof of concept crime fighting outfit."

"Please tell me you are not going to wear that out tonight..." Samantha groaned.

"It makes me feel confident." Penny lowered her raised hand. With both curled fists resting on her hips, she posed in a defiant stance.

Samantha started to speak but stopped herself. She had been pushing the nurse to build up her self-esteem. Dr. Nichols did not want to dissuade her from something that boosted her self-worth. At the same time, Samantha did not want to go out in public with Penny Dreadful. She wanted a normal looking friend to have a few drinks.

Penelope disappeared back into her bedroom. Samantha waited, hoping that she had not shamed her friend into changing clothes, but then hoping she had. Eventually, Penny reappeared in a red sweater with a large purse slung over her shoulder. Tight jeans showed off her thin legs and short, wide heels clacked against the floor of her apartment.

"Are you happy now?" The nurse asked with obvious displeasure.

"I am happy with whatever you feel comfortable in." Samantha tried to mitigate the damage.

"That's not true. You just questioned my decision to wear the other outfit and now you're trying to save face." Penny crossed her arms waiting for a rebuttal.

"I really don't want to fight with you. Tonight is supposed to be about fun and blowing off steam. Wear whatever you want, I mean it." Samantha felt too tired to argue.

Penelope Daniels shrugged it off. "I've changed too many times and that costume is hard to get into. I'm ready to go."

Samantha stood and grabbed her purse. "We should take a cab, just in case."

"In case of what?"

Samantha paused. "Well, what if we have too much? I don't want to drive drunk or even tipsy."

Penny pulled out her cell phone. "Taxi it is then." A few minutes later, they were in the back seat watching the city slide by their windows. As they neared the bars and clubs, the lights changed color from white and yellow to garish green, blue, and red.

The driver let them out in front of a club called "The Cowgirl". Neither of the women had ever been there, but internet reviews suggested it as a female friendly club. The neon sign showed a busty girl with a 10 gallon hat striking a provocative pose.

Samantha's mouth twisted into a grimace. "This is female friendly?"

Penelope walked up to the door. "Let's give it a chance."

Samantha followed her co-worker inside. Loud music assaulted their ears as they tried to get their bearings. A large man at the door in a tight security t-shirt waved them through without checking for identification. As they pushed their way through a throng of people enthusiastically gyrating on the dance floor, Dr. Nichols took the nurses hand to prevent them from getting separated. In a bizarre turn, Penny confidently forced her way between the revelers while Samantha felt a growing sense of claustrophobia as strangers surrounded her.

As the bodies thickened, Samantha lost sight of Penny. Samantha felt her hand being pulled harder and as she emerged from the other side of the dance floor, she realized they had reached the bar.

Penny screamed over the thumping bass. "We need drinks if we are going to get on the dance floor."

Samantha shook her head. "Who said I was going to dance?"

Penelope enthusiastically waved at the bartender while still carrying on the conversation. "What if some cute guy asks you?"

Samantha turned around and scanned the crowd. Some of the men were attractive but she doubted anyone would approach her. Even if a guy did, she really did not think a man that frequented clubs would be long term relationship material.

Penelope held up two fingers and yelled "Cosmos" at the man behind the counter. He nodded and picked out two stemmed glasses. As he prepared the drinks, Penny flashed her driver's license at him though he had not indicated he needed to see ID.

Samantha stopped watching the crowd when she felt a libation shoved in her hand. He examined the red concoction and experimentally took a sip. She had cosmos before but everyone seemed to make them in varying strengths. This particular one was weaker, thankfully.

"The first one is on me. I tipped the bartender well. So if we want more, maybe he'll try to get us before some of these others."

Samantha was struck by the idea that Penny seemed too at home in this environment. "Do you come to places like this often?" She shouted as Penelope took a sip from her drink.

The nurse shook her head. "I don't go out much."

There was a split second pause as the extended dance mix ended and another started. Showing renewed excitement, Penny hurriedly downed her drink and set the empty glass on the bar. "I love this song! Finish your drink and let's dance."

Samantha set her almost full glass on the bar when Penny stopped her. "What are you doing? You can't leave an open topped drink unattended. Someone could put something in it."

Samantha picked it back up and took a sip. She could not chug the entire thing as Penny had done. "You go dance. I'll wait here."

Penelope shrugged and started swaying her hips and shuffling toward the dance floor. A moment later, she had disappeared in the horde of revelers. Samantha watched her go still baffled by the sudden change in her co-worker. Her eyes absently scanned the bar and a suspicious movement caught her eye. A man just accepted two drinks from the bartender. He set them both on top of the bar and pulled something from his pocket. He dropped it into the brightly colored mixed drink. His eyes darted with fear of discovery. Then he picked up his beer and the cocktail before disappearing into the crowd.

Samantha could not believe what she had just witnessed. She looked around for Penelope but could not find her. Should she tell the bartender? Was there anyone she could call to report him? Could she find him again in the wall-to-wall people? Her train of thought switched tracks. Maybe whoever received the drink would know better than to accept an opened container from a strange guy in a bar. Anyway, was it even her place to intervene?

As she stood contemplating, the song ended and Penelope came bursting out of the crowd with a sheen of sweat on her forehead. "You've got to come out there. It's so freeing to just lose myself in the beat."

Samantha's eyes betrayed her and Penny asked, "What's wrong?"

The concerned woman moved in close to Penelope's ear and communicated what she had seen. The nurse immediately flew into a rage. "We have to find this guy and stop him." She growled.

Samantha looked around at the surrounding strange faces. "How do we do that? I couldn't find you in this mess."

"I don't know but we have to save this woman. How would you feel if you were in her position?" Penny seemed possessed by a manic energy.

Samantha felt fear seizing her. She did not want a confrontation with a morally bankrupt drunk. "Let's say we find the guy. What are we going to do?"

"We'll figure it out. Just give me a description, I'll help you look."

Samantha almost spoke but the man they searched for appeared at the bar dropping off empty drinks. She pointed as her mouth struggled to find the words.

Penny turned and saw the smug look on his face as he turned to return to his drugged date. Almost as a reflex, she snatched a beer bottle off of the bar and lunged toward him. He was not facing her as she started bludgeoning him with the bottle.

Dr. Nichols watched in horrid fascination, expecting the glass to shatter but proved more resilient than movies had her believe. She watched the bottle descend and ascend at the end of Penny's flailing arm. Each impact caused the victimizer turned victim to sink further toward the ground as he struggled to remain standing. It looked like her friend was hammering him into the ground like a nail and the overall effect struck her as comical.

When she saw the blood, Samantha snapped back out of her trance. She grabbed her friend's arm and pulled her away. Penelope came willingly, having spent her anger in one massive burst. Most of the crowd still struggled to process what they had just seen and the two women slipped away without being stopped. As they passed a garbage can, Penny casually dropped the bloody bottle into the trash.

Outside on the street, they briskly walked away from the club as Samantha tried to hail a taxi. One quickly pulled up and they jumped in. Penny gave her address and the cab started moving. As the ride commenced, Samantha blurted out what she had been burning to ask since the assault. "What the hell happened?"

Penny shrugged. "What was I supposed to do, politely inform him that what he was doing was wrong? Maybe he just didn't realize he was a piece of shit?"

Samantha nervously glanced at the oblivious driver. "That was at minimum a concussion. I had no idea you had such extreme measures within you."

Penelope gave her an ugly look. "Do you think Douglas would have let him get away with that? Your ex may have made you bitter but he inspires me in a way that your goofy self-esteem exercises do not."

Dr. Nichols stared at her co-worker with a mixture of awe and fear. Penny Dreadful had existed as an idea and as a proof of concept costume, but Samantha had just witnessed her birth into the real world.

Chapter: Amateur Firemen

In Clearwater Springs, Douglas fired up the Corvette and watched his son sit in the passenger seat. The youth whined, "Why are we going out?"

"I'm going to show you the sights." Douglas replied.

"This town is tiny. How many sights can there be?"

"Then this shouldn't take long." Doug gave a smug grin. "I thought you'd want to see where I grew up."

Jacob crossed his arms. "I saw it the first time we were here. It stuck in my mind since it was such a memorable trip."

Doug remembered it well. He had cracked a case involving a missing child and it also marked the first time he had witnessed Jake's power in action. Somehow, the boy had reflexively stopped a bullet. The idea that his adopted child could have died that night sent shivers up his spine. How had he been so careless with the boy's safety? After that, Doug tried to shield the boy from any action and of course, the young man resented him for it.

As the car cruised in to the city limits, Douglas slowed to a crawl and pointed. "There's the fire station where your grandpa worked. I got to hang out in there after school."

After another block, he motioned out his window at a brightly lit restaurant. "That's the drive-in. You want a burger and fries?"

"Nah." Jake had been eating his grandparents' amazing cooking and still felt stuffed from dinner.

"A milkshake?" Doug tempted.

"No, thanks." Jake watched the drive-in go by and marveled at how many pick-up trucks were in the parking lot. He never saw that many in the city. "Does everyone here drive a truck?"

Douglas laughed. "In these parts, you're not a man if you don't drive a truck."

"You don't drive a truck." Jake wryly pointed out.

"I drive a 'vette. I'd say I'm winning at life in comparison." Mr. Lawson defensively stated. "By the way, there's where I went to school." He pointed at a dimly lit building away from the road.

Jacob peered out his window but could only make out the outline of the structure. "Wouldn't this tour have been better in the daytime?"

"I thought you may want to get out of the house. It's kind of crowded in there." Douglas turned off of the main drag and cut through a residential street.

"I like having lots of people around." It went unspoken but Jake had spent so many years feeling alone, he relished every moment of company his new family provided.

Doug missed the comment, too absorbed in trying to figure out what he was seeing ahead of them. When his eyes made sense of the scene, he slammed on the breaks and handed his phone to his son. "Call 911 and tell them there's a fire on Sycamore Drive. I don't know the house number but they'll see it when they get here."

With that, Doug flung the door open and grabbed his cane. Hobbling up the sidewalk at the fastest pace he could manage, he headed straight for the front door. Smoke disappeared against the dark sky but the orange glow emanating from inside the home convinced Douglas that he was right. He turned around and sank to his knees and put his hands flat on the ground. With his good leg, he kicked backward like a donkey connecting with the door right under the knob. Wood splinted and it swung wide.

Jake ran on to the porch behind him. "Let me help! We can clear the house faster with two of us."

Douglas used his cane as a brace and painfully stood up. "It's too dangerous. I can't let you walk into a burning building."

Jake cried out in disgust. "People could be dying in there! I'm faster than you. I have two good legs and superpowers!"

Doug peered inside and sighed. "Okay, you stick to the first floor and get out as soon as it's clear."

Jacob shook his head. "I'm faster. Let me get the second floor. You'll take forever going up the stairs with your leg."

Mr. Lawson gave him a stern look and with a commanding voice, declared, "I am your father. You will stick to the first floor where you can get out quick if the fire spreads."

Jake grimaced. "Fine." He ran inside and feverishly looked around for any unconscious person to pull out. Behind him, Douglas mounted the stairs and began his ascent. Jacob did not see anyone in the living room. The kitchen was ablaze and he could not manage to peer inside due to the radiating heat. Instead, he checked the hallway and found a closed door. He gripped the knob to test for heat. It was cool to the touch so he swung it open. It was a master bedroom. The sheets covered two unmoving figures.

"Wake the fuck up! The house is burning down!" Jake ran and jumped on to the bed bouncing several times.

Both bodies sprang awake with terrified expressions. "What the...?"

"No time! Get out now!" Jacob screamed every syllable in an effort to move them.

The middle aged woman cried out, "Zoe is upstairs!"

Jake continued shouting. "My Dad's up there. He'll get her. Go, go, go!" The couple ran for the door and Jake followed behind. "Is there anyone else?"

"Just our daughter, upstairs." The husband replied.

As they exited the hallway, Jacob felt his stomach knot. The fire had spread past the bottom of the stairs. They had a line to the front door but Douglas was trapped on the second story. Racing the flames, the trio ran out into the night. As they stopped in the yard, Jake turned around and looked with worry at the windows high above him.

"Please make it." He whispered his prayer as he watched billowing smoke rise into the sky.

Douglas tapped his way down the hall stooped over to avoid the rising smoke. When he reached a door frame, he would check the handle for heat and open it when it was safe. The fire seemed to be just downstairs at the moment but he could hear a growing roar from the spreading inferno. He discovered a linen closet, the bathroom, and a room that looked to be used as storage. Finally, he swung open the final door and saw a bedroom that looked to belong to a young girl.

Even in the dark, he could see the bright colors and stuffed animals on the bed. He stepped inside looking for the child but the covers were thrown back and the bed was empty. He remembered his father saying that most kids that died in house fires were found under the bed or in the closet. In their fear, they vainly tried to hide from the fire. Douglas dropped to the floor and peeked under the bed. Using the glowing screen of his cell phone as a flashlight, he only found dust bunnies and lost toys. He rose to his feet, groaning as he put weight on his bum leg. Scanning the room impatiently, she saw the closet door. Using his cane to quickly hobble over, he looked inside. Curled up at the bottom of the closet was a young girl. She looked to be a preschooler. Douglas dropped into a squat and made eye contact.

"Hi, my name is Einstein and I'm a superhero. What's your name?"

The girl sat in silence too afraid to speak. Doug continued despite her lack of response. "Well, there's a fire in your kitchen. Did you know that?"

She nodded. "I wanted water."

"You saw the fire?" She nodded again and Douglas reached out to pick her up. "Okay, well I need to save the day. So can you come with me?"

Clutching a stuffed bunny to her chest, she refused to move.

"Okay, what's your name? We need to make friends fast." Douglas tried to sound non-threatening despite the knowledge that flames were licking their way higher with every second.

"I'm Zoe." She spoke in a meek voice.

"Nice to meet you Zoe. Time to rescue you." He tucked his walking stick under his arm and scooped her up. He grunted as he stood without the use of his cane. "Okay, let's go." With each shaky, pain-filled step, he walked out of the room and into the hall. Then he felt gooseflesh crawling across his body. The hallway was black with smoke but he could feel the intense heat from fire that had made it to the second floor.

"Zoe, we've got a change of plans. We can't go out the front door." Doug turned around and staggered as fast as possible back to the girl's room. Once inside, he set the girl down and pulled the window open. A fine screen blocked the exit but Douglas pushed it out and let it fall to the ground. He could see two adults and Jacob staring up at the window. He threw his cane out and watched it land in the lawn below.

Turning around, he picked up the girl again and held her close to his chest. "Don't be afraid." He urged her before stepping up to the window and turning so that his back faced the opening. If he jumped out, his legs would buckle. He would fall forward and possibly land on the girl. If he jumped and landed back first, he would take the brunt of the impact but the girl would be spared major injuries. He tucked his chin to his chest to hopefully avoid hitting the back of his head on the ground and flung himself backward out of the window. His last thought was "Please let the girl be okay".

Jacob watched as a screen fell to the ground, then a moment later as his father's cane followed. Then, Douglas Lawson, adopted father, came tumbling out of the window with a bundle held tightly against his chest. Jacob ran forward flinging his arms up in the air begging whatever God was in the heavens that his father would be unharmed. To his surprise, Douglas' body began to slow and eventually touched down on the ground without a sound. Jake ran over and looked down at his father. "Are you alright?"

Douglas opened his tightly shut eyes and looked up at his adopted son in wonder. "What happened?"

"I guess I slowed you down." Jake looked at his hands in disbelief.

"Thank God. Jake, meet Zoe." Douglas shook the girl to signal that it was safe. The girl unfolded herself from a fetal position and stood up. As her parents saw her, they rushed forward to hug her. Mother and father began showering her with kisses and crying thank you to both Douglas and Jacob.

The sound of sirens in the distance caused Douglas to stand and remark, "I think we should go before we have to answer questions."

Jake agreed and plucked his father's cane out of the grass. Together, the pair went back to the car. Still coughing up smoke, Douglas pulled away from the curb and headed toward his father's house.

Chapter: The Nightly News

The next day, Penelope sat on couch watching television while Samantha paced nervously around the apartment. "Sit down. You're going to bother the neighbors with the constant clomping around."

Samantha hissed. "I'm not being that loud."

"Well, you're annoying me then." Penny snapped back. "Just sit down and let's watch the news."

Samantha huffed and threw herself down beside the nurse. "I've never made the news before. This should be mortifying."

"We didn't make the news." Penny matter-of-factly stated. "Hush, it's starting."

Samantha crossed her arms to prevent them from shaking. She knew that any moment a police officer would knock on the door to inform them that they were going to have to go downtown. She had spent all of the previous night and all of the day worried about it. Being arrested for assault would definitely kill her career. Not only that, her last interaction with Dr. Straub had been confrontational. So she could not count on him to vouch for her character.

The anchors appeared on screen. They talked about political figures. They covered sports. The broadcaster cut to a man explaining the weather while pointing to a green screen map. There was no mention of their scuffle at The Cowgirl.

"See, I told you." Penny stated with satisfaction. "A fight in a bar is not going to make the news."

"And now from the little town of Clearwater Springs, some unbelievable footage of a house fire and the man who saved the family trapped inside." The camera cut to a man on a lawn in the light of day. "I came outside to see what was going on and had my cell phone with me.

There didn't seem to be anything I could do to help. So, I decided to get some footage on my camera phone. I've never seen anything like that."

The camera cut again to grainy night time footage of a house. The autofocus struggled to adjust to the changing light conditions due to the dancing flames. Finally, the focus steadied and everything became clear. An object fell from a window. Moments later a man fell out. Instead of plummeting to the ground, he seemed to float down as easy as a feather. When he landed, a teenage boy ran to him and helped him stand. The pair briskly walked to the street and stepped inside a white and blue vintage sports car and sped away.

The footage cut to the family. The father teared up as he spoke. "I don't know who they were but they saved us. It was a miracle." A microphone hovered in front of the little girl's face as interviewer asked, "Did the man tell you his name?" She nodded as she answered. "But I don't remember it. But he said he was a superhero."

As the camera returned to the newsroom, one of the co-anchors spoke. "A little girl claims that a superhero saved her, but the question remains 'is this footage for real?' Was it a real life man with extraordinary powers or just a good Samaritan and some camera tricks? Until the heroes are identified, we will not know for certain."

Samantha stood slack jawed at the screen. She could not see faces in the cell phone video but she recognized that car and the limping gait of the man who drove it away. "Douglas is at his parents' house."

Valerie had just poured another glass of Bourbon and sipped it. The warmth and the familiar flavor comforted her as she brooded over what a mess had been made. Her conman was dead. Her electronics expert was in a hospital with no memory, as was the doctor that invented the memory destroying elixir that she was running out of. Not only that, the last attempt on Douglas Lawson's life had been a failure. Arturo already accused her of being weak. Now she had to work up the nerve to give the execution order again. That meant another day of waiting for word that her lover had been killed. It was part of business, but it did not change the fact that she had grown accustomed to having Douglas handy when she felt lonely.

As she sat to wind down for the evening, she lamented that now he was in hiding and she was left with an empty bed. Pointing the remote at the television, she changed the channel to the local news. After a few insipid stories, the report of a strange sighting in Clearwater Springs caught her attention. Watching intently, she began to smile. Lawson could not hide from her. His inability to stay out of trouble had highlighted his location. Picking up the phone, she dialed *Bestia*. "Get a team together. Not just a lone junkie this time. I know where Lawson is and he won't see us coming this time."

Douglas scrolled though a list of court cases on his laptop carefully reading each description. With Valerie back in Kios and nothing to do in a small town, he had ample time to research Martin Ramsey's cases for a possible suspect. He knew that Devildriver or *Bestia* committed the act, but he did not know who hired them. From what he had gathered during his case tracking down Dr. Bernard Miller, the doctor had hired them to do a job but when they saw additional opportunity, they turned on him and took over his project.

It stood to reason that someone had probably hired them to murder Ramsey. As he looked through the list of cases prosecuted by Ramsey, he noticed that most of the list consisted of smaller crimes. Then he saw the big one. It was a felony and one that turned his stomach, the rape of a female cadet. A soldier named William Kessey stood accused. Doug's gut twisted into a knot and he delved into the case. Kessey was the son of a prominent general. General Kessey publicly declared no favoritism would be shown and requested the harshest punishment for his child. By all accounts, the young soldier showed no remorse and was unapologetic. Entitled and misogynistic, he embodied the worst of the old army. Even his father feared the allegations of nepotism and distanced himself. The trial ended with "Billy" Kessey going to Fort Leavenworth prison.

Douglas continued reading but none of the other convictions seemed extreme enough to warrant that level of vengeance. As he felt the eye strain of staring at a backlit screen for hours, Desiree entered the room and cleared her throat. "You should come into the living room. You'll want to see this."

Lawson stood and followed her out. The parents, Clifford and Maylene, sat together on the couch both with stern expressions. Jacob stretched out on a leather recliner with a smile plastered across his youthful face. Gaston was standing, waiting on Douglas to enter.

"You made the news with your exploits." The Frenchman ominously stated.

Doug looked at the TV screen and only saw the anchors speaking about a piece of cellphone camera footage that had previously played. "No one questions whether this strange man saved the day, but what has not been answered is whether this video has been faked."

Douglas looked expectantly at the room full of friends and family. "What did they show?"

Desiree sighed. "A video of you falling out of a window and then slowly floating to the ground. It is the most unnatural looking thing I have ever seen. It looks like bad movie effects."

Jacob defensively interjected. "I'm working on my control. It was a pretty stressful time."

Douglas shrugged. "Maybe people will assume it's a hoax."

Clifford stood up, fists clenched. "People will figure out who it was and then you will have a media circus around you and Jake. If it comes out that he's the one that stopped your fall, they may even take him away to study." Cliff took a deep breath. "Your showboating is going to get your family torn apart."

Doug looked at Jacob. "No one is taking you away. How are they going to recognize me? It was dark and I probably didn't look into the camera. Hell, I didn't even know there was a camera."

Cliff cried out. "It's a small town and your car is in the shot! How many vintage Corvettes do you think drive around in Clearwater Springs? I'll answer for you. One." He held up an index finger to drive the point home. "You went out in the most conspicuous vehicle possible."

Doug rubbed his forehead in frustration. "I didn't plan on anything happening. Would you rather I let the girl die?"

Cliff's face softened. "Of course not, you did a very brave thing, but you need to prepare for some consequences. They may not come. People may not figure out your identity, but they might. Then, you and your boy are going to have to be ready."

Douglas Lawson paced the room for a moment as his brain turned over the various plans. His face brightened as if an idea had struck him. Finally, he addressed the room. "If anyone comes looking for me, I won't be here. I'm going to Kansas to interview a suspect in the case I'm working. He's a prisoner at Fort Leavenworth. I'll be off the grid the whole time I'm driving down and back. By the time I resurface, the media blitz will be over."

Jacob launched himself off the plush chair. "Let's go!"

Douglas shook his head. "I don't want to march you into a prison, no matter how controlled the environment. You can stay here and hang out with your grandpa and grandma. Gaston, Desiree, which one of you wants to ride with me?"

Neither made a move to accept. Hesitantly, Gaston raised his hand. "I will go." He spoke with resignation.

Douglas clapped. "Excellent, if it's as easy to figure out who I am as everyone says, we'll leave in the morning and miss the hordes of reporters."

Gaston grimaced and Jacob sulked. With the next day decided, Douglas went back to his room, smiling.

Chapter: A Prison Visit

G aston sat in the Corvette listening to classic rock. No matter where they traveled, Douglas could find his favorite music on the radio. Every area had its own station, usually with some kind of predatory animal mascot. The volume made his ears hurt but Lawson insisted it had to be that loud to be heard over the engine. Looking out the window at the passing corn fields (sometimes wheat), Gaston thought about the complicated relationship with Desiree. He felt elated but guilty. He finally had proof of her affection and felt relieved that his feelings were reciprocated. However, having the object of his affection came with a price. He had to suffer her pain, no small amount considering her life as a mercenary. Or he had to transfer his pain into her. He had no off switch, only varying levels of directing the flow of suffering. As much as he wanted to be with her, every touch hurt one of them.

"Hey sourpuss, you're less talkative than normal." Douglas turned the music down to converse.

"I'm thinking."

"About?" Doug asked.

"It's about Desiree."

"And?"

"And I don't know if I can keep seeing her that way." Gaston spoke as if someone had twisted a knife in his gut.

"Why the hell not?" Lawson seemed honestly annoyed by the statement.

"Because I hurt her or she hurts me whenever we are together."

"Welcome to life." Doug snorted. "Everyone hurts each other eventually. The point of a relationship is to give each other enough good times to make the pain worth it."

"You speak like a hopeless romantic." Gaston meant it as an insult.

"Keyword is 'hopeless'. But really, what's your other option? You'll spend the rest of your life wondering if you should've taken the chance. At least now, you know."

"But I feel guilty that it has to be that way."

Doug took his eyes off the road to berate his friend. "She's knows what being with you entails. You're telling me you feel guilty for a decision she made?"

"Yes." Gaston pointed back at the road. "Watch where you're going."

"Get over yourself. You think you're so damn adorable that she can't resist you? She's a super fit badass woman. If she wants to get laid, she can. If she wants to be with you, then it's because she wants to be WITH YOU!"

Gaston sat in silence for a moment before speaking again. "How long until we reach the prison?"

"You're in luck, just a few miles." Doug looked straight ahead and kept his hands clenched on the wheel.

Gaston glanced over at Douglas with a rarely seen expression of hope. "Do you really mean what you said about her wanting to be with me?"

Douglas did not crack a smile. "I can't lie for shit. What do you think?"

"You are being uncharacteristically vulgar today."

"I'm a little on edge. I never expected my Dad to find out about my second job of crime fighting. I also don't particularly love his judgments of how I'm raising Jacob."

"Your father is quite an imposing figure." Gaston nodded, happy to change the subject from his love life.

"Try growing up with him. Everything is black and white in his mind. Right is right and wrong is wrong. There's never any gray area." Doug complained.

"You're that way too." Gaston defended the absent father.

"Maybe." Douglas came dangerously close to an admission.

"You are. I believe life is sacred because I am Catholic. You have a rule about no killing without this Church telling you so. Why? You agree that they are scumbags. Why not let Desiree put a bullet in each one?"

Lawson shook his head. "I am not an executioner. Everyone has a chance to be redeemed."

"You sound almost religious." Gaston chimed.

Douglas shrugged his shoulders. "My parents are. I just don't know."

Gaston looked at his boss with true concern. "You may want to decide what you believe before you face off against *Bestia* and Devildriver. You need to have your soul right with God before anything happens."

"You are assuming I will die. That's a vote of confidence." Doug derisively laughed.

"These men are ruthless. They have already tried multiple times."

"I know that, Gaston and I'm terrified. You don't think I know how ill-equipped I am to face off against them? Fisticuffs are not my forte." Douglas watched the yellow line in the middle of the road and grew uncharacteristically silent.

Gaston felt obligated to fill the void. "That's why you have Desiree."

Douglas gave a weak smile. "You two make a fitting couple, yin and yang, the pacifist and the mercenary."

Gaston blushed. "*Fermes la bouche.*"

Arturo sat in the back of the van, content to let his hired help do the driving. Several more people were packed in with him along with a few shotguns and a rifle. Most of the men present had pistols hidden somewhere on their bodies. They had stocked a reasonable amount of ammo. Considering the plan involved creeping up on the house in the dead of night and executing everyone in their beds, Arturo did not imagine that reloading would be an issue.

Honestly, he felt cowardly killing Douglas and whatever other guests happened to be present. It had shocked him how quickly Valerie Gossard had turned back into Raven. "Go ahead and kill his parents and son. They shouldn't have to grieve for his loss. That's just unfair."

Bestia had not worried about his ability to kill Douglas but he secretly hoped one of his mercs would take care of the child. He knew Devil would have no qualms about it but the lunatic was too volatile to trust on a mission requiring stealth. Instead, he had outsourced the job to some people he knew. They were not high class hit men like in the movies. These were just low level criminals that had a reputation for not being bothered by killing. More than one of them got their start by shooting during a robbery and realizing that the resulting death did not affect them in a meaningful way.

Arturo used to count himself among their number until Lawson's kid rushed him at the bridge. He had faltered when he thought about having a child's blood on his hands. Devil had not hesitated though. Somehow, the psycho still failed to kill the boy. *Bestia* had to beat a hasty retreat and the loss still stung his pride. Luckily, that was about to be remedied.

"What's the plan, boss?" One of the men asked him.

"Get inside as quietly as possible. Kill everyone. No survivors. There will be an elderly couple and possibly a child in addition to the main target. So if you feel like you don't have the sack for it, speak now."

No one moved or uttered a word. "Good. We shouldn't have too much to worry about. My intel says that the house is remote. We will have the element of surprise in addition to more numbers and a bigger arsenal."

One of the braver hired-hands asked, "What did they do to land on your shit list?"

"Does it matter?"

The gunman shrugged. "No, just curious."

"The main target interfered with a previous job. He denied me a big payday. Then he compromised one of my guys and got him killed." *Bestia* felt his hands clench into fists, remembering that Raven had ordered him to kill Valentine. He had not particularly liked Scott, but the man got results. In Arturo's book, results trounce personality.

"I get that." The reason seemed to satisfy everyone in the van. Arturo could not wait. By the end of the night, Lawson would be dead. Raven would go back to being the hard, cold bitch he had signed on with. Now, if only he could find a pretense to kill Devil, all would be right with the world. He smiled, imagining a new lease on his life of crime.

Douglas and Gaston walked with the warden through the cold echoing hallways. Each tap of his cane sounded off the walls more distinctly than the trio's footsteps. They had narrowly avoided getting tossed out immediately but after explaining their purpose, the administrator (Warden Gould) had agreed to let them see William Kessey.

"Mr. Lawson, I can allow you approximately ten minutes. However, 14:30 is the prisoner's outdoor activity. We run a very tight ship and I am letting you speak with him purely as a courtesy. Now, if you could get someone in here with a little more authority, I would be happy to give you as long as you like. Between us, this prisoner struts around like he's the cock of the walk, and because his Daddy's a General, he gets his way with the other prisoners. Even though they're in here, most of them still have respect for the rank."

They walked up to a visiting room door. "He's being brought in right now. There will be two armed guards present for the entire duration of your conversation." Warden Gould finished his speech and swung the door open.

Kessey already sat waiting for them. The guards flanked him by a few feet on each side. The prisoner smiled with his eyebrows narrowed like a predator evaluating prey.

Douglas walked in, trying to minimalize his limp. "Good afternoon, Billy." Douglas plopped down in the chair and Gaston silently followed beside him. "My name's Doug and I've got some questions for you."

"Call me William. I don't answer to Billy." Kessey looked at Gaston with suspicion. "Do I know you guys?"

Doug leaned back, trying to appear poised and relaxed. "We're not here to play games. Scott Edwards spilled everything."

William smiled. "I'm sorry. Who is that?"

Douglas considered the possibility that Kessey did not know the names of everyone involved. "He's one of the people you hired to kill Martin Ramsey." Doug made sure his voice left no room for indecision. He had to appear confident in his belief.

"Why would I do that? The case is over. Killing a prosecutor won't get me out of here any sooner." William looked him in the eyes with a stare that said "Don't push me."

Doug pressed on. "For you, it's not about in prison or out of prison anymore, Billy. You couldn't stand the idea of losing. The prosecutor showed the world what you really were and you couldn't take being made to look a fool, the same way that girl shot you down and you couldn't handle it. So you assaulted her. You raped her to show her what a man you were. Then, you expected your Daddy to save you but he sold you out. He'd had enough of you bringing shame upon his family. Blood is thicker than water most of the time but the General decided your blood was so tainted, he had better stick with H_2O. Face it, Billy, not even your own father could put up with you!"

Kessey jumped up with lighting speed. "I said don't call me that!" He reached out to choke Douglas but the guards were already on him. They pulled him back down to his seat, pinning him against the chair.

William thrashed around screaming, "Raven will kill you! I'll tell her and she won't put up with your shit! You and your friend are dead!"

The warden opened the door. "That's it, Mr. Lawson. I can't have the prisoners getting riled up. Guards take him out to the yard. I'll escort our guests out!"

Douglas rose with Gaston and they exited first, Warden Gould following behind to keep himself between the two visitors and the prisoner.

In the hallway, Gould ripped into Doug. "What the hell is wrong with you? You ask for a favor and then try to start a fight! Most of what I do is keeping these animals calm so they don't kill each other or a guard. And you're doing everything you can to upset that man. Now those soldiers are going to have to keep a close eye on him to make sure he doesn't take it out on someone in the rec-area."

Doug responded in a tone that was apologetic but defensive. "I'm sorry, sir, but I knew that if he lost his temper, he would say something we could use. I'm just trying to make sure Captain Martin Ramsey has justice done for him"

The warden's face softened. "Son, I can understand that but I need you to go."

"Okay, I'm leaving." Douglas turned and walked away. Gaston kept in step with him. As they neared the exit, Doug turned to him with a proud smile. "I sure pissed off Kessey, didn't I?"

Gaston didn't make eye contact and pushed his way through the door into the sunshine. "What was the point in that?"

"We got a clue out of it. There's someone out there called Raven, who commanded Scott Edwards to seduce Priscilla Ramsey and knows William Kessey." Douglas wilfully ignored the level of anger he had caused in the prison.

"How would Kessey get in touch with Raven from inside of a military prison? I need to find a way to look at the guest logs to see who has visited him."

Gaston shook his head. "I doubt anyone signed in under the name Raven."

"But how many visitors could this scumbag have gotten recently? It should be a short list of names to track down." Douglas countered.

Unable to agree, Gaston came back. "Do you think that the warden will be inclined to let you look around after that incident?"

Lawson shrugged. "It can't hurt to ask." He spun around and hobbled back toward the entrance.

"They're not going to tell you anything!"

Gaston watched as Douglas walked back inside and disappeared from view. He paced back and forth under a cloudless Kansas sky. The sun beat down on him and just as beads of sweat started to form, the door flung outward and Douglas exited with a sour expression on his face.

"How did it go?" The priest smugly asked.

"No help in there." Doug kept walking toward the car. "It's not a problem. I'm going to look up Kessey's lawyer and see if I can get any information."

"I have only been in this country a handful of years but I am sure that there is confidentiality between a lawyer and client."

"Maybe I can just get a list of witnesses, transcripts of the trial, anything to help." Doug flung his unoccupied arm out in exasperation, while the other firmly gripped his cane. "I'm grasping at straws here. I just keep hitting dead ends. I'm losing it Gaston. Last time I was on the heels of Raven and Devil and *Bestia*. Now, I don't even know what my next step is."

Gaston walked over and put a hand on Lawson's shoulder. "I know it is hard, but you've already saved so many lives. Maybe you are just not meant to solve this case. You are not infallible." Gaston wanted to say more, but he could not fully explain himself in the moment.

Douglas looked at his friend with regret. "The idea that I can make mistakes does not ease my conscience when people have lost their lives."

"I understand that, but it is time to give up for today. We can drive back and start again tomorrow." Gaston gave a small squeeze and let go.

"Let's stop at a restaurant. I could use some comfort food." Douglas shrugged. "I guess I'm a stress eater."

Chapter: Night-time Assault

Arturo had forgotten about the darkness of a country night. As such, he had forgotten to bring night vision goggles for his men. Urban environments were usually well lit, hindering the effectiveness of such equipment. Other than lacking the NV headgear, the men were well prepared. Small arms were in holsters or just tucked into belts, knives were in easy to reach sheaths. One of the men cradled a shotgun in case the stealth approach failed. Arturo surveyed the group. Everyone wore dark clothing and eagerly waited to start the infiltration.

"*Hombres*, I need to stress care and professionalism. We are facing a target that is lucky. He has already escaped multiple attempts on his life carried out by skilled operators."

"It's because he hasn't met us yet." One of the men boasted.

Bestia chuckled. "Maybe, but you still need to take this assignment seriously. This guy has dodged too many shots to be considered a creampuff. Now let's go." He swung open the back doors to the cargo van and the men filed out. They fanned out and looked across the grassy field at the silhouette of the house in the distance. Steel toed boots trampled through the knee high brush. All of the lights were out and as they grew closer, the silence convinced them that all of their victims had fallen asleep.

One of the men broke off from the group and tried the doorknob. It was locked. In a low hiss, he whispered, "Need a pick."

Another of the hitmen tiptoed up and knelt by the door. He produced a small pack of locksmith tools and began his work. An audible click was followed by the breathless words "we're in." Then a flash of light and an explosion splintered the wood of the door and ripped half of his face off. The body tumbled backward and gunfire erupted.

Desiree stretched out on the couch with a thin flat sheet and a thicker blanket covering her. Before settling down for the night, she had positioned Clifford Lawson's shotgun within reach under the coffee table. She was not tired and waited. Despite Douglas' assurance that nothing would happen, she felt a storm approaching. The people that wanted the Sentinels stopped would see Doug on the news and it took no effort to search for someone's hometown. Most people even volunteered that information on social media sites. Raven, Devil, and *Bestia* would have no trouble tracing Lawson to Clearwater Springs.

Tossing the bedding off, she paced through the living room occasionally peeking through the windows. Wandering by the kitchen, she caught a glint through the glass. Stepping closer and peering into the darkness, she saw humanoid shapes swaying through the tall grass outside. The shapes were fanned out and walking with a purpose which made her think of a hit squad. Rushing from the window, she grabbed the shotgun and went down the hallway knocking to wake the other inhabitants. Confused mumblings emanated from the bedrooms. The first door to open belonged to Jacob.

"What's going on?" His eyes were wide and his voice clear. A lack of grogginess indicated that he had not fallen asleep yet.

"Do not turn on any lights. Just listen to me for a minute." Desiree commanded as the door to the elder couple's room opened. She turned her attention to Clifford and Maylene. "Sir, we've got incoming attackers. If you have any additional weapons, please load up and come to the kitchen. They are approaching from that side and will probably try to enter through the back door. Don't turn on any lights; we need to keep the element of surprise."

Maylene grabbed her husband's arm. "Don't go out there. Let her handle it. She's a trained soldier."

Cliff gingerly peeled her fingers from his bicep. "What kind of man doesn't even take part in defending his own home?" he asked in a soft, soothing voice.

Jacob excitedly followed a few steps down the hallway until the adults turned and stopped him. Clifford Lawson used his stern fatherly voice to dissuade the youth. "This is going to be very dangerous. I need you to hang back and protect Maylene just in case they get through us."

Jake opened his mouth to object when Desiree interrupted. "Douglas wouldn't forgive me if I took you into battle with me. It's not that I don't think you are capable. I just don't want my boss to be mad at me."

Jacob looked back and forth between the two searching for a weak link. Neither face betrayed any sympathy and he choked back a bitter laugh. His two guardians came from environments where people did not shy away from unpleasant tasks. He knew he could not guilt either of them in to changing his or her mind. "Fine." He growled with frustration.

Since that was settled, Cliff looked at his wife. "Call 911 right away and get them over here. You know where I keep the thirty-eight. If anyone comes through that door that's not family or Desiree, you shoot."

Maylene nodded with understanding. Jacob stayed in the hallway but looked into his grandparents' bedroom. "They won't get by me." The boy swore to her with conviction that she felt was bluster more than substance.

In the kitchen, Desiree crept forward with the shotgun readied. Behind her, Cliff leveled a rifle at the door. He knelt down and steadied the weapon. A silhouette moved in front of the back door. As the sounds of someone working the lock made it to Desiree's ears, she pointed the barrel at a window pane shielding the lockpicker's head.

When she heard the click of success, she pulled the trigger. Glass shattered and a thump of dead weight hitting the wood of the back porch rang out in the night. Four remaining gunmen opened fire on the house. Bullets ripped through wood, windows, and sheetrock. Clifford Lawson returned fire as the attackers backed away from the house trying to find cover.

The loud crack of a high powered rifle filled the kitchen and a body outside was flung to the ground. Cliff knew in the low light, his best bet of taking out targets was to aim for center mass and he had succeeded in downing one of his assailants.

The three remaining black shapes melted back into the high grass. Other than an occasional stray shot and a voice crying "retreat", the property was quiet.

Cliff peered into the darkness for a long while before asking, "Do you think they're gone?"

Desiree lay prone on the floor with the shotgun pointed toward the frightened hit men. "They could be regrouping."

When nothing happened and they eventually heard approaching sirens, both protectors started to stir. Cliff lowered his weapon. "I don't think they'll come back tonight. The police will be here most of the night taking statements and looking at the crime scene."

Arturo reached the van cursing whatever God had decided to let him walk into an ambush. "*Puta madre!*" He spat repeatedly as he fired up the engine and pulled out on to a country road. He did not trust any of his surviving companions to drive with so much adrenaline flowing through their systems. It would be too easy to speed and get them pulled over if they encountered a cop. They needed to get back to Kios without incident or the night would go from shit to a cluster fuck. Failure was bad enough. Failure and incarceration would get his ticket punched by Raven.

The two other men sat in the back dejected and shaken by the firefight. "What the fuck happened? I thought everyone was asleep!"

"Obviously they weren't." The other man snapped.

"*Cállate!*" Arturo shouted back. "I need to concentrate on driving. They've probably called the police already."

The headlights illuminated the road ahead when a sudden blurry brown shape darted out. The van swerved to avoid a deer which stopped and stared into the oncoming lights. The frightened animal fled back into the woods as the driver corrected the vehicle's course. As the random shouts subsided, one of the surviving gunmen asked "What the hell?"

"A deer, a stupid deer." Arturo commented to his passengers. "I hate the country." He snarled to himself.

Red and blue flashes appeared in the distance. Arturo's heart beat faster and he focused on the road and not letting his foot further down on the accelerator. He wanted to pass them quickly but did not want to appear in too big of a hurry. The sirens grew in volume until the noise was a deafening roar and then quickly faded into silence as three patrol cars flew by.

Bestia watched his mirrors for any sign that one of the cars broke off and turned around in pursuit. Relief flooded through him when they disappeared from sight. Satisfied avoiding detection, his pride partially recovered from the sting of failure. "Well boys, I think we're in the clear."

Chapter: Can't Go Home Again

Douglas and Gaston slowed as they neared the turn for the Lawsons' driveway. A fleet of vehicles threw flashing lights across the landscape. The mixture of red and blue turned the yard into a morbid carnival. The Corvette pulled in and coasted slower until it barely moved at all. A uniformed police officer appeared at the window shining a flashlight in through the glass. Doug rolled it down and asked, "What's going on, officer?"

"Let me see some ID." The cop shot back, ignoring the driver's inquiry.

Doug fumbled through his wallet and pulled out his license. "I'm Douglas Lawson and this is my friend Gaston. This is my parents' house. Could you tell me what's happened?" He nervously glanced at the house seeing an ambulance that was not in a hurry to leave. His stomach knotted and he took slow, deep breaths trying to stay calm.

"Where are you coming from?" The officer continued as he studied the plastic card.

"We went to visit a friend. Look, can you just tell me if everyone is okay? My parents and my son were staying here."

The officer handed the ID back. "Your parents and kid are fine. Pull up a little more and park. Some of the field around back is a crime scene."

Doug said heartfelt thanks and put the car back in gear. As soon as the window was back up, Gaston asked, "He did not mention Desiree."

"Let's not jump to any conclusions. We'll find out what happened in just a minute." He killed the engine and engaged the parking brake. Both men swung the doors open and stepped out on to the dewy grass.

As they neared the house, a few former classmates that had joined law enforcement recognized Douglas and let him through. His mother and father stood in the living room. Jake sulked by the fireplace. Desiree stood in the kitchen, surrounded by grim faced detectives.

When Cliff and Maylene saw their son, they threw their arms wide and hugged him. During the fierce squeezes, Doug choked out "What happened?"

Clifford released his flesh and blood and shook his head. "I told you people would figure out who and where you are. Some armed men tried to break in. Luckily, your friend warned us in enough time to ambush them." He flicked his head toward Desiree.

"Why is she singled out?" Doug tried to read her expression but had no luck. Desiree was granite and her face gave up nothing.

"Everyone is very interested in her. She's in the United States legally but almost a ghost. Her electronic footprint is sparse to say the least. That's got everyone's radar up." Cliff gave his son a shrewd look.

"Hey, some people just don't spend all day on the internet." Doug defended her, before turning to watch his son pace. "Why does Jake look so pissed?"

"I made him hide in the hallway instead of joining in the attack. There were lots of wild shots. I didn't..."

"You don't have to explain." Doug patted his father on the shoulder. "I would have made the same decision. Thank you for keeping him safe."

Gaston walked in to the midst of the detectives and blurted out, "Desiree, are you hurt?"

She finally cracked a smile. "I will be fine as soon as these men quit harassing me."

The detectives turned their attention to the new arrival. "And who are you?" one of them asked.

"I am Gaston de Paul and both of us work for Mr. Lawson. As a matter of fact, he assisted us with the process of becoming U.S.

citizens. Is there some reason you are detaining this woman longer than the rest?" His tone contained an unverbalized accusation.

"No, we're just trying to figure out how she fits in to all of this. You see, everyone else over there has the same last name." The lead detective condescendingly spoke to the Frenchman. "Luckily, your girlfriend here was backed up by the family or she'd already be cooling it back at the station." He turned to face Desiree. "If you want to make life easier, wait until they get inside the house before you shoot them. It's less work for us." Then he shooed her away with his hand.

Gaston's eyes were wide. "How many men were there?"

"Five total, but we only took out two. I killed one and Douglas' father killed the other." She paused for a moment and gave a small, satisfied smile. "It was a bonding experience."

Gaston knew of her past but had never seen her in the midst of battle. He was aware of her skill and her cold nature when it came to survival, but the actual enjoyment of battle had not entered his mind. He had assumed that being drawn to violence was her cross to bear, not a hobby.

"You enjoyed yourself?" He muttered with shock.

"It beat staying up all night waiting for something to happen. Also, there are now two less men that want to kill our boss." She walked away from Gaston to join the Lawson family in the living room. Gaston stood dumbfounded and rooted to the spot.

In the other room, Douglas walked over to Jacob. "Hey sport, you okay?"

Jake glared at him. "You didn't let me go with you to the prison because I was supposed to be safe here. When we're attacked here, I'm sent to hide with Grandma. You do realize I am the most powerful person here, right?"

"And the most humble." Doug added in a sardonic tone. "Your Grandpa, my Dad, owns the house so if he wants to shoot intruders and make you wait in the hall, that's his decision. Desiree is a mercenary. She gets paid to take risks. She also has years of experience. Tell the truth, when the gunfire started, did you jump?"

Jacob guiltily looked at the floor. He had flinched at every shot fired. He did not know they would be so loud. Even through a few walls, it sounded like thunder.

"Imagine if you'd been out there with the noise and flashes and smoke. It would have been so much worse. You have to train to mentally handle stuff like that." Doug hugged the boy. "It's not because I don't think you can help. It's because I can't risk losing you. I know I've told you that before but I have to keep saying it until you finally understand it."

Jake returned the hug. "If you want me to use my power to help people, let me train with Desiree."

Douglas squeezed his eyes shut, trying to fight the realization that the attempts on his life would not stop. How many failed assassinations had he dodged so far? There was only one solution that he could stomach.

"Desiree, please come over here." He let go of his son and turned to face his employee. When she stopped in front of him with an eyebrow raised in curiosity, Douglas informed her "We are going to war. I need Jake trained for battle."

Gaston snuck up behind and Doug could also see his parents eavesdropping. "We're going back and we're shutting down Raven, *Bestia*, and Devildriver for good."

Desiree's eyes gleamed with anticipation. "Does this mean...?"

Douglas Lawson nodded. He felt tainted as he replied but he saw no other option. "They have tried to hurt my family and I will not stand for it. Use any means necessary to stop them."

Clifford Lawson nodded in approval. Maylene held her husband's hand and kept a worried but stern expression that everyone interpreted as consent. Only Gaston looked pained. His eyes moistened as he thought, "No Douglas, this is not your way."

Doctor Samantha Nichols sat in on the administering of the antidote to the third victim of Dr. Bernard Miller, the Memory Thief as some members of the press had dubbed him. Edward Stamps had been homeless and a veteran. Dr. Nichols hoped that he showed more gratefulness than Emma Tillman who immediately began swearing at them for bringing back all the pain from which the protein blocker relieved her.

As the pharmaceutical reps watch the grizzled older man take his shot, Samantha wished that she had a time machine. She would travel back to before she contacted Doug Lawson a year ago. He had infected her nurse friend with his delusions of crime fighting. Now, Penelope frightened the doctor. Samantha spent most of her work day dodging Nurse Daniels, a.k.a. Penny Dreadful. The outburst of violence during their girls' night out had terrified Nichols. She became a doctor to help and to heal. The idea of using force to curb problems with people made her chest feel constricted. Even in college when Douglas would foolishly confront people at parties, she would feel a wave of panic. Her family had never handled the direct approach well.

Stamps took the pain of his shot silently. When it was over, the lines in his face relaxed, slightly less tense. His gruff voice crackled with curiosity. "How long until we see results?"

"Five to thirty minutes." An emotionless voice answered from under a mask. If it had not been for the movement of the throat muscles, Samantha would not have even known which doctor had spoken. The drug had worked successfully on both of the other victims and there was no reason to believe that this time would be any different. The faith in the cure created a drop in attendance. With Frank Waltrip, the first target of the mad doctor, the room had been packed from wall to wall with doctors, lawyers, public relations specialists, and a bevy of other professions. Now, three doctors (not counting Dr.

Nichols) hovered around Mr. Stamps. Freeman Pharm only sent one lawyer who stood leaning against the wall out of the way. He looked disinterested but his keen eyes hiding behind his spectacles locked on to the patient. His intense gaze searched for any abnormalities.

Samantha thought through the devastation that Dr. Miller had caused. "All because one man couldn't handle rejection." She muttered under her breath. She wondered when they were going to get around to administering their serum to the Memory Thief. Once Bernard Miller had regained his memories, the court would be ready to try him for his crimes.

Samantha found herself questioning whether Douglas would attend the trial. She imagined that his heroic delusions would force him to attend to watch justice dispensed. She pictured him entering the courtroom dressed in the only suit he owned, tapping his cane as he walked up the main aisle looking for a seat. Of course, Jacob would trail behind him, not wanting to be left out regardless of how boring the proceedings would be. If Bernard received a conviction, Doug would smile with satisfaction and feel validated. Penny would probably take off work just to watch her new mentor gloat.

Samantha tried to clear the fantasies out of her head and focus on the patient. One of the doctors broke off from the group and walked over to her. He pulled his mask down and smiled at her.

"What do you think is going to happen to him after this?" Dr. Nichols asked.

"Freeman is going to try to give him a settlement in exchange for signing a piece of paper saying he won't sue. Dr. Miller was no longer employed by them and was acting on his own but they'll pay out a little just to avoid the courtroom. That's why the bored lawyer has been waiting in the wings the whole time." He pointed to the man against the wall that Samantha noticed earlier.

"When is Freeman going to cure Miller?" She asked with no real interest in attending.

"Not sure of the date, but there's also another victim, if you want to call him that. One of the terrorists that tried to destroy that bridge a while back was dosed with the protein blocker after he was captured. Someone smuggled it into his food or drink. He can't testify against his buddies because he can't remember them."

Samantha felt her heart leap. "When he's given the antidote, will the police have a brand new witness and be able to put the rest of his gang away?"

"Should be able too, assuming he wants to cooperate. I don't see why he wouldn't. Instead of trusting him not to talk, his friends robbed him of who he is. When I snapped back, I'd be pissed."

Samantha smiled. Maybe this whole dangerous situation would be behind Douglas and his merry band of crime fighters soon.

Seemingly, reading her mind, the doctor added, "Maybe things will finally get back to normal around here. Domestic terrorists, mad scientists, and some guy on the news that could fly…"

"Wait, what?" Samantha looked at him in surprise.

"The guy that jumped out of a window with a child in his arms and floated to the ground."

Of course, Samantha had seen the footage. She had spent an entire evening online repeatedly watching the video. "Oh yeah, I did catch that on the news." Curious, she asked, "What do you think of the flying man?"

"It's entertaining, obviously going for a comic book superhero thing, but too amateurish. The way the guy is falling and then suddenly decelerates like something caught him, fake. If he could really fly, why wouldn't he come down at a constant rate? Trust me, it's a hoax."

Samantha nodded. "You're probably right. No such thing as superheroes, right?" She felt a pang of guilt as she agreed with the stranger. Somewhere along the way, she had started to believe in Douglas' madness. It felt like betrayal, but she didn't owe him any allegiance. Then she kicked herself for flip-flopping.

Chapter: Best Laid Plans

R aven stopped by the coffee shop. It was open but only the young college girl was there. Valerie asked her if she had heard from Douglas.

"Mr. Lawson said he would be back today. I can't wait. It's been a madhouse without any help."

Valerie briefly wondered how Cindy the barista would react when news of her Lawson's death reached her. Raven knew that *Bestia* had failed, but she also knew that she was going to take matters into her own hands. If everyone else failed, she would do it herself. A voice in the back of her head seductively whispered, "Let Devildriver take care of him. Save yourself the grief." She pushed that thought away. As much as Douglas had to die, he had provided her with enough good times to not deserve that fate. Devil would make it messy and brutal. Valerie knew that she could execute him with mercy. After all, her empire was a business. She was not a sadist.

"Would you be a dear and get me a mocha latte?" Cindy nodded at her request and went to work.

Valerie sat down at a table and thought through her options for eliminating her boyfriend. She picked up a local magazine that the previous patron had left on the table and thumbed through it. A full page advertisement caught her attention. "Pink Passion Breast Cancer Gala: Gambling, Dancing, and Decadence. All for a good cause!" Then a smile spread across her lips.

An idea popped into her head almost fully formed. There would be an abundance of cash on hand for winner pay-outs. The biggest people in the city would be in attendance. With a little forward planning, a small contingent of armed men could handle security and make off with the money. If Douglas Lawson were in attendance, he could become a casualty of a robbery gone wrong. He would show up if she wanted to go. It would be their final date and this time he would die. She would guide him into the kill box and succeed where Arturo had failed time and again.

Cindy placed a cup on the counter and cleared her throat. "Miss Gossard, your drink is ready."

Valerie smirked. "Please, call me Valerie. Miss Gossard makes me feel old." She stood and slipped her coffee into an insulating paper sleeve. "Please, as soon as Douglas gets in, have him call me." That would give her some time to start planning with *Bestia* and Devildriver.

Gregory Phillips described it as waking from a nightmare only to realize he was in a new one. One moment, he had no idea who he was or what he had done. Then miraculously, his memory returned, fully intact. He knew it was not a real miracle. It was a chemical compound in a syringe that they pumped into him. The shocking part was that the change was instantaneous. Memories flooded back as if a dam had burst. He was Gregory Phillips. He had built a device that, when tuned correctly, could shake a building to pieces. He had been captured by a team of vigilantes. Members of his crew had tried to save him but ran when the cops arrived. While in custody, he ate a meal that disagreed with him. One of Raven's minions had poisoned the food with a memory inhibitor.

Now he would likely die. Raven would have him assassinated when she discovered he was in police custody with all of his knowledge returned to him. Luckily, he had not been returned to general population. He had guards outside the door in a Bryers hospital room. The only people who knew he was here and his condition were doctors and a handful of police.

Detective Sudduth came to visit him minutes after the doctors had left. Sudduth had tried to scare him with a story about one of Raven's con-men that had been captured. The truck transporting him was attacked and left a smoking wreck. Sudduth cryptically added, "He was a goldfish and we are hunting shark. We want the head honcho. The gunmen that hit during his transfer weren't concerned about the condition of the cargo. Do you really think they broke him out to welcome him home or just to make sure he couldn't be a witness for the prosecution?"

That story rattled Greg more than he wanted to admit. It sounded plausible and was in keeping with Raven's methodologies. He could visualize *Bestia* and Devildriver cutting through the armed guards amid the acrid smoke and the roar of gunfire. The poor sap that they broke out probably wished that he had been left to rot in prison. Devil probably relished in torturing the man, just to be sure of what he told the police during questioning.

"Here's what I'm proposing: we let you break out of custody. We would make it look realistic. You crawl back to Raven and regain their trust. You are our inside man and help us take them down. That's the only way you are ever really going to be safe. If they find out you're cured, you know what they'll do." Sudduth kicked back in his chair looking nonchalant. "Of course, you can always refuse. We'll make an announcement that one of our witnesses is cooperating with us and we'll wait for them to come after you." Then he sat up and looked at Gregory Phillips with a piercing gaze. "One way, you are bait. The other way, you are the infiltrator. Come on; take your destiny in your own hands."

Gregory had never been composed of stern stuff. That's why he chose a life of tinkering with gadgets rather than conquering like the alpha males he suffered under in high school. But, he was damned either way if the Detective was being above board. Why not take charge for once, be the guy that everyone relied on?

Shaking with fear, Phillips said, "Okay."

The problem with the plan was that Gregory had no idea how to contact them. "I had a phone number programmed into my cell. Everyone on the team had a disposable cell that was business only."

Sudduth shook his head. "There's no way you just happened to escape with the very same phone you had when you were captured. All you're going to have is a prisoner jumpsuit and your wits."

"I can go to one of the safehouses that I knew about but there is no telling how long I will have to wait for someone to try to use it. They may have completely abandoned it since I was in custody and knew its location."

Sudduth sighed. "You don't have any other way of contacting them?"

"No, they came to me at my store when they needed something." Greg was just as exasperated. If this plan didn't work, his recovery would be hinted at in the press and he would have nothing to do except wait for his executioner to show. He did not relish that thought.

"I guess the safehouse idea will have to do. They should come looking for you, though. So I don't think you'll have to wait long." Clarence knowingly stated.

"Why is that?" Greg felt apprehension skittering across his face.

"Your escape is going to make the nightly news." Sudduth beamed at him.

Penelope Daniels worked her shift like a good nurse, but itched for it to be over. She wanted to go home and put on her Penny Dreadful clothes. Though she wanted others to see her in it, she would not leave her apartment. The outfit was too conspicuous. She would just model in front of the mirror for a bit. She liked the way it looked on her and moreover, it made her feel stronger. She was unused to feeling powerful. She knew it was just a subconscious reaction but she still relished it.

Her work on the superhero costumes was all she had to look forward to now. Ever since the incident at the bar, Dr. Nichols had avoided her. With no more girls' nights out to occupy her and only so many hours allowed at the hospital, the designing and sewing expanded into her go to activity. She wished that she could do more to help Mr. Lawson though. What she really wanted was an active role in his crime fighting.

As she made her rounds, Penny entered the wing where they cared for the comatose patients and felt a tickle at the back of her mind. Gaston de Paul had a comatose friend. What was the history behind the man that he and Mr. Lawson would always visit? Samantha had told her the story, trying to impart how delusional her ex-boyfriend was. Sean McGuire had been a patient at Bryers hospital for years because Douglas and Gaston had fought him or something like that. The end result is they put a man in a coma in their "misguided quest for justice" (as Samantha called it).

Penny wondered what would happen if Mr. McGuire recovered. He would probably be pissed. More than that, he would want revenge. A bad guy with a personal axe to grind against the hero sounded like the makings of an archenemy. If he never woke up, it would save her favorite vigilantes repeated battles against their greatest villain.

Then she had an unsavory thought pop into her head. What if she made sure that Sean never woke up? It would be easy for her. She could make it look like an accident or natural causes. No one would ever have to know and she could aid the cause. Her feet moved of their own accord, guiding her to the unconscious man's bedside. She fluffed a pillow longer than she needed and then tightly gripped each end. Slowly lowering the cushion, she froze inches from his face. The eyes were closed and the face slack and relaxed. He may have been a criminal, but he was defenseless. "This was not how a hero saves the day. This is not how Mr. Lawson would do it." She slipped the pillow behind his head and walked away from the bed, slightly ashamed at what almost transpired.

Chapter: Casing the Joint

Valerie finished her tour of the convention center making note of entrances, exits, security cameras, and other pertinent information to succeeding with an armed robbery. She visualized where everything would be set up for the gala. If she focused, she could see the spaced out blackjack and poker tables, the roulette wheel, and the craps table. Slot machines would be absent. People attending such events do not want a solitary gaming experience.

Raven pictured the attendees in their gowns and tuxes, sparkling jewelry, and coiffed hair. She could also see the added security for an event with tons of on-hand cash, rent-a-cops in starched brown uniforms pacing the floors and hanging out by areas of ingress and egress. She wanted the score to be easy but was a realist enough to know things never go according to plan. The job to kill Martin Ramsey had soured due to Devildriver. It was one of the few failures she could blame one of her men for and not the interference of her boyfriend.

As if on cue, her work phone vibrated. She recognized the number as *Bestia*'s phone. She held it up to her ear and heard his light accent instruct her to check the local news for a jailbreak. She swallowed. Dr. Miller and Greg Phillips had no memories. William Kessey was incarcerated in Kansas. Why would that make the local news? She hated surprises. She survived by eliminating all the variables that she could. Whatever new speedbump had risen in her path, she would mow it down.

"Just tell me what I'm looking for." Her clipped voice commanded him.

"Gregory Phillips is out. A traffic accident allowed him to escape custody."

Valerie's voice suddenly contained apprehension. "How is that an issue? He doesn't remember us."

Arturo's voice gravely informed her otherwise. "Apparently, Dr. Miller's former employer has developed a cure. He is in full control of his faculties."

"Bugger all!" She groaned.

"We need to find him." Arturo prompted.

"I know bloody well what we need to do." Valerie snapped. Stopping to collect her thoughts, she asked. "What safehouses did he know about?"

"The garage on 71st."

"Get some eyes on it. I don't care who. We need to grab him as soon as he shows." Valerie barked orders.

"How do we know he'll go there?" *Bestia* tried to follow her thought process.

"He can't go back to his shop or his apartment or his family. The authorities will know about those locations and will be watching. The only place he knows he can lay low will be one that the police don't know about because he couldn't tell them." Valerie impatiently explained.

"What if he gave it up as soon as they cured him?" Arturo countered.

"That's why you have a pair of eyes watching from a distance. If he's being followed, you'll see someone tailing him." Exasperated, Valerie concluded. "Just get it done." She hung up and cursed the world around her for its failure to comply.

Outside on the sidewalk, she angrily stomped her heels all the way to her car squirreled away in a downtown parking deck. After finding her vehicle, she nestled into the leather seat and tried to relax. She had a map to draw up and she had extra guns to recruit for crowd control. She would be the "inside man" for lack of a better term and crowd control would be risky with just Devil and *Bestia*. There were

so many entrances and exits that covering everyone would be difficult. The cannon fodder would mean a smaller cut of the profit. On
the other hand, she would have many more executioners to choose
from when someone needed to put a bullet in Douglas' head.

She pushed the button on her dash that turned over the engine.
Some days she wondered if it would be easier just to get a straight job.

Greg Phillips watched the building from a distance. For all intents
and purposes, it looked abandoned. He felt under his shirt where the
small microphone sat taped to his chest. He felt like a bit player in a
weekly crime drama. He would be the character that is discovered
to be a rat and executed to show how ruthless his bosses were. The
thought made him shudder. He didn't even rank as a main character
in his own story. He was sweating profusely and no one was even
working him over. Greg crossed the street and finally ended up on the
same block as the safe house.

"God, I'm such a loser." He declared to no one in particular. He
walked down to the end of the block and eyed the door to the garage.
It looked undisturbed. He reached the intersection and loitered by the
crosswalk before walking back the other direction. No one jumped
out of an alley with a gun. No cops popped out of the woodwork to
tell him he was doing it wrong. All in all, he felt as if the entire event
had become boring.

Sighing, he walked over to the door and tried the handle. To his
surprise, it was unlocked. As the entrance widened, he peered into
the darkness. Thin shafts of light from the sparse windows caught
particles of dust as they danced on the new current of air he had created. A small fleet of vehicles filled the floor space, some covered with
protective tarps, others with a thin layer of dust. One car stood out
though. Freshly wiped down, a solid black Dodge Demon gleamed
as if it had been freshly waxed. His restored memory provided the

information. That car belonged to Devildriver and he would kill whoever put so much as a fingerprint on it.

"Forewarned is forearmed." Greg decided that whatever he touched inside this place, he would avoid that car. He walked around absently and finally sat down in a small closet sized office. Large windows allowed him to see the entire garage floor. One rickety office chair waited behind a particle board desk. He sat down and closed his eyes against the cloud of dust that he generated. How long was he going to wait here, for days? Here five minutes, he was already bored.

As he waited, his imagination filled the blank spaces in his mind. *Bestia* would probably be the happiest to see him. Arturo had given him a speech about always improving and adding on to the skill set. An employee that showed worth and proved value would always be in demand. And in a job where getting fired could mean ending up in an unmarked grave, being irreplaceable was mandatory.

Raven would be indifferent to his return as long as she thought he posed no threat. He had no doubt that he would die if she thought he had flipped. He worried about her ordering his execution. "Better safe than sorry." He felt his heart flutter. He put his hand to his chest and felt the wire. He was in real danger.

Greg Phillips stood and sprinted to the bathroom. In a panic, he pulled his shirt over his head and threw it on the floor. He clenched the microphone in his fist and ripped it off. The tape gave way and stung but he curled the transmitter and wires up in his hand and looked in the garbage can. About to drop it in, he hesitated. No, someone would see it when they came in here. He looked around and saw a window on the outside wall. "Perfect." He pushed it open and dropped the equipment outside. If he had the layout of the building right in his head, the device would me hidden in an alley behind the garage.

Feeling free and slightly safer, he walked out of the restroom and back to the semi-cozy office chair. He leaned back and took a deep breath. He could be killed anyway but if *Bestia* found a wire on him, he'd be dead for sure. At least now, he had a chance to talk his way back into their good graces.

He watched the door expectantly but as time dragged on, he started to doze. His eyelids fell and then he started snoring. He jerked awake when the door swung open. Night had fallen while he napped and the street outside was dark. The figure that entered filled him with fright. Devildriver saw him staring and started walking straight towards him.

Greg held his hands up in a gesture of surrender. "It's cool. It's cool. Call Raven or *Bestia* and let me talk to them."

Devildriver did not slow down and in a mere moment towered over the seated man.

"Jesus Christ, please don't kill me!" Greg tucked his chin to his chest and closed his eyes.

He felt something press to his ear and then heard ringing. Was that a cell phone? A male voice with a light Hispanic accent spoke. "What is it?"

"Uh, um, this is Greg. I escaped and need help." His voice shook as he had been convinced Devildriver had beelined toward him to satisfy an urge to kill.

"How the hell did you get Devil's phone?" Arturo asked in surprise.

"He…gave it to me." It came out sounding unsure, like a question.

"Okay, put Devil on."

Greg looked up into the black pools that Devildriver called eyes. "He wants to talk to you."

The scarecrow like specter put the phone to his ear and listened. "No, I didn't see any law enforcement." His gaze bore holes into the poor frightened Phillips. "I understand. Yes, the one where I keep my car." His mouth barely moved and his voice contained no inflection. "Understood." Devildriver hung up and shoved the cell into the pocket of his black jeans. Without another word, he walked away from the terrified man and over to his car.

Greg tried to steady the shaking hands but could not. That freak was so hard to read. Anything could be floating through that homicidal head of his. Greg just praised God that he had survived another encounter with the weirdo.

Pressing his luck, he tried to engage Devildriver in conversation. "So, *Bestia* is coming?"

Devildriver popped the hood on his car and started examining the engine compartment with the eye of a surgeon.

After a protracted silence, he added, "So that was a yes, no, maybe?"

Devil stopped and gave him a withering look. "He will be here when he is here." The flat voice sounded alien and threatening. Greg shut up. Devil continued to work on his car in silence while Greg contemplated his future.

Chapter: An Unusual Discovery

On a mission, Gaston walked into the coffee shop with Desiree watching from the sidewalk. Her eyes vigilantly swept the environment for potential assassins. Douglas would be the primary target but Jacob needed some things from the apartment. It would be safer for the other members of the Sentinels to retrieve them.

Cindy greeted the Frenchman. "Hi Gaston, did everyone have a good vacation?" He curtly nodded and walked behind the counter to access the stairway to the second floor. She continued talking. "Ms. Gossard wanted to know as soon as Mr. Lawson was back."

Gaston felt seething rage at Douglas. The man who wanted to go by the code name "Einstein" was too dumb to find a solution that did not involve murder, vigilante justice, and execution. Gaston wanted to lash out at the man and explain that there would be blood on everyone's hands. The priest knew something about the difficulty of truly washing away a sin and Douglas insisted on finding out the same lesson the hard way. Gaston lashed out at the only person handy. "Then call his cell phone and tell him. I am not a secretary."

Cindy appeared stunned. After the shock of the verbal assault wore off, she picked up the shop's phone and dialed Mr. Lawson. She had seen Gaston's snide comments before but he had always spared her his wrath.

"Mr. Lawson, Ms. Gossard came in here and wanted you to call her as soon as you were back in town. I just saw Mr. Gaston and he said you were here." Her voice shook from the fight or flight response her body engaged.

"Okay, I'll call her." A long pause stretched out until Cindy started to hang up. Douglas' voice returned. "Are you okay? You sound different."

Cindy swallowed. "I'm fine. I just had a customer snap at me."

"Don't let it bother you. There's one rotten banana in every bunch." His voice carried a sense that he had sat through many beratings.

"I know. It was just unexpected." As she spoke, Gaston sullenly appeared and walked out the door with a suitcase in hand. With a wounded heart full of confusion, Cindy watched him leave.

On the sidewalk, Desiree walked beside him. Ever vigilant, she monitored the environment as she spoke. "How long are you going to stay mad?"

"I'm not mad" he said in an angry tone of voice.

"Sure and I'm a pacifist." Her sardonic reply caused him to glance at her with a flicker of disdain.

"He is betraying his ideals." Gaston finally admitted his anger. "He is betraying the mission he convinced me to help him with."

Desiree looked at her short-term lover with pity. "He was an idealist, but there comes a time where reality has to be accounted for. He has survived on sheer luck so far. But luck runs out and he will die unless he rises to the challenge."

Gaston shot back. "Rising to the challenge means becoming a monster himself? Once he commits certain actions, he cannot come back from it."

"This is a war. He needs to destroy his enemy or he will be destroyed." Desiree scowled at him.

"An eye for an eye makes the whole world blind." Gaston dropped the quote with vitriol.

"Pacifists get trampled under the boots of the powerful. I've seen real horrors on a scale that would crush your faith. I'm not talking about petty street crime or even a murder. I have seen fields of rotting bodies." Desiree grabbed Gaston by the arm, forcing him to stop and look her in the eyes. "Some people are animals and have to be treated as such."

Gaston shrugged, pulling his sleeve free of her grip. "Everyone's life has value, even the 'animals' that you want to put down."

"Douglas has seen reason. Why won't you?" She called after him as he walked away.

"You call selling out your ideals and condoning premeditated murder 'seeing reason'? I would hate to see what you think pushing the envelope looks like." Gaston kept moving so he did not have to see her.

Douglas walked from his car. One hand held the phone to his ear and the other wielded his cane. He had gotten a message to call Valerie and being the dutiful boyfriend, immediately called. She answered after a few rings and sounded perturbed.

"Everything okay, sweetie?" Douglas prompted.

"I'm fine, just having a work issue. An associate is causing headaches." She muttered without conviction.

"Cindy said you wanted to talk to me. You know you can just call me directly, right?" He followed the sidewalk forgetting to keep aware of his surroundings.

"I know but I was already there for my daily caffeine. Plus I was going to be busy for the next several hours. I knew if you picked up the phone, we would talk for a while."

"I guess you're right. I've got a lot to tell you. There was an attack on my childhood home." Douglas conversationally mentioned the event as if it were not a big deal.

"Oh my God, is anyone hurt?" She modulated the amount of surprise to sound authentic.

"No, I was on my way back from following up a lead in the Ramsey case. My father and the rest of the Sentinels took care of the threat."

"What lead?"

"I talked to a prisoner named William Kessey. He had a strong motive to kill the prosecutor that put him away. He even let the name Raven slip when I was questioning him." Douglas proudly recounted his success.

Valerie felt her mouth go dry. "What else did he say?"

"That was about it, a short conversation."

She knew that she had to get in front of his discovery that she knew Kessey. It would be best for her to volunteer the information so that she looked transparent. "Kessey? I think I worked on that case recently. He came to my firm to handle his appeal."

Douglas nearly dropped his phone. "What?"

"He wanted us to represent him while he appealed the decision. We couldn't help him and he's still in jail." Valerie gave him the information, almost by rote.

"This whole time...you knew my suspect?" His mind strained at something that was just out of reach.

"My firm is a good one and his father is a general. They sought us out because of our record and reputation. It's not that unusual. We can afford to pick and choose our cases."

"Then why represent such a scumbag?" Douglas lost the train of thought and now focused on his girlfriend being in close proximity to the degenerate.

"General Kessey wanted his son out but couldn't do it publicly because of the black eye the boy gave the army and the general's testimony. My boss wanted to score some points with a prominent general and assigned it to me. It's not like I volunteered." Valerie fluidly rattled off her explanation.

Douglas quickly followed up with more questions. "Did he say anything that could help me out, any names of co-conspirators?"

Valerie let legitimate disgust creep into her voice. "No, he spent most of our meetings trying to flirt and making crass remarks."

Lawson accepted that comment at face value. It sounded true enough. "I can't believe the coincidence." He spoke rhetorically but Valerie started to sweat.

"It is a small world and we both run in circles that involve lawbreakers." Valerie reasoned.

"Yeah, enough about that. What did you want to talk to me about?" Douglas felt like he had missed something important but since it was not coming to him, he changed subjects.

"I was going to ask you out on a date." Valerie added a flirting lilt to her voice.

"You know I'm going to say yes." Doug laughed.

"There's a gala for breast cancer research; dinner, dancing, gambling." Valerie tried to not sound too eager for him to accept.

"Well, I do love breasts." Doug made a show of thinking it over. "Eh, I guess I'll go."

Valerie smiled though her voice dripped with sarcasm. "Don't get excited on my account."

"You know how excited I can get on your account." Douglas laughed.

Valerie could not wipe the grin from her face. He was wrapped around her finger. "It's a date and don't bother to bring your wallet. This time, it's my treat."

"I don't feel right about you paying. It's not how I was raised." Douglas protested.

"I said it is my treat. I want to do this for you, no argument." Raven had to let Arturo and Devil know that the job was a go. The target would be present and they would be rid of "Einstein" forever. Her poor boyfriend would die in front of her and this time, nothing would stop it. If she had to pull the trigger herself, Douglas Lawson was a dead man.

Chapter: Hotel Bar Revisited

D r. Nichols sat at the hotel bar that Dr. Straub had introduced her to. She nursed her cosmo while waiting for a guest to arrive. She sipped the pinkish concoction and scanned the door. She had not been waiting long when in walked the reliable Stuart Straub. After their last meeting, he greeted her with obvious reservation.

"Hello, Dr. Nichols." Stuart's voice carried professionalism tinged with hope.

"Hello, Dr. Straub." Her tone was conciliatory. "I am sorry about the way we left things. I was having a rather bad day."

The middle-aged man gave her a smile. "I have to confess, it surprised me when you asked me to meet with you."

Samantha shrugged. "I need to talk to someone and you are the closest thing I have to a friend right now."

"Ouch." He put his hand to his chest as if he had been mortally wounded. "I'm glad I rank so highly."

"I'm serious. I don't communicate with Douglas and I don't feel comfortable around Penelope anymore."

"The nurse you hang around with?" Stuart asked.

"Not so much now." She stirred her drink with her finger before confessing. "I saw her hit a guy in the head with a heavy piece of glass. It scared me, mainly because she was so unremorseful."

"The shy one? That sounds unlike her." He looked at her skeptically.

"Douglas infected her with his crime fighting dreams." Samantha looked at the salt covered napkin sitting under her drink.

"Is Douglas really that bad? How can he run a small business and have time to jump across rooftops."

"He can't jump anymore. Leg injury, remember? He pays other people to do the running and jumping for him."

Dr. Straub shook his head in disbelief. "Are the people he employs rational?"

"For the most part. I can't decide if they are fully bought in to his plan or if they are just using him for a paycheck." Samantha felt herself opening up to her mentor. "I think Gaston is the real deal. I'm not sure about Desiree. I haven't spent enough time around her. They boy though, Jacob, he's fully committed and thinks he has superpowers." She drained the last of her drink in one long pull and set it back on the bar with a clack. "You know what? I am starting to believe him. That news footage is damn weird. Douglas falling out of that window with that little girl in his arms…"

"Wait, Douglas and the boy are the ones on that video clip of the house fire?" Stuart's eyes widened. "You think it's legitimate? I heard some video experts commenting that it was faked footage based on the uneven fall rate of the guy holding the little girl. He described it as if a wire suddenly caught and slowed down the hero's descent."

"Doug is crazy. He wouldn't stage a fake show because he believes it for real." Samantha countered.

"So your argument is to leave a delusional man running around unsupervised?" Straub eyed her suspiciously.

"Well," she blushed. "He's a better person now compared to when I met him. His delusion makes him genuinely want to help people."

The bartender handed Stuart a highball glass containing a clear concoction. The doctor lifted the glass to his lips and took a large swallow. "You know, I think you are going to be a fine psychiatrist."

"Why do you say that? I just said let the guy be crazy." Samantha asked, dumbfounded.

"You can't help people that don't want your help. The only thing you can do is try to calculate the needs of your patient. If Mr. Lawson did want to be cured, do you think it would be the best thing for him?"

"I'm afraid he will get hurt standing up to some criminal if he doesn't get help." Samantha replied.

"Plenty of people who aren't delusional get hurt trying to fight off a home invader or a mugger." Stuart looked at his protégé waiting for a reaction.

"They don't go looking for it. Douglas does." Samantha grimaced.

"It's just an observation but you've already said that he's a better man. You also pointed out that he has a close knit support group. It looks like there is already a contingent that thinks the delusional Mr. Lawson is the one that they prefer."

"I know and I do too." Samantha looked down at her empty glass. "Damn him! He admitted he needed me. He rejected me and then came to me for comfort in lieu of his girlfriend. I was the one he would call in the middle of the night."

Stuart smiled. "You are still in love with him."

"Ptttthbt." She made a random noise while sticking out her tongue.

"Eloquent." He laughed. "You didn't deny it though."

"What chance do I have against that stuck-up lawyer bitch?" She looked her mentor in the eyes. He could see the hurt behind them.

"You really love him. He knows that deep down but maybe you should remind him." Dr. Straub drained the last of his drink. "I've got to head home but I wish you luck. Don't forget, no one knows how you feel unless you communicate it. Come on, you're a psychiatrist. You know this stuff." He patted her shoulder before walking away from the bar.

Dr. Samantha Nichols looked at the mirror behind the bar and saw a sad looking woman staring back at her.

Penny walked out of the hospital in her scrubs with a large purse slung over her shoulder. It had been a long shift but she was free to focus on her own pursuits again. She had put the finishing touches on a costume for Jacob and was quite proud of the outfit. As she planned out the last alterations, her phone began ringing.

She looked at the display and saw the name Samantha Nichols. Hurriedly, she answered it. Despite rushing to accept the call, Penelope paused to make sure her voice was nonplussed. "Hello?"

Slightly slurring her speech, Samantha replied. "Hey, I am free tonight and thought you may want to hang out. I've had some stuff on my mind."

Penny thought of the almost finished costume waiting at her apartment. "I had plans." She coolly stated. "Besides, I got the impression you have been avoiding me."

"I just needed some alone time to think through some things." Samantha tried to gloss over that she had been intentionally avoiding the nurse.

"Uh-huh." She sounded unconvinced. "I guess you could come to my place."

"Uh, yeah. I'll come over." Samantha sounded slightly hesitant.

Suddenly perking up, Penny ordered her friend. "Bring over a bottle of wine. We'll celebrate."

"What are we celebrating?" Samantha slowly asked.

"I'm finishing my latest outfit."

"You already have one that you can't wear in public. Why do you need another?"

Penny replied, shaking her head. "It's not for me. It's for Mr. Lawson's kid, Jake."

"I'll meet you there and you can show it to me." Samantha offered.

"Kay,kay. I'll see you in a bit." Penelope felt lighter now that her friend had started talking to her again.

A short bus ride later, the nurse walked to the front door of her building and saw Samantha Nichols sitting on the stoop with a bottle of red wine cradled in her hands. "I'm sorry; it's a pretty cheap vintage." The doctor called out to Penny.

"It's okay. It's for getting drunk." Nurse Daniels flashed a smile as she passed her. Samantha stood and followed her friend into the building.

Inside the apartment, Penelope rolled out the male model form and proceeded to show off a leather hooded jacket. Around the cuffs and trimmed around the hood, orange flames curled back like on the hood of a hot rod. "I wasn't sure what kind of weapons Jake uses. So, I just gave him a bunch of multipurpose pockets. If I knew he liked a knife or a boomerang, I would sew in a specific holster."

Samantha laughed. "A boomerang?"

"Hey, they are dangerous." Penny warned her.

"I'm sure they are..." Samantha waited a moment before continuing. "I'm not trying to make you feel bad, but if Jacob gets hurt, how will you feel about helping him?"

"What do you mean?" Penelope seemed shocked.

"If he puts on your costume and goes out fighting people, what if he gets seriously hurt or killed?" Samantha tried to drive home the seriousness of encouraging Douglas and his son.

"I just make clothes. I'm not responsible for what anyone does while wearing them." Penny acted taken aback.

"But when you give him this uniform, you are implying that you are okay with his actions." Samantha stressed.

"I am okay with it. I want to help them more but I don't know how to fight." Penny seemed unsure of why her friend was concerned.

Samantha shrugged and gave up on getting through to her. "What do you have left to do?"

Penny immediately became more animated. "I am going to do some more fire around the bottom of the pants legs. That's the last step."

Samantha placed the wine on the countertop and reached in to a drawer, producing a corkscrew. "I'll open this so it can breathe before we dive in."

Full glasses slowly disappeared only to be replaced and emptied again. Penny held back so that she would not make a mistake, but

Samantha indulged even more. As the evening ticked away, she passed out on the couch.

Dr. Nichols woke up to the sound of a shutting door and whispering voices. She lazily opened her eyes, still feeling the effects of all the alcohol she had consumed. Penelope stood at the entrance to her apartment talking to a hobbling man.

Suddenly, Samantha was off the couch and on her feet. "Douglas? What are you doing here?"

He looked tired, as if sleep stopped coming easily. Despite the obvious exhaustion, he grinned like a fool when he saw her. "It's been too long."

"You look like hell." Samantha stated before considering the insensitivity of her comment.

"You look drunk." He immediately shot back. "But yeah, I haven't been sleeping in a real bed. My apartment and my parents' house are no longer safe."

"Is everyone okay?" Samantha felt her chest tighten. She had always liked Clifford and Maylene Lawson.

"No one on our team got hurt. We've taken down a few of their guys." He nonchalantly spoke. "The one I faced off with is in jail. Desiree and my father killed some of them." His face fell in disappointment. "I never wanted us to become judge, jury, and executioners. Things just spiraled out of control. I guess I was a little naïve."

Samantha stepped toward him and wrapped him up in a hug, her inhibitions temporarily lowered. "I'm so sorry."

He returned the embrace and asked, "No I told you so?"

"That's coming later. I want to really enjoy it." She playfully added.

"Don't relish it too much." He laughed.

"Why didn't Penny just drop off the costume?" She eyed the nurse suspiciously. Could Penelope have masterminded trying to get them back together?

"The apartment is compromised. Anyone that knows about it could follow us back to the Bulwark."

"What's that?"

"It's our hideout."

"Your secret base." She giggled. "I bet Jacob thinks that's amazing."

"He does actually." Doug added.

"So, what does your girlfriend think about you hiding out?" Samantha inquired.

"Valerie's not a big fan but she lets me do what I want."

"That's so egalitarian of her." Dr. Nichols sardonically replied.

"Uh-yeah, I guess it is. How's your love life? Penny said the two of you had a girl's night out bar hopping. Did you meet anyone?"

Penny interrupted. "I told him everything, Sam. He is okay with it."

Samantha forgot the initial question and focused on lashing out. "She could've killed that man!"

Douglas shrugged. "I don't think the world would miss a piece of shit that would drug his date and then rape her. Did you miss the part where I told you a couple of days ago members of my team killed some guys? At least Penny won't have to go through the years of holding back because of some antiquated moral code."

"Antiquated...?" Samantha Nichols' face flushed red with rage. "A moral code is what keeps you from becoming them! It's why the police have to follow procedures. It's why everybody gets a trial. We don't want to sink to their level!"

"We?" Doug snorted. "You cut me off from your professional help and your friendship."

"Because I care about you and can't stand the idea of you getting hurt!" She shouted back at him.

Penny stepped in between them. "Einstein, let me get the suit for you. Cataclysm will want to try it on."

Curious enough to subdue her anger, Samantha asked, "Who's Cataclysm?"

"It's Jacob's code name." Doug spoke in cool, controlled tone.

Addressing the nurse, he added, "Yeah, I'll let you know what he thinks and if there are any alterations needed. If you are serious about crime fighting, you may want to take up a self-defense class. I know a good Brazilian Jujitsu teacher. Tell him I sent you." He pulled a card out of his wallet and handed it to Penny.

The nurse swapped the card for a folded stack of clothes and thanked him.

Douglas looked at Samantha. "I really, truly am glad to see you... even if it devolved into an argument again."

Samantha gave him a melancholy wave. "It was good seeing you, too." With that, he was gone.

Chapter: Revelations

Douglas walked into the Bulwark and handed the newly finished costume to his son. Jacob excitedly unfurled the leather clothing and ran off to try change. He disappeared into the office where he had set up his cot and sleeping bag and shimmied his pants off to put on the uniform. Examining the flames sewn on to the hooded jacket, he marveled at the quality. It could've been a prop from a blockbuster super-hero movie. He looked around for a mirror but could not find one.

He walked to the restroom and stared into the mirror. "I look so cool!" He exclaimed as he flexed and watched his reflection. He wondered how he looked while using his power and held out a hand. His toothbrush floated out of the holder and began to spin end over end. Focusing on the task, he only caught a glimpse of himself but he looked intense. His furrowed brow sat above piercing eyes. He concentrated on aiming the toothbrush handle on the hole as he set it back. His accuracy kept improving.

Jacob wondered what other superhero things he could watch himself doing. A smirk crossed his face. If he could move objects by focusing on them, why couldn't he focus on moving himself? Flight was a standard superpower in the comic books. Almost everyone could do it.

Jake closed his eyes and focused. He visualized two hands scooping him under the arms and lifting him off the ground. Pain radiated through his armpits as his weight rested on narrow invisible supports. Grunting in annoyance and hurt, he stopped concentrating and fell a few inches. He shuffled his feet on the bathroom floor and tried again with a different technique. Instead of pulling himself up, he thought he'd push this time. He imagined a platform under his feet slowly rising. Eventually, the top of his head brushed the ceiling tiles and he stopped. Opening his eyes, he could see his legs dangling in front of the mirror. "Hahaha! He cheered and fell back to the floor. "Holy shit, I can fly!"

The excited teen ran into the garage looking for any kind of audience. Gaston looked up from a book he had been reading to see what the commotion was about. Before the Frenchman could ask any questions, Jacob shouted. "Watch this!"

The boy rose off the floor in a smooth and controlled motion, levitating. He continued ascending higher into the warehouse when a voice called out. "Be careful, Jake."

His father's voice surprised him and he opened his eyes. Realizing he was twenty feet above hard concrete, he faltered and fell. On his way down, he focused on hands catching him and he jerked to an excruciating halt. He still hovered eight feet high and slowly sank to the ground.

Gaston and Douglas were beside him. "Jake, are you okay?" He father worriedly whispered to him.

"I'm fine. I just need to learn to block things out better." The boy felt embarrassed at trying to show off and failing.

"That was impressive. When did you figure out that you could do that?" Doug asked.

"Just a minute ago, in the bathroom."

Doug dryly added, "I don't think I was doing anything as constructive in the bathroom at your age."

"Gross." Jake replied before starting to levitate again. "Keep talking to me though. Say the most distracting things you can come up with."

"Uh, a gorilla playing basketball…green eggs and ham…great balls of fire."

Jake started to giggle and his height dipped several inches but he quickly recovered. "See? I've got this."

Gaston whistled with appreciation. "Your skills are growing magnificently."

"Do you think I'll be ever to fly like in the comics?"

Doug shifted uncomfortably. "I don't know. If you hit a bird, it could kill you. They can take down planes."

"What if I have a windshield?" He grew quiet for a second and then piped up. "I could focus on pushing the air in front of me away."

"Would it be enough to save you from an errant bird?" Doug worriedly asked. The boy had just discovered an entire world opening up to him.

"I'll push really hard." Jacob convincingly begged.

Doug smiled. "We'll take it slow and train. Don't take off until we really get this thing hammered out."

"I promise." Jake answered with a twinkle in his eye.

Doug tossed out a compliment. "The uniform looks really good on you by the way."

"Thank you for having that lady make it. I love it."

"No problem." He looked at Gaston. I think I'm going to hit the sheets. It's been a stressful few days and I'm worn out."

His son and the Frenchman gave him a "good night" in unison. Doug disappeared into the office and picked up a paperback novel. He flopped down onto a bare cot and began reading.

Holding the book above his face with one hand, he quickly tore through the flowing prose. He had always been a fast reader to the point that teachers had doubted him in school. The rate at which he consumed literature endeared him to the librarian but few other people. He could appreciate the story, the character development, and the use of language. Every once in a while, he would discover a phrase that he would fall in love with.

As he read the description of a main female character, he became enamored with the wording. The author had described her as "a raven haired beauty". The turn of phrase made him think of Valerie's jet black hair. Valerie was his raven haired beauty. Then his stomach knotted and his heart skipped a beat. Valerie. Raven.

Doug dropped the book and bolted upright. "No, no, no, no, no!" She had encouraged him in the beginning but as soon as he was a threat to Raven, she had become much more negative. If she was in the employ of *Bestia*, she would have been able to furnish the location of his residence to them. She would have been able to tell them the town in which he grew up. She would be the perfect spy to feed information to them.

Einstein was not as smart as he thought. His chest constricted with anxiety and shame. He stood up and paced back and forth across the small room. "Son of a bitch, this can't be true!" Suddenly, he felt like he was falling down a hole and it was too dark to see the bottom.

Valerie sat in the office chair watching a standing Gregory Phillips. She glanced over to Arturo. "Did you check him for a wire?"

"Of course. He's clean." The muscled man answered. Greg felt vindicated that he had tossed the mic and transmitter.

"I really should kill you just to be sure." Raven watched the chubby man squirm. "But I think you may be able to help me with a new score. How quickly could you build a cell phone jammer?"

Greg jumped at the chance to be helpful. "It's no problem at all. I've built them before just to take to the theater. I hate when people play with their phones during the movie."

"Good, we're going to hit a target with a big crowd and I would hate for someone to get a call through to 911." Valerie never stopped staring at him with a freezing gaze.

"I've got you covered. It covers all common US broadcasting frequencies." Greg tried to assure her.

"What is the effective range?" She asked.

"It really depends on how portable you want to make it. Get me access to an electronics store and I can throw any kind together in less than a day." He smiled a see through smile trying to convince her he was just part of the team.

She watched him for what seemed like an uncomfortably long time. Then she nodded at Arturo. "Get him what he needs to build one with a two hundred yard range."

Bestia nodded. "Thy will be done." He roughly grabbed the obese man by his arm and hissed. "We're going shopping."

As they left the garage, Valerie was left with her thoughts. In a short amount of time, she would be on a fatal date with her boyfriend/archenemy. She tried to project herself into the future to feel how Lawson's death would affect her. She would never admit it to Arturo, but she had grown fond of Douglas. He could be amusing, sometimes with a juvenile innuendo and other times with a dry wit. He was generous in bed, always deferring to acts that pleased her most. He had a sense of purpose and a drive that stood independent of other people's opinions. She thought he could be slimmer, maybe a little more muscular. That was really her only complaint. It was shallow but she considered herself to be slumming it when she was with him.

Yet, Ms. Gossard still kept seeing him. She told herself that it was part of the job, keeping tabs on a potential threat. She knew that reason to be false. When they met, the police still considered him a bumbling fool wasting their time. She could have walked away and wrote him off. However, she went out with him. Then went out with him again. And again. Before she knew it, weeks had passed and they were a couple in everyone's eyes.

It was not a bad job though. Raven had a warm body at night if she wanted it. Lawson had learned what she liked and obliged. She never worried that he would try to take advantage of her or that his affection was part of a long con. Aside from talking about her criminal enterprise, she did not have to keep her guard up. It felt good to just relax with someone.

As she sat in her office chair and closed her eyes, Valerie thought about how she missed him when they were apart for more than a few days. After their next date, she would be without him for good. She would be there to see to it. Her eyes flew open as it dawned on her that this time he really would die. Valentine, *Bestia*, or Devildriver could fail but she never would. A chill ran through her as she realized that she was going to kill the man she loved.

Chapter: Groundwork

G regory Phillips could not stop sweating. Partly, he was prone to sweating more in general and he was overweight. So the stress sweat was lost in the mix. None of the other mercenaries batted an eye at the pit stains on his shirt as he unveiled the jammer. His voice shook as he explained to the few faces he recognized and tried to block out the other gunmen.

"Ms. Raven, *Bestia*, Devil." He nodded at each as he addressed them. "This jammer is easily portable and covers 1850 Megahertz through 2690 MHz. That covers most 3G and 4G, also a host of other possible US cell technologies."

"English please, or Spanish." Arturo smirked.

"Um, when I turn it on, you can't use your phone." Greg replied with more lip than he intended.

"The mouth on this one." Arturo shook his head with amusement. "How hard is it to operate?"

The truth was that the device had a few dials on it but they were for show. He could flip a switch and as long as a component did not burn out, it would run without an operator until someone turned it off. Of course, the poor Mr. Phillips did not want them to know how expendable he was. Ever since he was discovered in their safe house, he had not been allowed to leave. Some of the hired guns stuck around to guard him. Meals were brought in periodically. It was like prison but with even more fear for his life.

"I'll need to be on hand to make adjustments, monitor it, and repair it on the fly if necessary." He rattled off this list by rote. He had practiced it most of the morning.

Raven shifted and re-crossed her legs. "It can't be that difficult.

I'm sure one of my men could stand in for you. I know field work did not pay off for you last time." Her voice stayed prim and proper despite the undercurrent of menace.

Deciding that the only way to make it through the day was extreme confidence that they needed him, he affected a surety that he did not feel. "How many of you know about cell triangulation, oscillating frequencies, or the window of time for re-soldering wires?" He glared at the room of career criminals waiting for someone to step up. "If you want people to get a lucky phone call through, just let one of these yahoos try to work the jammer. The only thing guaranteed to get jammed is a cock in your ass in a federal prison."

Some of the men stole furtive glances at Raven. She cracked a smile. "You forget, I would be in a women's prison. Too few cocks for my taste. I guess you are coming with us. Would the infrastructure at the Kios Convention Center be an issue for your jammer?"

"No." He realized the location of the heist, but had no way to relay that information to the police. He had tossed his wire out the bathroom window. While he had not moved to a new building, he also had no way to escape his captors and go get it. He wondered if they were even listening at this point. If he ran out the door and shouted it into the microphone, there could be no one on the other end.

Valerie interrupted his train of thought. "Very well. Pack it up. You won't even have to come inside with us."

Greg shook with fear. As soon as the job was over, he was going to end up dead in a ditch. He had to find a way to alert the police.

After the presentation, Raven left. Most of the gunmen trickled out. Devildriver crawled into the back seat of his car and fell asleep. Arturo sat in the office looking over a sketch of the convention center floor. He was as unsupervised as he was likely to get. Scooping up a paperclip and a pack of dental floss from the office and bathroom, respectively, he went to the window where he had disposed of the wire. Tossing his makeshift fishing hook into the alley, he hooked the microphone wire and slowly started to reel in the electronics. When the dental floss became taut, he gave a steady pull. He felt the floss sliding through his fingers and he looped it several times around his fingers. As he tried again, he could feel the paperclip struggling against the weight of his surveillance equipment. The malleable metal could not bear the load and bent out of shape. The wire stayed outside and he pulled in a mangled improvised hook. He looked forlornly at the failed paperclip and thought "My fate was in the hands of this little crappy office supply."

Chapter: The Final Date

Douglas sped along in his 1963 corvette with a beautiful woman beside him. He wore a tuxedo but left his hair disheveled. His right hand worked the manual transmission with such flair that the lady accompanying him easily realized that he was showing off. He took turns sharp enough to slide her against the door and would look out of the corner of his eye to gauge her reaction. Remarkably, she seemed unperturbed and unimpressed. He searched for any signs of nervousness on her face. He wondered if he was crazy for suspecting her. She seemed so at ease.

Valerie glanced at the driver. "Your shop must being doing very well for you to risk so much tonight, the ticket price plus you are expected to gamble. I offered to pay."

Doug smiled at her, even though he was not feeling jovial. "It's no big deal. It goes to a good cause."

"I did not realize that breast cancer research rated so highly on your list of worthy charities."

"What can I say? I love breasts." Douglas looked to see if she found the comment funny or disgusting. Then he had a vague memory of previously making that joke.

Valerie laughed. "You look cultured, dressed as you are, but then you open your mouth."

Douglas looked back at the road, satisfied that she had not taken offense. "Well, I have to say, you look ravishing in that little black dress. When some people dress up, you can kind of tell they're not comfortable, but you look just as natural in that as the t-shirt and jeans you wore when we met." He felt awkward being so open with a woman that may have given information to his enemies.

"Thank you, kind sir." She flicked her straight black hair back and rested her left hand on top of his while he worked the gear shift.

Douglas pretended to not notice her hand. "So, are you much of a gambler? I thought I'd ask since the theme is casino night."

Valerie shrugged. "In life or at cards?"

Doug perked up. "Oh, philosophical, are we? Both. You've piqued my curiosity."

"I'm not into most card games. I'm too good at reading people for it to hold any appeal." She flatly stated.

"Wow, that is cocky." Doug appreciatively smiled. "Do you think you could read me? What am I thinking?" He raised an eyebrow in mocking challenge.

Valerie slapped his hand. "You're thinking dirty thoughts. Now behave. I'm trying to fully answer your query." She paused to remember the original question. "In life, I do take more risks. In baccarat, poker, or any other game of chance, the risks and rewards are easily calculated. It is a number. In life, the risks and rewards can be anything at all. When I took a chance in playing a game of chess in your quaint shop, I had no way of knowing that it would lead to being driven to a black tie event in a vintage American sports car."

"Good point." Doug found himself falling hard for her black hair, azure eyes, and the spirit of this woman despite the fear that she was a snake lying in wait. "We are almost there." He lamely added, unable to follow up the conversation with anything that sounded intelligent.

The blue and white 'Vette cruised through a circular drive and stopped in front of a waiting valet. Banners proclaimed, "4th Annual Night at the Casino Breast Cancer Fundraiser". Spotlights waved back and forth reflecting off of clouds and occasionally disappearing into clear portions of the night sky. Within seconds, the valet had taken Douglas' car to be parked in the underground lot with the Aston Martins, Bentleys, Lamborghinis, Ferraris, and Rolls.

The well-dressed cafe owner extended his hand to the lady and together they ascended the steps to the trio of large double doors serving as the front entrance. A uniformed usher stood by the threshold collecting tickets and directing guests to the "bank" to purchase chips.

"Welcome to casino night. Sir, Madame, may I see your invitations?" Nodding at each person he addressed, the greeter held out a white gloved hand.

Douglas handed over two white cards with gold leaf lettering and trim. The doorman stepped aside and pointed to the right. "You may visit the bank for chips or apply for a line of credit."

Douglas said thank you and tipped the man a twenty. Inside the vestibule, Douglas headed for the bank and winked at Valerie. "How much should I convert to chips? I must warn you, I'm felling lucky tonight."

Valerie lightly touched his hand. "Not too much. I would hate to think that a single night out with me put you into financial hardship."

"Come on, Val. It's for charity." He looked at her with a pleading grin. "Don't spoil my good deeds."

Valerie felt a twinge of doubt. The casino's bank would be robbed within the hour and most of Douglas' money would be inside. Despite his assurance that he had money to lose, she kept envisioning his empty coffee shop and the well-used look of all its furniture.

"You bought the tickets. Allow me to buy some chips." She offered. In a few hours, the money would just come right back to her.

Douglas tried to protest but his date wedged her way between him and the window. "Excuse me, could I exchange this for three hundred in chips?" She slid three bills under the clear partition and accepted her chips in return. "Thank you." She said to the well-dressed cashier.

When she turned around, Douglas tried to give her a hard stare but she noticed the corners of his mouth struggling to suppress an amused smile. She allowed him to save face by directing the conversation to another subject. "Black Jack, Poker, Roulette? What game would you prefer?"

He reached out and took her hand. "Let's warm up with black jack." In the main room, the couple strolled around examining the tables and stopped for a hand of 21. Douglas misjudged and busted with twenty three. In truth, he was trying to show off and took more of a risk than he normally would have.

Valerie whispered. "I think the dealer is on the level. I was watching his hands the whole time. So, how did you lose that hand?" She teased.

Douglas whispered back. "It's going to breast cancer research. I'm not trying too hard to beat the house."

Valerie gave him an appreciative squeeze on the shoulder. Suddenly, the score that she had planned with Arturo did not look so appealing. In theory, they had planned to rob the richest of the city's upper crust who only held "Night at the Casino" to assuage their consciences by wasting money on a bourgeois pastime, but Douglas' naïve assertion that every dollar he gave up helped someone else ate away at her. She may have also been dreading the eventual murder of her boyfriend as well.

Suddenly, Valerie had to get away from this table where she knew Douglas would continue throwing away money. She leaned in close where the dealer could not hear her. "If we continue our tour of the convention center, I will make sure that you get a surprise." She infused her voice with a seductive intonation.

Douglas pocketed the rest of his chips and addressed the dealer. "Sorry, the lady would like to powder her nose and needs an escort." He walked away with the raven haired woman in a satin black dress and looked over several other tables as he passed by. Eventually, his date led him out of the crowded floor and into a hallway. Elegant brushed metal plates posted beside the doorways displayed the room names throughout the length of the hall.

Walking a few doors down, Doug noticed a door ajar that led into a darkened conference room. "Quick in here." He whispered with a sense of urgency. Then he ducked out of the hallway pulling Valerie in behind him.

In the eerily silent, unlit room, talking in a normal volume seemed wrong. So, in a hushed voice, she asked, "What is it?"

Nonchalantly, Doug said, "Oh, nothing. I just wanted some privacy for this." She felt his lips pressed against hers and his body followed suit. She reached around him and felt the fabric of his tux as she ran her hands up his back. She pulled him closer until she should feel his body heat burning through her dress. She groped around with a free hand searching for the edge of the conference table in the unlit room. The tips of her fingers brushed the smooth top and she positioned her body to gingerly fall back onto the table. Douglas climbed on top and hovered over her until she wrapped her thighs around his waist. Gripping the edge of the table, he could feel her grinding against him. Despite both of them being fully clothed, Valerie thought the date was going well...aside from the coming death.

Despite their experience, the four men assigned to Devildriver showed signs of nervousness. Auditioning for tougher jobs did not bother most of them. Fundamentally, they understood that a big heist or a life or death gunfight required people with a proven track-record. Truthfully, they were nervous about the driver. The other guy *"Beastia"* had come across like a typical business oriented mercenary, but Devildriver seemed...off, somehow. They hadn't seen his face since both men were wearing masks when they arrived and the actual recruiting was never done face to face. However, the driver's voice and manner had set them all on edge.

One of the recruits laughed to break up the silence. "So, we're going to have a big haul tonight? Think we'll get to plug any yuppies?"

Another one shrugged. "Don't make none to me. Live rich man or dead rich man, I'm still getting' mine."

The third man interjected. "You're actin' tough over nothin'. As soon as you point a gun at one of those pampered aristocratic types, they piss themselves."

The masked gunmen looked over their weapons and tried to kill time as Devildriver steered the van through heavy Saturday night traffic. Finally, he pulled the van through a rear service entrance. He had planned to avoid the brightly lit front with the valets, doormen, and onlookers even though it meant a longer trek through the interior of the building. He turned to the masked gunmen in the back and called out, "Phillips."

One of the mercenaries raised a gloved hand. "That's me, sir."

"Knock out communication." He commanded.

Greg stumbled as he tried to stand and move toward a large black hard-shell case. He stepped on the toes of a boot trying to wedge himself through the seated soldiers. "Sorry" he sincerely mumbled.

He finally reached the case and unclasped the silver locks. Swinging the lid up, he flipped a switch and started adjusting a set of old fashioned analog dials. "You know," He said to no one in particular. "I could have bought a cell phone jammer but figured it would be harder to trace back to me if I just built my own."

One of the gunmen seemed surprised. "You built that from scratch?"

"Oh yeah, it's easy. All you need is a voltage controlled oscillator, a tuning circuit, noise generator, and some kind of RF amplification system."

"Dude, I have no idea what you're talking about." Another merc added.

Devildriver silenced them with his unnatural voice. "Enough talking. Flip the switch on the jammer." He looked at the other men. "We rush in." He produced a two way radio. "Team 1, we are in position. Signal when ready."

Arturo's crackling voice came through. "We are ready. You are cleared for action."

Devildriver nodded at Greg who flicked a small metallic switch over to the crudely labeled "on" position.

The driver pulled out another two way radio and handed it to the electronics expert. "We will communicate with these. You stay here and make sure the equipment continues to function." It was the most speaking he had to perform in ages and his throat was already sore from the effort. The pain did not trouble him near as much as having to interact with the people he had been forced to lead.

The rear double doors of the cargo van swung open and the gunmen filed out. Seconds later, masked men sprinted through the service door and began the assault.

Arturo Gomez had arrived in a separate van with the personnel evenly split between them. It was part of the getaway plan to have two vehicles, just in case a weak link broke and they had to distract the police. Both teams ran through the building herding any stray civilians toward the casino main floor.

Bestia and his subordinates spilled into the casino with five members of the kitchen staff at gunpoint. The first party goers to notice screamed. One of the robbers shouted "Shut up! This will go down real easy as long as no one does anything stupid!" More people caught the disruption and by the time Devildriver entered with his men, nearly the entire room had their hands in the air. One man had ducked behind a craps table and furiously punched 911 into his cell phone. Nothing happened. One of the thieves walked over and shoved the barrel of his sub-machine gun under the caller's nose. The man with the cell phone out dropped it to the carpet and lifted his hands in submission. At gunpoint, he stood and walked over to the accumulating crowd of prisoners.

"Trying to be a hero?" Arturo asked the room. "You know that most heroes get their medals posthumously." The voice did not yell or even convey aggression but did hold resolve that the words spoken were not idle.

Two mercenaries ran over to the casino's bank with two large black locking cases. "Fill 'em up!" One of them shouted at the teller while unclasping the locks and swinging the lid off as the other criminal covered the charity volunteer with the MP5.

Two more members of the gang broke away to patrol the halls looking for anyone they missed. The cell phones were jammed but if a hostage could get to a land line, he or she could call the police. In a matter of minutes, the agents had taken possession of the city's largest charity event of the year complete with a list of distinguished and valuable guests.

Arturo looked around for Raven and Douglas Lawson. Neither person was on the casino floor as was planned. He whispered, "Damn you, Valerie."

Douglas and Valerie stopped their heavy petting when a scream erupted from the casino area. Doug looked up and focused, trying to determine what had just happened outside their room. He turned his head back to his date and smiled. "I guess someone just hit the jackpot."

She smiled back. "Are you afraid that we'll be caught?"

Doug laughed. "Please, I'd give 'em a show if anyone walked in on us."

Despite her coy facial expression, Valerie knew that the scream did not belong to a lucky gambler. She had counted on being on the main floor when her team arrived but Doug had distracted her. She did not care about whoever had screamed. In her mind, a victim that incurred the wrath of an armed assailant got what he or she deserved. However, the plan could have gone smoother. Douglas was supposed to be out on the casino floor where he could become a casualty of the robbers. The solution was to convince him to walk out with her and get taken hostage quickly and easily.

When he bent his head down to kiss her, Valerie whispered. "The night is still young. We don't have to move so fast. Let's really savor the tension. Let the expectation build a little more." She accentuated her last few words by running her fingers up his back.

Douglas slid off the table into a standing position and reached out to help her up. "Okay, I can handle anticipation."

When she had finished getting off the table, Valerie began adjusting her dress. Her face grew serious and some of her concern resurfaced. "Douglas did you bring me here tonight to show off?"

He looked confused and his heart leapt up into his throat. "Show off? I'm not following you."

She explained. "The price of the tickets, the reckless opening bet. It's like you are trying to convince me you are wealthy."

Doug grimaced like he had just tasted something unpleasant, though inwardly he was relieved. "I bought the tickets because I thought you'd have fun. I wanted to gamble because the money goes to a good cause." He turned somber. "I don't want to be with someone who thought my view of the world is so warped that I would try to buy her affection."

Valerie believed him and knew that his estimation of her would permanently fall if she did not do something to rectify her unintentional insult. She glided forward and snaked her arm around his waist. "I just don't want you to hurt yourself financially. I know you can't mind the shop as efficiently while people are trying to kill you. Between a neglected business and the money you are spending while in hiding, I worry." Then she kissed him roughly, catching his bottom lip between her teeth then releasing. "Let's go back to the party."

Douglas allowed himself to be led to the ajar conference room door. He stepped ahead of her to open the door as he believed a gentleman should. When he pulled on the knob, he looked into the hall and saw no one.

Doug turned around with a devilish grin and spoke in a fake

British voice. "No one has seen us. You need not fear your reputation m' lady." He took her by the hand and they walked out together.

"My accent is much better." Valerie giggled.

"I wonder why that is." Douglas mocked.

As they neared the end of the hallway, both of them saw the armed men milling around the card tables. Douglas immediately jumped back against the wall pulling Valerie with him. Unsure of the situation, he could only stare at his date with wide eyes. "There are men with guns in there!" He spoke in a panicked whisper.

Chapter: Unexpected Violent Outbursts

*B*estia paced while several new recruits loaded the cash into large black cases. In theory, the whole robbery should have taken a matter of minutes but this was not a typical smash and grab. The boss insisted on a maximum payout. All patrons had to be rounded up and kept within range of the cell phone jammer. That meant a little bit of tension filled the time with the city's elite.

Arturo scanned over the masked faces and found Devildriver by the man's creepy eyes. The getaway driver had a singular stare that unnerved so many people. Did anything ever cause those eyes to change, to show an interest in something? Arturo doubted it. Even in the midst of murder, Devil looked bored.

The Mexican-born gunman could not figure out what made Devildriver tick, other than that car. Surely, the automobile enthusiast did not spend all of his earnings tuning that vehicle. He would have run out of upgrades already. Not only that, but Devil didn't even spend money on a house or an apartment. He slept in the car. He did not buy new clothes. Day in and day out, he wore the same darkly colored, worn attire. He did not stockpile weapons. When he needed to kill, he just used whatever was handy. It was like his entire world revolved around his black 1972 Dodge Demon. He even gave it an affectionate pet name, "Lilith".

Valerie called Devil her getaway driver but he rarely acted in that capacity. Mostly, he acted as an extra gun. Arturo wondered why someone with such a narrow focus would choose an unrelated, high risk occupation.

Bestia had allowed his mind to stray from the task at hand long enough. He looked over his efficient team doing its work. The recruits were performing well. No one had questioned or back talked Arturo. The only point that concerned him was Valerie's absence from the hostages. That indicated that not everyone was accounted for, and as long as the party goers could possibly alert the authorities, they were all at risk. Plus, he wanted to kill Lawson.

A middle-aged couple sat by a black jack table in the shape of a half circle. The female rested her back against the cool, polished wood as she cradled her pregnant belly. Pleadingly, she called out to one of the mercenaries. "Please just let us go." Tears broke free and rolled down her face. "I'm going to have a baby in three weeks. Just let us go."

Her husband knelt beside her and aggressively whispered. "Shut up! You're going to get us all killed."

Unable to control her voice, she shouted. "Why did you make me come here? I told you I just wanted to stay home!"

Everyone watched the developing argument. Arturo moved forward to shut the husband up and restore order when things escalated faster than anyone could predict.

The husband growled back at her. "You didn't want to come tonight? Well that's too bad! I'm not going to let that little bastard in your belly ruin the rest of my life!"

Before anyone could blink, Devildriver appeared by the man's side. Arturo opened his mouth to yell "Stand down" but Devil had already palmed the side of the man's head and slammed it into the sharp edge on the dealer's side of the blackjack table. The pointed corner hit the victim in the temple and cracked his skull. When Devildriver let go, the fatally wounded husband fell the short distance to the floor and a gaping wound leaked blood and brain fluid on the carpet.

Screams erupted. One woman fainted. A man in a tuxedo vomited. With quick thinking, Arturo play the unexpected death to his advantage. "Everyone quiet or we'll kill another hostage! That's what happens when you make a disturbance! Keep that in mind next time you want to distract us from our jobs!" Regardless of making the execution look like a consequence of not following the robbers' directions, Arturo Gomez was furious at Devildriver but couldn't reprimand him quite yet.

While his field commander spoke, Devil knelt in front of the pregnant woman. His face, hidden behind an expressionless mask, came closer to the lady. Her eyes did not focus and her breathing sped up. She quickly slipped into shock.

Then Devil gripped her chin firmly between his gloved thumb and forefinger. His monotone voice and vacant stare grabbed her attention when the screaming and crying of other hostages had failed to engage her. "Your baby is better off." Without further explanation, he let go of her and stood up.

Arturo approached him and leaned in very close. Whispering so no one else would overhear, he chided Devildriver. "Raven is not going to be pleased. We were supposed to avoid killing except for Lawson."

The getaway driver made eye contact and held it for several seconds until Arturo turned away. The Mexican cursed in frustration. Devildriver was so hard to read. Did the threat of facing their boss worry him? Impossible to tell. "However, what's done is done." He thought. "I wonder how the men I sent to round up the revelers are doing."

Douglas held Valerie's hand as he led her back down the hallway. He had started his retreat before the murder of the hostage. The screams were muffled but still convinced him that the gunmen weren't concerned with leaving people alive.

"We need to find a place to hide." Douglas tried to exhibit a take charge attitude but was secretly terrified. Even more upsetting than being afraid, his date showed less anxiety than him. It was further proof that she was guilty. She had betrayed him.

Glancing into an open doorway, Doug saw a large dining hall with silverware laid out for full service meal. Dinner had been included in the price of the ticket, but the catering staff sat with the other hostages in the casino room.

Valerie urged him into the dining area. "I can hear someone."

Douglas ran through the doorway, holding her hand. He glanced around wildly searching for any decent hiding place. "Quick, under the nearest table and don't move."

Valerie ducked under a white table cloth draped to the floor. After making sure her hands and feet were pulled inside, she waited for Doug to join her but he did not appear. Her ideal resolution involved giving away their position and peacefully rejoining everyone in the main hall. Douglas inadvertently ruined it. Why hadn't he slipped under the table with her?

Douglas heard the crackle of a two-way radio and dived behind the door that he had just entered. The gunman had gotten too close for Doug to risk hiding with Valerie. If he was right, she'd just use the opportunity to give away his position. As his heart pounded in his chest, Douglas thought of his only chance. "I've got to get the drop on this guy." His muscles tensed at the thought but he resolved to attack whatever came through that doorway.

The barrel of a sub-machine gun poked past the edge of the door. In an explosion of force, Doug threw a clumsy kick that succeeded in sending the MP5 twirling off. The mercenary lost the gun but quickly reacted. Instead of chasing the firearm, he turned at his attacker.

Douglas tried to block the multitude of strikes flying at him. Even when he managed to knock the fists away, his forearms were bruising at the points of contact. Most of the punches made it through his defenses to hit him in the face, chest, and stomach. The merc obviously had more experience with hand to hand combat and did not seem worried about the lack of a gun.

Douglas felt his body topple and his back hit the wall as he went down. He looked up at the figure standing above him and pulling a knife out of a black sheath strapped to his leg. As the gleaming steel blade revealed itself inch by inch, Valerie appeared brandishing a flimsy wooden chair from the dining set. She swung it hard through the air and brought it crashing into the thief's back. The chair broke apart and the figure staggered. Douglas used the momentary distraction to spring up and snatch a steak knife from the closest table top. The gunman lunged after him just as Doug wrapped his fingers around the handle and spun around to confront his attacker. Seeing the raging eyes behind the black ski mask, Douglas blindly shoved the blade forward sending it into the robber's throat.

Doug let go and stepped back watching the dying man's gloved hand paw at the protruding utensil. The victim slowly sank to the floor. Most of the blood disappeared into the black outfit but a large pool began to spread on the light colored carpet.

Douglas could not speak. His mind simultaneously celebrated and rebelled. He had just killed a man. The world swirled before his eyes and the sounds of breathing suddenly muted. His chest felt constricted like iron bands tightening across his torso.

Valerie watched in morbid fascination. Her plan had been simple. A nerdy, comic book obsessed goofball had invited her to a night of dinner and gambling. She had used the event as a way to eliminate a threat and line her organization's coffers with additional funds. She and her date were supposed to be hostages along with the rest of the fat and spoiled Americans. Instead, her coffee peddler attacked and killed one of her men. Now, the boyfriend she had made out with in an empty conference room sat on the floor sorting through the confusion of his first kill. He had surprised her. Something she had not foreseen, he turned out to be a killer. Even more shocking, when she had peeked out from under the table, she had instinctively jumped into the fray on the side of her date. Valerie had sided with a man she had planned on executing over one of her own soldiers. Ms. Gossard reached out to the dead body to pull the mask off. She needed to know if it was *Bestia*, Devildriver, or one of her expendable initiates.

Douglas' eyes caught the movement of her hand and he suddenly shouted. "No, don't do it!"

Valerie looked at his pitiful, conflicted face not understanding his objection. "Why not?"

Douglas shook uncontrollably as he spoke. "Please, if I see that face, I'll see it every time I close my eyes for the rest of my life."

Valerie debated for a moment. She really only cared if Arturo or Devildriver had left this mortal coil. The rest were expendable. The frame of the dead man did not match the stocky frame of Arturo or the scarecrow frame of Devildriver. She didn't lift the mask. The first kill could haunt a person forever, despite self-defense as a motive.

Brief flashes of memory hit her. Her mind's eye looked over rain-slick streets and a filthy man trying to pull himself up from the ground. She stood in front of him clutching her side, applying pressure to avoid more blood loss as his coarse voice pleaded. "Wait Birdie, we had a misunderstanding is all. No need to play so rough." She heard him but still silently slashed the thin sliver of metal across the man's throat. He gurgled and aborting his attempt to stand, fell back to the pavement.

Valerie snapped out of her daze and realized that she was staring at Douglas' kill, not hers. A steak knife extended from the man's throat. Her kill had been with a large nail file with an edge sharpened into a blade that she kept in her purse. Still, the similarity had sent her back to a dark time in London.

She turned to Douglas. "We need to hide." Why did she say that? The best strategy would be to let a guard find them and escort them to the casino. "We can hide in the lavatory." Her mouth betrayed her mind again.

Despite her original plan, she took Douglas by the hand and led him to the ladies room. He followed, reduced to a willing child by the shock of what he had done. She ushered him in and ran back to the dead man and took his two-way radio. She glanced nervously. Making up her mind, she pressed the button to talk. "One of your men is down. Dining room." Then she let go of the button.

She did not expect *Bestia* to respond. Radio communication needed to be kept to a minimum. Their frequency was not in the range for which her electronics guru had built his jamming device and theoretically could be overheard.

The radio crackled and Arturo commanded another faceless soldier. "Get over to the dining room. We want them alive." He had included the last order for his boss' benefit. The last thing he needed was the mastermind getting seriously injured by an overzealous hired thug.

Valerie held onto the radio and waited outside the restroom, debating whether or not to reveal Douglas Lawson's position. Second guessing felt so alien to her and she decided that her first instinct to hide with Douglas would prove to be the correct one.

Slipping back through the ladies room door, she whispered. "We need to lay low. I heard someone coming." She looked at the stalls as a hiding place but immediately dismissed the idea. They would have no room to maneuver if discovered. Instead, she entered the stall and looked up at the foam tiles that could easily move. "Douglas, come here."

Doug had been leaning in the corner of the room with a vacant expression. At the sound of her voice, a little life came back into his eyes. "What?"

Valerie urged him on. "I need you to climb into the ceiling. We need to hide in the crawlspace. Stand on the seat and pull yourself up." She pointed at the toilet. "I'll help you."

Douglas stepped onto the rim and braced himself against the side of the stall. Then he reached up and slid the thin foam panel to the side. Looking into the black rectangle he was supposed to enter, he floundered. "I'm not sure I'm strong enough."

"I'll help lift you! Just hurry!" Valerie impatiently snapped. She knew that time slipped away as they wasted breath debating. To emphasize the need for expediency, she reached out placing both hands on his buttocks and pushed upward.

"Geez" Doug lamely exclaimed. He gripped the painted frame, keeping each panel in place and heaved. His biceps strained, unused to lifting his entire body weight. With Ms. Gossard's help, he pulled his upper body into the darkness. Slowly, he pulled his legs up as well. He shuffled on his hands and knees until he turned around. Facing the hole, he reached down to help his paramour.

Valerie reached up to take his outstretched hand but heard the restroom door creak open. In a blind panic, she crouched balanced on the toilet seat. The sounds of footsteps clomping on the hard floor made her shiver. *Bestia* wouldn't have come himself and none of the new recruits would know her identity. If she had to take out one of her hired help, questions would be raised about how an unarmed 120 pound woman dispatched an armed thug. Her heart rapidly beat as she fought with herself. Go on the offensive or let it play out? Then she heard the stall doors open one by one, methodically starting closest to the entrance and working closer to her.

Chapter: Siege

Gregory Phillips watched his wristwatch and deciding that no one was coming back to the van to watch him, he turned off the cell phone jammer. Peeking through the windows and seeing no one, he opened the door and stepped out of the vehicle. It was now or never. He could get back into the van and do his job. There was still a high probability that he would be executed once the job was over. Or he could run for it, find a phone and call in a tip. The cops would surround the building and everyone would go to jail except for him.

He looked at the exit to the parking deck and he looked in the back of the van. "Should I stay or should I go?"

Greg thought back to that memory doctor tied to a chair being tortured by his bosses. He remembered how he had spent months in a psychiatric hospital with no memory after he had been captured on the bridge. The people that employed him were heartless monsters, efficient and ruthless. They would never trust him again after being in police custody with him memories restored. He was a dead man unless he could engineer their capture.

His feet started moving before his brain had fully weighed the options and he found himself sprinting toward the street outside. After entering the cool night air, he looked around for any random pedestrian. Seeing a couple holding hands and strolling down the sidewalk, he started running right at them.

"Hey!" He shouted in a panic. "Stop for a second! I need your help!"

The lovers turned to face him, frozen in surprise. Their faces registered alarm but they did not move.

"Please can I borrow your phone for one moment?" He panted, finally reaching them.

With shaking hands, the boyfriend offered his cell.

Clarence Sudduth watched cars surround the building. Men in tactical gear waited anxiously. The whole situation had gotten out of hand. When it became clear that Gregory Phillips had ditched the wire, Sudduth made the decision to not go in to the garage and grab him. Instead, surveillance was set up on the building. He had plenty of pictures of people coming and going. Well, more accurately the peons that he had tasked with staking out the building had pictures. Once people started showing up, there had not been time to review them before the whole group was on the move again. The elusive Raven had been photographed leaving only an hour before the rest of the gang had headed out in two separate delivery trucks. Not knowing where they were going or what they were up to, the police kept their eyes on the building while allowing a single tail to follow the vans and report back. Luckily, Gregory Phillips had gotten in touch with Sudduth shortly after the vehicles stopped.

Phillips had implored them to move immediately, that the big score was going down now. Clarence scrambled to assemble a large enough force to intimidate the bad guys into surrendering. Hopefully, the thieves would walk right out into an ambush. If the police had lain low enough, the men inside the building would not think they needed hostages. The civilians would be out of the way and the men would have no choice but to lay down their guns and put their hands in the air. Clarence doubted such a perfect confluence of events but the grizzled veteran could hope.

Detective Sudduth's radio crackled to life. "Clarence, we have your CI that called in the tip."

"Good. Is he talking?" The detective responded.

"He won't stop. He keeps trying to explain why he ditched the wire."

"Any intel on the people inside?"

"He says eight total. He specifically mentioned two aliases, *Bestia* and Devil."

Sudduth had hoped they were present. Both of them had repeatedly popped up whenever Lawson was around. Clarence thought he should inform Douglas that they finally had his enemies cornered. Before he could make the call, a fleet of news vans parked on the other side of the police barriers. "Son of a bitch!"

Douglas peered down at the masked man about to stumble upon his date who cowered, perched atop a toilet seat. The villain held a sub-machine gun as he flung open each stall with a well-placed boot. Doug's mind raced through alternatives before deciding the only solution was to dive bomb the merc.

The robber moved directly in front of the door hiding Ms. Gossard and rocked back to prepare for the kick. Above, Douglas lifted his upper body as much as the crawlspace would allow. As the criminal knocked the stall wide open, Doug brought both fists down onto the center of the foam tile that acted as a ceiling. He tumbled through the hole and performed a clumsy tackle on the unsuspecting gunman.

As both men landed on the floor, the mercenary's skull hit the edge of the sink basin directly behind him. The body went limp after a sickening crack.

Douglas watched the body expecting it to move. He watched in rapt horror until Valerie's voice forced him to turn around.

"He has a radio and a gun." She looked at him with awe. "I think you should talk to their leader."

Douglas raised an eyebrow. "Why?" He did not see the advantage in giving up the element of surprise.

"The best chance for a robbery to be successful is for the thieves to get out before it turns into a standoff with police. It's in their best interest to abandon the dead and leave with what they have. Besides, how long can it take to empty the safe? They are probably finishing up."

Douglas could not figure her out. Was she setting him up? If so, why'd she save him when he was locked in battle with one of the gunmen? He still wanted to believe in her. He wanted to be the nerdy guy that scored a beautiful, intelligent woman out of his league. He wanted her to really love him. Despite all his wants, a part of his brain kept adding and subtracting evidence that she was a fraud.

Valerie kept eye contact with him; her lips tightly pressed together in a neutral expression. Maybe the tension had gotten to him and he couldn't clearly think. Regardless, she had a point about time being a factor. If he notified them that guy number two would not be returning, the gang would not wait a few extra minutes expecting him.

Doug lifted the two way radio to his ear. He pressed the button and spoke, injecting a false nonchalance into his voice. "Hi there. Just wanted to let you know, I've taken out two of your men in the space of a couple of minutes."

The radio crackled. "Congratulations." Then silence.

"Not very talkative, *Bestia*?"

No noise came from the radio. Douglas turned to Valerie. "I don't think that accomplished anything."

Valerie shook her head. "They can leave without worry. They don't have time to sweep the whole building to find you and the two dead scouts. They will cut their losses and leave with the money."

"Allowing them to escape..." Douglas spoke with disdain.

"Allowing them to avoid a protracted hostage situation and ensuring the safety of everyone in that casino room." Valerie corrected.

Exasperated, he agreed. "You're right. It's just money...But this was a charity! What kind of person steals from charity?"

Valerie did not answer. Oddly, the look on his face made her feel a sense of shame.

The radio emitted a static and then Arturo's voice came over loud and clear. "Come to the main room and give yourself up or I start executing hostages. You know I will because we've already killed one."

"I didn't see it happen." Doug challenged.

"Would you like to speak to the pregnant widow? I'm sure she'll confirm her husband's death."

Valerie grabbed his forearm. "They are serious."

Douglas scrutinized her face. Was she playing him? He lifted the walkie to his mouth. "What happens to me if I obey?"

"We'll kill you and take off without another casualty. Listen up hero, it's a straight trade: your life for all the other hostages." *Bestia* sounded smug as he mocked Lawson.

Doug pressed the button. "I'm on my way."

Valerie shook him. "Did you not hear him? They are going to kill you!"

He dropped the radio and kissed her. "I know they are, but they'll kill innocent people if I don't. It's what a real hero would do."

"Stop playing a part! This isn't a game! You will die!" Valerie shouted into his face.

"If I don't, I am a coward and a murderer. I will have basically pulled the trigger on those hostages myself."

He broke eye contact with her and pulled out his phone. Quickly typing out a text, he shoved it back in his pocket.

"Did that go through?" Valerie watched him with fascination.

"Yeah, why?"

She bit her tongue. The plan was falling apart. The cell jammer had failed.

"Well hero, let's go."

Douglas shook his head. "No, you stay here. Stay hidden."

"Do you think I'm going to let you walk in there and die? I'm coming with you. We'll find a way out of this." Valerie patted his shoulder.

He cracked a smile and started walking toward the casino.

Gaston, Desiree, and Jacob felt their phones vibrate simultaneously. Each one had been in a different part of the Bulwark wrestling with individual demons. Gaston still fumed at the thought that Douglas had become corrupted. The man he knew had eroded into someone that sanctioned killing. Desiree thought about the deteriorating relationship with Gaston. What had she been thinking opening up to him? The warrior and the pacifist would never work. Their philosophies were diametrically opposed. Jacob practiced tossing a tennis ball at the wall and then blocking it from hitting him when it bounced back. A few times, the fuzzy sphere hit him when his concentration broke. Despite his age, he was driven to become everything the comic books taught him a superhero should be.

The buzzing of their cell phones grabbed their attention and separately, they gasped in astonishment. The unthinkable had happened. Douglas had been captured and was minutes away from execution.

Desiree sprang to her feet and ran to the armory. She grabbed an AR-15 and pre-loaded clips. She slipped on a belt with plenty of magazine pockets and prepared for war. Gaston walked in on her.

"What are you doing?" He asked.

"Saving our boss." She shot back. "You should come. You can use your powers to disable people. Flood them with pain and they'll go down in seconds."

"That's not how I use my power." Gaston flatly stated.

"Protecting innocent people isn't ethical enough for you?" Desiree glared at him as she slung the rifle over her shoulder.

"I am not a sadist. I don't like discharging pain into others."

"You were okay with letting a little of it go when I was sleeping with you. Saving people isn't as important as you getting laid?" Her voice cut him with its sharp edge.

Gaston opened his mouth to respond when Jacob's voice distracted them both. "I'm ready to go."

Both adults turned to look at the boy that had snuck up on them. Cataclysm stood before them in his full costume. His face obscured behind the hood pulled low and the flames decorating the trim gave the look of a villain or anti-hero. His childish smile ruined the effect and he appeared as a youth playing dress up.

Gaston dismissed Jake immediately. "You are not going. Douglas would kill us if we let you walk into such a dangerous situation."

Desiree stepped around the Frenchman and addressed the young vigilante. "Stay behind me and do as I say when I say it. If you hesitate or question me, you could get hurt."

"What do you think you are doing?" Gaston chased after the pair as they headed toward a vehicle.

"I'm taking backup to save Douglas. At least this boy has the balls to answer a call to action. Now join us or get out of the way. Every second we waste could mean Einstein's death."

"You are taking his son into a battleground. Do you think he'll be appreciative?" Gaston yelled at his brief lover.

"He'll be alive." Desiree quipped.

Jacob watched the whole proceeding with rapt attention. Adults could be so insane. "Time is wasting! Gaston, help or don't. Just don't keep us from going to him."

The boy snapping at him shocked Gaston into shutting his mouth. Meekly, he spoke. "Go while I call the police." Both his teammates took off like rockets, disappearing out the door.

Chapter: Gunfight!

D ouglas stepped into the main hall with his hands raised. Valerie entered behind him. Arturo smiled. "You are a man of your word. Believe it or not, I respect that. There are not many of us left."

Doug could not see through the mask but recognized the muscular frame and the voice. He had been afraid of hearing it again, but there he was right in front of him. He limped closer, making a show of his difficulty walking. He wanted to be underestimated again.

"No, lose the cane. I don't want you thinking you can get the drop on me with your makeshift weapon." *Bestia* trained the gun on him. "Unlike some love-blinded people, I have made it a point to study you and your methods. A trick cane disabled that junkie I sent after you. Fool me once..."

Douglas tossed the cane to the side and Valerie stepped in and offered her shoulder for support. Lawson's gray/blue eyes glinted with icy hatred.

"Awww, isn't that sweet? Do you think she's going to mourn you when you're dead?" Arturo mocked. The other robbers stared in confusion. They had not been informed that one of the hostages would have history with *Bestia* and seemed even more lost by the appearance of Raven holding on to the man that was an obvious enemy to Arturo.

Douglas felt his stomach drop as soon as *Bestia* began speaking. "Love-blinded people" and his sardonic comment about being mourned confirmed what he had been denying. Valerie worked for them. She had been a spy. She was not afraid of facing them with him because she knew she would be fine.

Douglas cleared his throat. "You think I'm a fool for trusting her, for trusting people? You have to trust people too. Those gunmen for instance. How do you know they won't turn on you for a larger slice of the pie? How do you know that your spies are giving you reliable information? Maybe they got a little too close to their targets. Maybe the act became reality." He stole a quick glance at Valerie. Her eyes grew moist and she almost imperceptibly shook her head.

Doug sighed and looked at Arturo. "She saved me earlier. She hit one of your men with a chair and distracted him long enough for me to grab a knife. There were so many nights that we were in bed together. She could have slit my throat in my sleep at any time. Why didn't she? The answer is simple. You lost control of her. She fell in love with me for real."

Valerie's mouth fell open. "You think I work with him?"

Douglas shushed her. "Drop the act. I just said that you had come over to my side. I've already forgiven you."

Arturo began to derisively laugh. "Yes, don't insult his intelligence. Einstein was always smarter than we gave him credit for." He pointed his weapon at Douglas. "Get on your knees."

Douglas obeyed.

Arturo stepped closer. "I've been looking forward to this for so long. I've wanted to kill you ever since I knew you existed. You've been a thorn in our side that everyone underestimated. The cops didn't believe you, until they did. I wanted you dead then but Raven told me 'no'. Then you started thinking you had some legitimacy with your stupid code name and your gadgets. You got lucky! Finding us on the bridge was nothing more than a lucky break and if the cops hadn't saved your ass, you'd be dead. I would have left you limp and lifeless on that bridge."

Douglas smirked. "But you didn't. You did a swan dive into the river, running away like a little bitch."

Arturo smacked the butt of the gun into Doug's nose and watched him fall onto his back. Towering above him, *Bestia* bellowed. "Tactical retreat!"

"Call it what you will." Doug gingerly felt his nose. "I saw you turn tail and run."

The barrel pressed against his temple. "Words, words, words. I'm sick of you and your constantly running mouth. I'll show you how a man of action deals with a problem."

Then the world grew loud.

Desiree and Jacob stood on the roof of a neighboring building. They looked at the convention center and stared down at the sea of emergency vehicles encircling it. "Are you sure you can do this?" Desiree asked Jacob.

Cataclysm answered. "I can. It's easier to move someone else or something else than myself. I can get you across no problem. I just don't know if I can follow."

"Do not follow. Gaston was right. Douglas would kill me if you came any closer. But you are saving the day just by getting me over there without the police seeing me."

Jake nodded. "Don't worry. I've been practicing."

Desiree took a deep breath and thought "Relax. This isn't any more risky than a HALO jump." Except instead of training and a parachute, she was relying on a strange boy with superpowers who was going to levitate her sixty feet over an army of police officers.

"Do you think you can save him by yourself?" Jake interrupted her thoughts.

"Of course, I'm not a criminal. I am a soldier. These guys may know how to point guns at civilians, but I know about war."

Jacob grinned. "That's so badass."

She felt her body rising and then moving forward. She tried to stay calm but as the roof dropped away beneath her, she tried to struggle against the invisible bonds that held her. It was like pushing against a brick wall and she eventual relaxed. "Save your energy for the battle."

Desiree watched the building looming closer and as she reached a window, smashing it opened with her assault rifle. She felt Jake let her go and she tumbled through the opening into the main casino hall. Screams filled her ears and as she plummeted, she saw a man with a gun pointed toward Douglas' head. To his credit, Douglas immediately capitalized on the distraction by pushing off with his feet and slamming into *Bestia*. Desiree lost sight of him due to the impact. She tried to break her fall on a craps table and felt the air leave her lungs. The element of surprise would wear off any moment. She needed to move. Even with no breath, she forced herself over the lip of the table and fell to the ground. A blast of sub-machine gun fire erupted as soon as she landed.

Scrambling to her feet, Desiree lifted the AR-15 and fired back. Everything seemed to move in slow motion. She adjusted for her target's panicked flight and squeezed off three rounds. The man fell back as a red spray flew from his chest. She did not catch how many total gunmen there were and knew the odds were against her.

As Desiree saw others take aim at her, she heaved the craps table on to its side. The wood would not stop bullets but at least they would not be able to see her. She peeked over the top of her cover and *Bestia*, Devildriver, and three unknown gunmen remained, five on one. "I've faced worse."

A few well-placed bullets splintered the wood around her and she ducked behind the table. They were going to keep her pinned down and flank her if she did not act. She popped from behind cover and fired. A spray of bullets came her way but the shots went wide. The gunmen were relying on using lots of ammo instead of taking the time to place their shots. She had more discipline than that. With a single pull of the trigger, the man on her far right spun and fell to the ground. They would not flank her from that side.

Arturo growled with rage. Lawson had managed to hobble away in the confusion and his men were preforming poorly. "It's just one person! Close in fast and she won't have time to..." Another gunshot and Arturo looked down at his abdomen. She had heard him directing his troops and targeted him. He had to admire her placement, center mass. He fell back clutching his stomach. Something strange happened to the sound after he had been hit. Everything seemed muffled, like he was hearing the world through an ocean of water.

Devildriver saw *Bestia* fall and shrugged his shoulders with resignation. Standing in full view of the female that picked off his teammates, he pulled out a pipe bomb and lit the fuse with a disposable lighter. He tossed it into the middle of the room and walked toward the exit. The survivors (criminal and civilian alike) ran for the doors.

Desiree saw the explosive land and she ducked back behind the makeshift barrier. The homemade explosive had been designed with anti-personnel in mind. A mixture of nails and ball-bearings shot out in a radius around the detonation point. After the smoke cleared, she stood and observed the battle field.

To her surprise, Douglas stood up. He had hit the floor and stayed low. Most of the debris sailed over his head. He walked towards her but stopped beside Arturo. He knelt beside the villain. When Desiree arrived beside him, she was shocked to discover that *Bestia* clung to life despite the gunshot and lacerations from the pipe bomb.

Arturo smiled a wicked smile and chokingly spoke. "You finally got me, but I've got one more trick up my sleeve to even the score." He grimaced as he swallowed. "Your girlfriend is the mastermind. She's Raven and she ordered your death." He laughed with malicious glee. "She wanted you dead, but didn't want to pull the trigger."

Desiree leaned in and whispered to Doug. "Do you want me to finish him off?"

Doug shook his head. "Get out of here. I bought a ticket and I'm supposed to be here. You will get arrested if the police catch you."

Desiree nodded and ran for the stairs. Her extraction plan was simple. Make it to the roof and let Jacob carry her back. When she was gone, Doug sat on the ground beside the injured man. "Hold on and you can pull through this. You just need the will to fight."

Arturo looked at him in confusion. "Why do you want me to live? I tried to kill you."

Douglas looked the man in the eyes. "I don't want anyone to die. I want you to live and redeem yourself. If you die, there's no more hope but every moment you keep going, there's a chance for you to turn things around."

Arturo chuckled. "You are an optimist. I'm going to die a professional killer. Nothing you say or do can change that."

Douglas started to argue, but Arturo started speaking again. He lapsed into Spanish and Douglas was not able to understand most of what was said. The words tumbled out, then came haltingly, and then stopped all together.

The police entered, guns drawn and rushed over to Douglas since he was the only conscious person. He stood up slowly, raising his hands. He announced, "The man at my feet needs medical attention."

Chapter: Recovery

Valerie walked into the garage she had designated as the rendez-vous point after their mission. The location had been known only to her, Devildriver and *Bestia*. The surviving recruits would see it for the first time after they made the cut. The fact that multiple prop-erties had been used for the operation should have impressed upon them that they had not joined a fly-by-night operation.

Ms. Gossard scoped out the personnel taking a mental invento-ry. Devildriver rested sitting with his back against his favorite car, a black Demon. Two of the recruits glanced around nervously waiting for this new arrival to say or do something. The other survivors just disappeared, probably put off by how everything had gone massively pear-shaped.

One of the gunmen looked at Devildriver and flatly stated, "He snapped and killed a civilian for almost no reason."

"What is 'almost' no reason?" Valerie sardonically asked.

"The man was arguing with his wife after we told the hostages to shut up."

Valerie stormed over to Devildriver and looked down at him as he rested against the rims of his front tire. "Is that why you killed him?"

The getaway driver just shrugged. He did not even lift his head to make eye contact. Several moments passed before it became obvious he would not give any further answer.

Valerie knew that the new employees watched her. She also knew that Devildriver had to be kept in check. Despite her worry that he would give in to another random outburst of violence, she needed to punish him. Slowly reaching into her pocket, she pulled out a set of keys. She looked down on the vacant black pools that passed for his eyes and she scrapped the key across the Demon's fender leaving an ivory scar across the onyx surface.

Devildriver's eyes burst into fire as he sprang to life. With an inarticulate howl, he caught Valerie with both hands and as he jumped up, twisted his body around 180 degrees to slam her onto the hood of his car. Her body hit the sheet metal creating a loud thump and then a creak as it bent back into place.

Devil screamed into Valerie's face as he pinned her down. His voice lost its bizarre monotone and he briefly sounded like a man, a real human. His frenzied shouts carried the twang of someone raised in the Deep South and no one witnessing the spectacle immediately grasped that the voice they heard issued from their very own boogeyman.

"You promised me! You promised me that you would help me find the people on that list!" He cried as he tried to choke the life from his employer.

He abruptly cut his rant short and his hands fell from her throat. Valerie had jammed the barrel of a handgun into his abdomen, forcing him to release her and back away.

"If I kill you tonight, you'll never find them either." Valerie's voice cracked and she coughed a few times. It hurt when she spoke but she had to regain control. When she swallowed, she imagined that felt similar to forcing down a giant ball of unrefined cotton.

Devildriver growled. "Do you really think one bullet will stop me before I cut your throat? You've seen what I can do."

Raven could not let him off the hook. "Don't try it, Devil. I've watched you work and I know why you didn't kill me the first time we met. You have a weakness." The two new recruits looked terrified. One veteran member was dead and the boss had just pulled a gun on another one. She needed to get her employees under control now. "Devil, the man that I found tried very hard to hide himself. I just received his alias. Take my computer. It has the identities of the men you are looking for."

Devildriver stepped away and grabbed her laptop from the office. He silently walked to his car passing within inches of Ms. Gossard. He slid into the front seat and started the vehicle. The roar of the engine echoed off the garage walls as he revved the V8 beast. Using a remote control in the cabin of the Demon, he opened the door. The chain and gear kicked into motion and as soon as he saw enough clearance, the dark traveler and his coal black car rocketed out into the night.

Valerie Gossard rubbed her neck. "I've just released a monster."

Doctor Samantha Nichols sat in the lounge sipping a latte from the cafeteria. She needed to get up and check on her patients but she was enraptured by the television. The news had been covering the attempt to rob a breast cancer charity event. They had interviews with survivors and attempted interviews with tight lipped police officials. Finding out what really happened had been problematic because the stories wildly varied. Some talked about a SWAT team breaching and everyone running for it in the confusion. Others said a lone vigilante smashed through a skylight and single-handedly took down the thieves. Someone else said the ringleader suicide bombed the event when it was evident they were surrounded.

Samantha wondered if the truth would ever come out. Her cell phone buzzed, rattling against the table top. She picked it up and looked at the display. Douglas Lawson. Why was he calling her?

She put the phone to her ear and politely said, "Hello." To her surprise, Gaston spoke.

"*Bonjour*, do you have a moment to speak?"

"I suppose." Gaston reaching out to her struck her as unusual. She was intrigued by what was so important it over rode his introverted nature.

"Are you aware of the attempted robbery of the charity gala?"

"Of course, it's all over the news."

"Douglas was there. He is physically fine but killed two men in the process."

Samantha felt as if she had been punched in the gut. The fact that Doug had been in yet another situation where his life was in danger did not surprise her near as much as the idea that he had killed two men. The police had stated that the assailants were armed and highly organized.

"What happened?"

"He was just released from police custody. I don't know the details of what happened but I do know that it was in self-defense." He paused. "There's more. Valerie Gossard turned out to be working with the criminals responsible for the memory victims, the bridge attack, and the casino night robbery. Between wrestling with her subterfuge and the taking of two lives, I think he will need a therapist."

Samantha did not know how to respond. She had no idea how she would react to a betrayal of that magnitude. In her experience with Douglas, still waters ran deep. He could appear impassive but beneath, he was all rushing emotional currents.

"Gaston, I can't be his therapist." She rushed to excuse herself.

"He needs you." Gaston quickly replied.

"There are other therapists besides me." She reasoned.

"No, he needs you." He stressed the last word before adding, "And you still love him."

"I can't be that close to him, watch him suffer, and feel the way I do. I couldn't be objective."

Gaston's voice grew gruff. "He doesn't need objective. He needs sincerity and passion and someone that really knows him."

"Do I really know him anymore? We've spent years with no contact and then limited contact because he had a possessive girlfriend."

She could hear him pleading. "Even after years apart, you still loved him. You knew he had a woman and yet, you managed to maintain a connection. Can't you see you are his saving grace?"

Samantha clutched the phone like it was a lifeline. "I thought you hated me for not supporting him."

"How I feel doesn't matter. What matters is that Douglas recovers. Now will you help him?"

Dr. Nichols tapped the phone against her forehead as she struggled with the decision. "Gaston, do you know how hard this is?"

"Yes, I do, but you get used to the hurt." He grew firm. "Tell me you will be there for him."

Samantha bit her lip. Indecision gnawed at her. A streak of resolve ran through her and she acted before she could over think it. "I'll swing by and evaluate him. Then I'll decide whether or not to stick around."

"Thank you."

Douglas walked up the stairs to his apartment. He skipped the Bulwark and went to his bed instead of a cot in a warehouse. It did not matter that Raven knew where he lived. She had known for a while. She had stayed with him. They had made love in the bed for which he longed. Maybe there would be traces of her scent left behind.

He had begged for some space when Desiree, Gaston, and Jacob had rushed him with hugs and hurried questions. Well, Desiree had not tried to hug him. Jake wanted to know if he was in trouble. Douglas laughed and tightened his arms around the boy. "Of course not, you saved the day." Then he thanked them.

Gaston protested. "I did nothing. I stayed behind." Desiree gave him the evil eye after the admission.

"Never-the-less, you've been there for me and kept me safe for as long as I've known you. Now, I don't want to hear any more arguing. What I would like is to go home to my bed and sleep and I don't want you guys hovering over me and making a fuss." He waved them off. "I just need to rest."

Of course, they let him go. How could they contradict the wishes of a man who had just taken two lives, been betrayed by the woman he loved, and survived a gunfight culminating in a bomb blast. He had earned a little indulgence.

In his bedroom, he pulled off his shirt and looked down at the layer of fat hiding his abs. "How did I think I could attract a woman like Valerie? Of course she was playing an angle."

The phone in his pocket vibrated and he answered without thinking. A chipper voice greeted him. "Hey Einstein, it's Penny Dreadful."

He had to laugh to himself. "I don't think I'm going to go by 'Einstein' anymore."

"Oh, you found a better name?"

"No, I'm just not as smart as I think I am." Doug thought of how thoroughly his girlfriend had duped him.

"You should stick with the name. You're plenty smart. Anyway, I was just calling to let you know that I started that martial arts class you recommended. Sensei says I'm a natural." The enthusiasm in her voice was infectious.

"I'm happy for you."

"It won't be long and I'll be able to join you. I'll start working on a costume for you on my next day off." Penny rattled on but Douglas was lost in his own thoughts.

Absently, he dismissed her. "That's great. Let me talk to you tomorrow. I'm feeling pretty tired." He ended the call and collapsed on to the bed, still wearing his slacks. His eyes stung with tears as he thought about Valerie telling her underlings that Douglas Lawson had to die. His stomach roiled as he closed his eyes and could still see the steak knife sinking in to an unguarded throat. His body begged for sleep but his mind raced too many thoughts. He rolled over on to his back and blinked away the salty tears. He was a fool, a jester, a laughing stock.

Then he heard Samantha's voice. "I let myself in. You left it unlocked."

He sat up and saw her in his doorway. "Why did you come here?"

"Gaston called. He told me everything." She stepped closer.

"I'm fine. I just want to be alone."

"I can understand that. It's been a traumatic few weeks. You've had attempts on your life. You went into hiding. You took lives while defending yourself. You've been betrayed. It's a wonder you are functioning so well."

He spat the words like they were poison. "I thought so highly of myself but the whole damn time…I've been playing the fool."

Samantha sat on the bed beside him and slid her arms around him. "Emotion clouds judgement. There are worse things to be a fool for than love." She kissed him on the cheek.

Douglas threw himself back on the bed and covered his eyes with his forearm so she would not see him crying. "Why are you here?"

"To make sure you're okay." She lay down beside him and draped her arm across his chest. "Go to sleep. I'll watch over you."

Douglas obeyed and rolled on to his side. Motionless, he felt her warmth press against his back and her arms give him an affectionate squeeze. He closed his eyes and tried to drift away. Through a mixture of exhaustion and a familiar presence, he finally fell asleep.

Epilogue

Douglas Lawson heard his cashier call his name. "Boss, the phone's for you."

He walked over to Cindy and took the receiver. "Thanks." He directed it at her before putting the handset up to his ear. "Hello, this is Douglas, owner."

A crisp British accent made his heart stop. "Hello, lover."

"What the hell?" He blurted.

"Don't get too worked up. I am calling with a business proposition." Valerie Gossard cooed in his ear.

"Why in God's name would I want to work with you?" He snorted.

"If you don't, many people will die. We're on the same side this time."

"And what side is that?" He muttered.

"Devildriver is no longer in my employ. The man is a psychopath that is responsible for more death than you know. Now that I am not there to keep him under some semblance of control, the bodies will start stacking up and I don't know how far he will take his bloodlust."

"Why do you care? You're a monster too." Doug accused her.

"No one is a monster quite like him." She coolly responded. "Save the day or not, just let me know what you want to do. But I know where his targets are and more importantly, who they are. Help me put him down."

"You didn't answer why." Doug retorted.

"Maybe I feel guilty. Maybe I want to tie up loose ends. Maybe I missed you. What do you say? Want to work together?"

"I'll just call the cops and have you arrested." Doug threatened.

"You probably would. You have this annoying sense of justice.

However, I know who Devil really is and what made him. I'm betting curiosity will be more of a driving force than seeing me again. Haven't you always wanted to know what makes a monster?"

Douglas felt his heart skip a beat. There was no doubt Devil would kill. Everything Lawson had seen pointed towards someone with no regard for human life. Despite his curiosity, he found himself saying, "Sorry, I'll find him and take him out but if I see you within a mile of me, I'll take you down too."

Her curt voice shot back. "Oh sweetie, you'll never see me coming..."

"You know where I am; I'll be waiting." He smiled at the thought of finishing off Raven's organization. He looked over at his cashier. "Cindy, I'm going to take a vacation. I'll hire some extra help to see you through my absence."

"Where are you going?"

"Hunting." He said with no trace of a smile.

To Be Continued...

CPSIA information can be obtained at www.ICGtesting.com
Printed in the USA
BVOW08s2200130915

417242BV00002B/324/P